T0367822

GOD'S BASIC DOCTRINES

Caleb MacDonald

authorHOUSE®

AuthorHouse™
1663 Liberty Drive
Bloomington, IN 47403
www.authorhouse.com
Phone: 1-800-839-8640

Scripture taken from the New King James Version. Copyright 1979, 1980, 1982 by Thomas Nelson, inc. Used by permission. All rights reserved.

Published by AuthorHouse 06/02/2014

ISBN: 978-1-4969-1394-4 (sc)
ISBN: 978-1-4969-1392-0 (e)

Library of Congress Control Number: 2014909511

Any people depicted in stock imagery provided by Thinkstock are models, and such images are being used for illustrative purposes only. Certain stock imagery © Thinkstock.

This book is printed on acid-free paper.

Contents

Introduction

G od's *Basic Doctrines* is all about God, his Son Jesus, the Holy Spirit, and man. The man who wrote this book came to know God personally at the age of ten in 1963. The author, Caleb, has walked with God for fifty years, gaining a wealth of experience and knowledge. He now is passing along some of this knowledge and wisdom to you.

What Caleb found so shocking during these fifty years are all the false teachings or doctrines that have been incorporated into the church today. Caleb was horrified to discover that very few true doctrines are taught today. The church is so watered down with junk that even God is unable to be himself in any assembly. In *God's Basic Doctrines,* Caleb shares what the Bible is truly teaching. He takes the time to reveal all the scriptures about the basic subjects of Christianity. At the same time, Caleb exposes many of the false teachings that have been adopted by the modern church. Once you read through each chapter, you will agree with Caleb about what is truly taught in the Bible. Caleb leaves no doubt about what is taught in the Bible.

God has now called Caleb to be a prophet to all the earth, beginning in America. Part of this calling includes revealing what is false. *God's Basic Doctrines* teaches the truth about the Bible and exposes some of the heresies and false doctrines. The first disciples warned the first church that destructive false teachings would arise. Two thousand years have passed since this warning, and the modern church has evolved into a sick mass of trashed doctrines. Millions of people are searching for God, and the church can't show anyone how to get to God because of all the false doctrines. Caleb attacks these doctrines and also shows the truth. Doubtless, Caleb has gained a lot of clergy enemies because of exposing these false teachings.

This book was written for the millions who want to know the truth about God and then decide if they want to go on to have a relationship with him. Caleb also warns the millions that there is a price to pay for this relationship. The cost of knowing God can be daunting.

This book is intended for those who have accepted Jesus into their hearts. The book was written for those who have never known about maturity and growth in God's kingdom. The book was written for those who have not gotten much beyond accepting Jesus into their heart. This book is for those who have just come to accept Jesus into their lives and who want to understand more of how God works in his kingdom and how to utilize the basic principles of a foundation in God.

This book can also to be used by those who have been wondering what Christianity really is about. It will provide a very descriptive explanation about what Jesus taught and what God's kingdom entails. *God's Basic Doctrines* will definitely give every reader a thorough knowledge of who Jesus and God are all about.

Once you've finished the book, you will have a very different understanding about God. This book will shake and rattle your beliefs as they have never before been challenged. You will learn how much false trash we have all been fed by the church. You will gain a very clear understanding of what is taught from the Bible. You will have an extremely accurate view of God's world.

CHAPTER 1

A Foundation

Throughout this book I will be quoting lots of Bible verses. This is so that the reader doesn't have to use a Bible as a separate companion alongside this book and thereby require much more time in looking up verses. I use the New King James Version for most all of the verses used in this book. The reader is more than welcome to use their favorite Bible version alongside this book. For those who are more interested in accuracy or the use of several translations you will find the use of a lap top computer to be quick. Much of this book was written with the use of the software "Quick Verse 10". With this software you can have several Bible versions that can be used simultaneously. You can also purchase other add-on software or Bible software programs that offer many versions of the Bible as an aid to studying the Bible. Many of these software programs work as an add-on to "Quick Verse 10."

> Therefore, leaving the discussion of the elementary principles of Christ, let us go on to perfection, not laying again the foundation of repentance from

dead works and of faith toward God of the doctrine
of baptisms, of laying on of hands, of resurrection
of the dead, and of eternal judgment. (Hebrews
6:1–2, NKJV)

The subject that I deal with in this chapter is not
mentioned as one of the basic doctrines in Hebrews 6:1–
2. I'm going to include the Bible as part of one of the
basic foundational doctrines in Christianity. In the New
Testament time, there was no Bible as we know today. All
that existed in the first-generation church was the Old
Testament and letters that where written to various churches
scattered across the earth.

It was taken for granted that the first believing Christians
had access to the Old Testament books and these letters
(epistles). Thus the subject of written scripture is not part
of the basic doctrinal requirements listed in Hebrews 6:1–2.
Just because the Holy Scriptures do not mention the Bible
and salvation in Hebrews 6:1–2 as two of the basic doctrines
does not mean that the Bible and salvation are not part of
the basic doctrines.

For believers today, the Bible plays a critical role in
the development of maturity and fundamental beliefs
of Christianity. Because of the major role of the Bible,
I choose to teach about the entire Bible as part of the
development of a believer in God. In the second chapter,
I teach all about salvation. In the rest of the chapters, I
teach about the six remaining basic doctrines mentioned
in Hebrews 6:1–2.

In the Bible, there are a few references that mention
a foundation. This foundation is what I want to use as a

true life structure in everyone's lives, including my own. It is extremely critical that anyone who wants to get to know God and become powerful in his kingdom must have a correct foundation. I'm amazed by how few Christians take the time to learn from someone who knows about the Christian foundation. I'm even more amazed by how few pastors and teachers instruct new Christians about Christian foundations. It is extremely critical that anyone who wants to get to know God and become powerful in his kingdom must have the correct foundation.

Any time you intend to learn something or build something, you will need a platform or a foundation. You will need a solid base to work upon. If you're going to produce a product, you will need a factory. If you are going to build a business, you will need a fundamental amount of money to start it. If you want a good, lasting marriage, you will need a foundation of basic understanding and knowledge of relationships.

The Bible uses buildings as an example of a spiritual foundation in God. God wants us to build ourselves into fully mature Christians. Building a proper foundation in God is the act of building and growing into that fully mature spiritual man or woman of God. The Bible compares a believer's life to the construction of a building and also to a farmer, but for now, I will use the analogy of a building. Every believer is called to first build and later be used in God's service. You will not find, in the entire Bible, God using immature or baby Christians to perform his great deeds. You will find God using mature people to perform his wonders and deeds among men and women.

But you, beloved, building yourselves up on your most holy faith, praying in the Holy Spirit. (Jude 1:20, NKJV)

For we are God's fellow workers; you are God's field, you are God's building. According to the grace of God which was given to me, as a wise master builder I have laid the foundation, and another builds on it. But let each one take heed how he builds on it. (1 Corinthians 3:9–10, NKJV)

In whom you also are being built together for a dwelling place of God in the Spirit. (Ephesians 2:22, NKJV)

Rooted and built up in Him and established in the faith, as you have been taught, abounding in it with thanksgiving. (Colossians 2:7, NKJV)

To build a solid and secure building requires a good foundation. A poor or weak foundation will not support much weight of the materials used in a building. A strong and solid foundation will support a lot of weight of the materials that are used in a building. The same principle applies to a believer's life in God's kingdom.

In past centuries, men used a large cornerstone to begin a foundation. The Egyptian architects used this first. The cornerstone was one massive, solid stone. The bigger the stone that was used, the better the foundation. The same parallel is used in Christianity.

Jesus Christ is referred to as the main cornerstone of Christianity. Without Jesus, you cannot build anything in God's kingdom. Jesus is the required cornerstone to anything that is done within God's kingdom. Anything done outside of Jesus is religion—man's attempt to appease God through man's own efforts.

> Now this I say, brethren, that flesh and blood cannot inherit the kingdom of God; nor does corruption inherit incorruption. (1 Corinthians 15:50, NKJV)

> For no other foundation can anyone lay than that which is laid, which is Jesus Christ. (1 Corinthians 3:11, NKJV)

> Therefore, it is also contained in the Scripture, "Behold, I lay in Zion a chief cornerstone, elect, precious, and he who believes on Him will by no means be put to shame." (1 Peter 2:6, NKJV)

> Therefore, thus says the Lord GOD: "Behold, I lay in Zion a stone for a foundation, A tried stone, a precious cornerstone, a sure foundation; Whoever believes will not act hastily. (Isaiah 28:16, NKJV)

God the Father and the Holy Spirit also make up the foundation having a vital role along with Jesus as being the corner stone. The basic subjects of this foundation are: salvation in Jesus, the Bible, faith, repentance, baptisms, laying on of hands, the resurrection of the dead, and eternal punishment. It all begins with Jesus. That is why he is referred to as the chief or main cornerstone. Jesus is like a door to the kingdom of heaven. To get to God and all that he has for us, you have to go to Jesus first.

Therefore, leaving the discussion of the elementary principles of Christ, let us go on to perfection, not laying again the foundation of repentance from dead works and of faith toward God of the doctrine of baptisms, of laying on of hands, of resurrection of the dead, and of eternal judgment. (Hebrews 6:1–2, NKJV)

13When Jesus came into the region of Caesarea Philippi, He asked His disciples, saying, "Who do men say that I, the Son of Man, am?" 14So they said, "Some say John the Baptist, some Elijah, and others Jeremiah or one of the prophets." 15He said to them, "But who do you say that I am?" 16Simon Peter answered and said, "You are the Christ, the son of the living God." 17Jesus answered and said to him, "Blessed are you, Simon Bar-Jonah, for flesh and blood has not revealed this to you, but My Father who is in heaven. 18And I also say to you that you are Peter, and on this rock I will build My church, and the gates of Hades shall not prevail against it. (Matthew 16:13–18, NKJV)

The direct translation of verse 18 explains that Peter's name means small rock or pebble. Rock means a large rock. In verse 18, Jesus is telling Peter that his name means small rock. Jesus is using the word rock in reference to himself. Peter is a pebble, and Jesus is a large rock. Why does Jesus use this analogy? God can't use a pebble for a foundation. God requires a large rock for a secure foundation.

The entire point of these verses is that Peter finally understands through revelation that Jesus is the Messiah, the Son of God. With this revelation to Peter, Jesus is saying that He Himself is like a large rock to build the church of God upon. This statement probably sounded very strange to Peter and the rest. Then Jesus gave them an insight to their calling.

A revelation in the Bible is when God speaks to a person and reveals a fact or certain bits of information. A revelation is God's voice within a person. A revelation is when God is speaking to you personally. I go into more detail about how God speaks to someone in the chapter about faith. This subject is also discussed in the book: *America's Resurrection – A Modern-Day Prophecy.*

Each and every time that God speaks, New Testament believers call it a revelation from God. It is like a being in a classroom after reading the assigned chapter, but you still don't understand the theory being explained. When the professor goes into more detail in the lecture, you suddenly come to understand the theory. This is a revelation in the classroom. A revelation from God is when God speaks to you personally, and you suddenly gain some facts about the kingdom of God from God himself.

> And I will give you the keys of the kingdom of heaven, and whatever you bind on earth will be bound in heaven, and whatever you loose on earth will be loosed in heaven. (Matthew 16:19, NKJV)

Jesus is trying to show the disciples that God desires to use them to build the church of Christ. They probably didn't understand verse 19 until later.

The point of this passage is that Christ is the cornerstone for Christianity and that select people are called to be builders while the rest make up the entire structure of Christianity in a church. I might also mention that God desires to dwell in the midst of his church in the hearts of men and women.

Every believer has a specific task to make up the church structure or church building. The church building is not a material building; instead, it is made up of a group of believers. Each believer is just as important as another. The more people who believe in Jesus, the bigger the church of Christ. As believers grow and mature, they will be shifted to other parts of the building structure.

Whatever the duty or calling, church members are vitally important to the health of the church building. As a member increases in maturity, so will the calling and responsibilities of that individual increase. The more members of a living church, the more powerful the church becomes; God can use His church to destroy Satan's structure as well as convince the world about God. As the church becomes larger, God can pour out more power through his church.

A good solid foundation in every believer's life is the main key to building a powerful church. With a weak foundation, the entire building will be weak, cracked, and unstable—eventually crumbling and falling apart. I have personally witnessed this crumbling and falling with many believers and several new churches within my first fifty years of life.

In whom you also are being built together for a dwelling place of God in the Spirit. (Ephesians 2:22, NKJV)

> For we are God's fellow workers; you are God's field, you are God's building. (1 Corinthians 3:9, NKJV)

So, how does a person build his or her spiritual life? How do you build your life in God's kingdom? What must believers do to build our lives in God? How do we build upon the foundation of Jesus?

Three Steps to Each Phase of Building

There are many phases of building upon the foundation in God's kingdom; in fact, there is no end to building. For each phase that a believer undergoes, there are always three steps that occur. As you begin to build upon Jesus's rock, you will notice these three steps occurring and reoccurring in every phase you encounter. These three steps are also signs that you are building correctly. I call these three steps "The Revelation Steps."

I'll use the verses mentioned above in Matthew 16:13–18 for an illustration how these three steps occur. In the first step, Peter has a direct personal confrontation with Jesus as did all the disciples.

> When Jesus came into the region of Caesarea Philippi, He asked His disciples, saying, "Who do men say that I, the Son of Man, am?" So they said, "Some say John the Baptist, some Elijah, and others Jeremiah or one of the prophets." He said to them, "But who do you say that I am?" (Matthew 16:13–15, NKJV)

Jesus speaks to them all directly. Jesus did not single out Peter. Jesus spoke to all the disciples in the past just like in this direct personal confrontation. This is what is required for step one. You have to have Jesus, God, or the Holy Spirit speak to you directly. You must have a confrontation from one of the three.

For step two, there must also be a revelation within your spirit that accompanies what is spoken. A revelation from God is when someone receives an inner understanding within his or her spirit about what is being spoken. Only God can do this within anyone. You suddenly are experiencing a spiritual understanding that is coming from God himself. No one can understand what a revelation from God is like until they experience one for themselves. A revelation from the Father is the most wonderful and exciting experience that any human can ever experience. This revelation experience can last or linger up to two days. I personally live for the next revelation from God. Getting revelations from God is that exciting.

In verse 17, we read, "Jesus answered and said to him, 'Blessed are you, Simon Bar-Jonah, for flesh and blood has not revealed this to you, but My Father who is in heaven.'"

For the first time, Peter has a revelation from the Father concerning who Jesus really is. The Father puts the revelation of who Jesus is within Peter's spirit. Peter understands with his mind and his spirit.

Two things are happening within Peter at the same time. Jesus is speaking to Peter's mind, and the Father is placing this revelation within Peter's spirit. Every time God speaks to you, it will be to your spirit. God communicates to us through our spirits. By experiencing this, you will truly understand how God speaks to anyone.

In the third step, there is a personal acknowledgement of the revelation of what you just experienced. You will speak about the revelation you have experienced from God. You will find yourself confessing to others about your revelation—even though they may not understand.

> Simon Peter answered and said, "You are the Christ, the Son of the living God." (Matthew 16:16, NKJV)

I'll give a modern-day example. When someone accepts Jesus into his or her heart, these three Revelation Steps occur. Revelations begin when someone hears another preacher talking and telling stories about Jesus. You will hear other people talking about Jesus, but nothing really happens inside you.

One day, you will hear someone, usually a preacher, talking about Jesus and his role in people's lives. When this person speaks about Jesus, a revelation occurs within your spirit. God is revealing within your spirit about Jesus, and within a few minutes, you understand with your mind and spirit what is being spoken and revealed. It's not just with the mind; your spirit is involved now. You understand within your spirit who Jesus truly is and why he came to earth.

You will also know that you must respond with your mouth. You follow the preacher's instructions and confess your sins. In an instant, Jesus cleanses you of your sins, and you are clean within your spirit. You can't keep quiet about this experience because it's so exciting. You will speak to someone else about what happened. This example is the first of many revelations that God wants to bring into everyone's lives.

These Revelation Steps always occur this way for every revelation that you will ever receive from God. These three Revelation Steps are required for building your life in God's kingdom. This is how God establishes growth and maturity in your life and your spirit.

Growth and maturity are controlled by God and not by you. You must build God's way. When you begin building, God will do his part. I have seen tens of thousands of people try to build in God under their own initiatives. They never grow or mature. In fact, they always end up in false doctrines and usually fall away from God. They didn't receive revelations from God.

Building your life in God takes time and patience. The truth is that it takes years to build, mature, and grow in God's kingdom. There is no quick building program for your life in God. If you apply yourself to all the instructions in God's written Word (the Bible), you will be able to build a wonderful, successful life in God's kingdom. I will show you how to build this later.

Also be aware! Getting revelations from God will become very addictive. Each time you receive a revelation from God, you will be living in the ultimate ecstasy. Nothing in life is more exciting than revelations from God. The more revelations you have, the more revelations you'll want. And there is no end to receiving revelations from God. After a revelation, you move onto the next revelation. One revelation at a time is how you build on the foundation.

Understanding the Revelation Steps will help you understand one of God's ways of establishing a true foundation in Jesus. I will be referring to the Revelation Steps many times throughout this book.

Begin Building the Foundation in Jesus

> Therefore, whoever hears these sayings of Mine, and does them, I will liken him to a wise man who built his house on the rock: and the rain descended, the floods came, and the winds blew and beat on that house; and it did not fall, for it was founded on the rock. But everyone who hears these sayings of Mine, and does not do them, will be like a foolish man who built his house on the sand: and the rain descended, the floods came, and the winds blew and beat on that house; and it fell. And great was its fall. (Matthew 7:24–27, NKJV)

What is being painted in this passage? The difference is between a wise man and a fool. God considers a wise man to be the person who reads the Word of God and does what it says. There are various commands written in the Bible that we are all to practice. This involves hearing God's voice and reading the Word of God—and then doing what you're instructed to do. The fool just reads or hears the Word of God but does not do as instructed. I call the fool and the wise, hearers and doers. Being wise involves obeying all of God's words, not just part of them.

Also notice that there is mention of various storms that came along. This is part of real life. It is the same in your life in God. Spiritual storms are going to come along. Satan is going to try to stop you in every attempt at building a foundation or building upon the foundation. Like it or not, you're going to experience Satan and his horde of demons because you choose to mature in God.

Strengthening the souls of the disciples, exhorting them to continue in the faith, and saying, "We must through many tribulations enter the kingdom of God." (Acts 14:22, NKJV)

There are going to be many tribulations in your life in God. Most all these trying times will be from Satan. He is going to attack you mainly to keep you from God. I'm not saying he *might* attack you; instead he is going to attack you over and over and again and again. Satan's attacks are going to occur throughout the rest of your Christian life. In the Book of Job, you will see how serious Satan is. It is critical to build a correct foundation in order to survive so many tribulations or attacks. In *God's Advanced Doctrines,* I expound upon Satan's ways and why God has us suffer tribulations, but for now, I'm only interested in teaching you how to build a strong foundation in Christ.

You need to build a foundation before you begin to build a structure. When I first accepted Jesus into my heart, no one had told me that Satan was going to attack me. I quickly discovered that Satan is continually attacking God's believers. He can be relentless. I was never taught how to deal with such a powerful opposition. Even Bible school didn't deal with the power of Satan. I had to learn it on my own. Very few people know how to go to war against such a powerful enemy. You need a foundation to build upon to experience more of God and grow and mature in his kingdom, and you also need a foundation to be able to weather all the storms or attacks from Satan.

For we do not wrestle against flesh and blood, but against principalities, against powers, against the rulers of the darkness of this age, against spiritual hosts of wickedness in the heavenly places. (Ephesians 6:12, NKJV)

The Bible Is Part of the Foundation

You have Jesus as the cornerstone. You have the three steps to getting revelations from God. Now you must add the Bible—the Word of God.

A believer who has decided to practice the written Word and be a doer of the written Word must become a diligent reader of the Bible. You will have to become a lifetime student of the Bible. I have done this and still study the Bible. God has designed the Bible as a help towards maturity as well as a manual of instructions.

God designed the Bible only for doers. The Bible is only designed and written for the seeker and doer. For anyone else, it will be a mass of confusion. God designed the Bible to work along with the Holy Spirit and the believer. When the doer is reading and studying the Bible, the Bible becomes alive and full of life within your spirit. The Holy Spirit will unlock all the hidden meanings and secrets within the Bible.

I'm forever amazed how people are always trying to use Bible verses to try to persuade non-believers to become believers. This is the stupidest thing I have ever seen Christians do. And if you are one of the Christians who do this, then you're utterly stupid. The Bible is written for believers. It is a mirror for us to see ourselves and what we need to correct in our lives. Quoting verses of scriptures to non-saved people will only do more harm to them than good.

The church is always teaching believers to use the Word of God to bring sinners to repentance. This is so utterly false. Jesus said, "If I be lifted up, I will draw all men unto me." He didn't say if you quote verses of scripture, then men will come to God. Remember the three Revelation Steps? "No man comes to the Father unless he is drawn." you are to work with God. God has to first speak to an individual and do the persuading.

The Bible is intended for believers. You must read and read and read the Bible. This is part of your work as a builder on the foundation.

> It is the Spirit who gives life; the flesh profits nothing. The words that I speak to you are spirit, and they are life. (John 6:63, NKJV)

One of God's ways is that he hides himself. He makes himself difficult—but not impossible—to be found. You have to search for him and anything about him and his kingdom. The reasons he does this are explained in *God's Advanced Doctrines*. Knowing that this is one of God's ways about himself reveals you will have to seek to find him. Part of this difficulty will be in reading the Bible. The translation barrier can really mess things up, but we have all kinds of tools that can resolve this problem.

Another difficulty is coming across apparent mysteries of God in the Bible. God does some very different things, but there are reasons why he does what he does. As you build on the foundation and mature, you will come to understand his seemingly strange ways. It will all be very logical once he reveals these ways to you, but this requires maturity in God and a proper foundation.

> Because narrow is the gate and difficult is the way which leads to life, and there are few who find it. (Matthew 7:14, NKJV)

The entire Bible is designed for doers who are going to have to apply themselves to studying the Bible. When you study and work with the Holy Spirit, you will receive revelations about God. You will be utterly amazed and excited beyond anything you have ever thought possible. You will quickly discover how exciting God is and learn all about his kingdom. I will show you how to work with the Holy Spirit later. I have spent many sleepless nights marveling and rejoicing at the revelations that God reveals, and I'm not usually one to stay awake all night. I have discovered that God is the most exciting being in existence. The doer who does not give up will go on to do the difficult work and attain life in God.

> Ask, and it will be given to you; seek, and you will find; knock, and it will be opened to you. For everyone who asks receive, and he who seeks finds, and to him who knocks it will be opened. (Matthew 7:7–8, NKJV)

> But those who seek the LORD understand all. (Proverbs 28:5, NKJV)

> So now, brethren, I commend you to God and to the word of His grace, which is able to build you up

and give you an inheritance among all those who are sanctified. (Acts 20:32, NKJV)

God's written Word builds you up even to you gaining an inheritance from God. Wow! An inheritance!

All things that the Father has are Mine. All that are Mine I give to you. (John 16:15, NKJV)

And if children, then heirs—heirs of God and joint heirs with Christ, if indeed we suffer with Him, that we may also be glorified together. (Romans 8:17, NKJV)

All we have to do is built through studying the Bible and then practice it. By doing this, we gain an inheritance. That is one of our rewards from God. By being doers and practicing God's rules, we will gain an inheritance. I'm very much interested in gaining an inheritance. This is also called a promise from God.

You will soon notice that there are a lot of promises in the Bible. How wonderful can this be? It just gets better and better. God literally gives promises to doers of his Word. Understand that God is not a liar. This means that all his promises are true. A promise involves God's provision and requires our provision. Every promise has a requirement from each person. You have to take action and be a doer of each promise in order to cause the promise to work in your life.

- False Doctrine: Just claim the promises—and they will happen for you!

When you become a doer, you gain an inheritance and promises from God. Wow! How are all these things possible? Why should God do all this for doers? When you read the Bible, you will discover the answers to these questions.

This leads us to a most important understanding in our walk with God, which is the relationship between Jesus (the Savior) and the Bible. More precisely, this relationship explains how the Word of God interacts between your relationship with Jesus and the Father and the Holy Spirit. You have Jesus, the Father, the Holy Spirit, the Bible, and you the believer. All five must work together. All depend upon each other. All work in harmony together. Without one of the five, nothing will happen.

It is most important to understand that all five of these subjects work together. You must employ all five to grow in God's kingdom or build upon the foundation. Failure to actively participate in all five will not produce growth or maturity. Having knowledge of the Bible is not enough. It's not enough to just have Jesus. It's not enough to just have yourself. It's not enough to just have the Father and the Holy Spirit.

So now, brethren, I commend you to God and to the word of His grace, which is able to build you up and give you an inheritance among all those who are sanctified. (Acts 20:32, NKJV)

A key part of this verse is "which is able to build you up." It does not say that *it will* build you up. It says, "*Which is able* to build you up." This implies that you will have to be a doer, and if you do all that is written, you are going to be built up!

The promise is that if you do all of the provisions, you will be built up. I put this to the test in my life and can tell you that it truly works. The way it all works is that all five—the Father, Jesus, the Holy Spirit, the Bible, and you—work together.

The important part of the verse is that you are going to have to go to work. God is not going to do it all for you. You will literally have to do work. You will have to read the Bible and pray and study the Bible and pray and ask and ponder. When you do all this work, you will be rewarded.

Notice that it doesn't give you a certain time for when this happens. I have seen baby Christians who are twenty years old in Christianity that never grew or developed because they don't do the work. I have seen Christians grow to a certain point and then stop growing because they quit doing the work. Most growth happens slowly, over several years. This is normal in Christianity. A lot of growth depends upon the zeal you have and are able to maintain. Apostle Paul was this way. I'm this way. Sometimes you can grow at a faster pace than normal, but it all still takes time. There is no instant maturity with God.

But those who seek the LORD understand all. (Proverbs 28:5, NKJV)

As you gain revelation understanding, you grow. As you build, you gain many things in heaven and on earth. Most importantly, you become wiser. Also, it is important that you build. The principle is that you must do the building upon the foundation that I'm teaching in this book. God is not going to do the building for you.

You must seek the Lord. Sometimes seeking takes a lot of time and effort. Sometimes seeking requires a lot of effort or work; other times, it doesn't require so much work.

> But without faith it is impossible to please Him, for he who comes to God must believe that He is, and that He is a rewarder of those who diligently seek Him. (Hebrews 11:6, NKJV)

Notice the phrase "diligently seek." This does not say casually seek or sometimes seek. What does diligently seek really mean? You must be aggressive and not give up in your efforts to get answers. You may even have to add some fasting to your seeking. In Greek, diligently means being careful or thoroughly investigating. It means that you want to be sure that your answer is correct. Sometimes the answers seem to be delayed. There are reasons why there are delays to answers, but the one who keeps pounding away will get an answer. The one who gives up will never get an answer. You have to determine and set your heart that you will not give up.

I've talked to thousands of Christians who give up seeking when confronted with delays. There are many reasons why delays occur. If you're going to grow and mature, you are going to experience delays in getting answers to your questions. Delays can become very frustrating, but the faithful seeker will get an answer.

Understand that the subject of this verse is really dealing with getting faith from God, but it also is revealing a principle of how you get faith. It's this principle that I'm interested in and expounding upon. A diligent seeker is seeking faith. In Proverbs 28:5, the seeker will come to understand all things. This is the entire goal of the subject of maturity. As you grow and increase in God, you will understand each level of maturity. I liken it to climbing a ladder or climbing steps in a building. In order to be able to move onto the next step or rung, you have to understand the one you're standing on. This understanding must come through the three steps of revelation.

Some of the steps I had to move to required a long period of time. In fact, some of them took over a year to gain insight and understanding. That can become very frustrating. I'm not trying to discourage you, but I'm being honest with you. Keep knocking, seeking, and asking, and you will get an answer. I only wish I had someone who I knew, in my younger years, about maturing in God's kingdom to help me along.

As you build by praying and reading the Bible, you will soon realize that the entire Bible is true. You will soon learn that the Bible is in itself the supreme authority to all truth. You will come to see that the Bible is part of God and Jesus and the Holy Spirit. You will be in awe at how this can possibly be. The Bible is the written authority of God. Somehow God is intertwined with it. The Bible, for the doer, is literally alive with the life of God. This can only be experienced by the doer. To anyone else who is just reading it, the Bible will be dead. The Bible is written only for the doer. For doers, the Bible is alive and full of life. The Bible can truly become an amazing book.

At this point in this book of foundations, I need to go into more detail about the Bible, the written Word of God. The Bible is part of the foundation. The Bible is not mentioned in the verses that describe the basic foundation found in Hebrews 6:1–2. The Bible is part of the elementary principles of Christ.

You will come to see the importance of the Bible as part of the foundation. You need Jesus as the cornerstone. You also need the Bible. Then we will go on to see repentance, faith, baptisms, laying on of hands, resurrection from the dead, and eternal judgment.

> Therefore, leaving the discussion of the elementary principles of Christ, let us go on to perfection, not laying again the foundation of repentance from dead works and of faith toward God, of the doctrine of baptisms, of laying on of hands, of resurrection of the dead, and of eternal judgment (Hebrews 6:1–2, NKJV).

Notice the words, "the foundation of." This clearly reveals that we need a foundation. Notice also "the elementary principles of Christ." I've already shown what a foundation consists of. Now I need to describe "the elementary principles of Christ."

What are the elementary principles of Christ? One of these principles is the Bible. Another principle is the Word of Christ. Another principle is Jesus being the Son of God. Another principle is Jesus is the Savior of our sins, and there are a few more principles I will discuss later.

First I will define what a principle is. In the Bible, a principle is a truth about God. A principle is literally a fact about God's kingdom. It can also be referred to as a teaching, a doctrine, or an oracle. I use the word *principle* because I expound how the Bible works in practical applications of your life.

When I use the word *doctrine*, I'm referring to a general teaching in the Bible. I use the word *doctrine* to prove the existence of the Bible's principles as facts dealing with one subject. When opposing false doctrines, I use the word *doctrine* and not *principles*. I prefer to use the word *doctrine* when debating others who believe false truths of the Bible. Because of the use of the word *doctrine* in most other religions, I use the Bible's doctrines as arguments to counter the false doctrines that people have developed. For the purpose of this book, I will make use of the word *principle* because I'll be expounding upon the truths of the Bible's facts and facts about God, Jesus, and the Holy Spirit.

For example; Jesus is the savior of our sins. This statement is a true doctrine but it is a general conclusion of the fact of Jesus work. We humans must have a sinless person to take our place of judgment due to our sins in order to have our sentence of sin removed. This statement is a principle in that it is explaining the mechanics of how judgment of sin works.

The word *elementary* is found twice (Hebrews 5:12; Hebrews 6:1) in the New Testament. The Greek word *stoicheon* is also translated in the King James Version as *elements* and *rudiments*. In Hebrew, its meaning is clearly related to the elementary knowledge of Christian truth or doctrine.

Notice the use of the word *elementary* in Hebrews 6:1. *Elementary* is just what it means—very basic. In Greek, it is referred to the ABCs of a language. The basic or the beginning principles of Christianity are written about here in these two verses

> For though by this time you ought to be teachers, you need someone to teach you again the first principles of the oracles of God; and you have come to need milk and not solid food. (Hebrews 5:12, NKJV)

The use of first principles in this verse is the same as beginning or basic principles. As we mature in God, we go on to more complex principles. These more complex principles first require the basic principles to be understood. All this requires time and growth in God's kingdom. There is no way to speed up your growth in God's kingdom. As you learn principles, God will make them real to you through revelations. (Remember the three steps for a revelation?) This is part of the growth process. This is the practical application of biblical principles.

In Hebrews 5:12 (NKJV), we read about a group of Christians who didn't put the elementary foundation principles into practical application and never grew in experiential or revelation knowledge of God. They didn't utilize the foundation. As a result, there were still infants in Christ.

Let's now get back to the Bible as one of the elementary foundations.

God's Word (the Bible) contains thousands of facts. We are concerned with the authority of the Bible and the work or fruit of the Bible. Here is the major fact about the Bible: it is entirely true. No one has ever found the Bible to have one bit of falsehood. Every bit of the Bible came from God. God would move upon various men and women at different times in history and command them to write what he was saying or revealing to them. These men and women were instruments for God to write his words on paper (parchment in the past). So the real author of the Bible is God, not humans. Since God is the author, the Bible is entirely true, it carries its own authority. The authority of the Bible is based upon a characteristic of God himself. This characteristic is that God does not lie nor is there any falsehood in him. This is how we know that the Bible is entirely true.

A good example is in the first chapter of Genesis. Moses wrote about how the earth was created and all the events that led up to the creation of Adam and Eve. How did Moses know all about this working of God? He wasn't there to see it happen! In fact, no man was there to witness any of God's work in the creation of the universe up until the creation of man. How could anyone know this information about God? Through revelation, God revealed what he created to Moses, and he later commanded Moses to write it on parchment. There may have been others that God revealed all this to as well, but Moses was the first to be commanded to record it. This is not man's doing; it is God's doing. God is the author, not man.

Jesus answered them, "Is it not written in your law, I said, you are gods'"? If He called them gods, to whom the Word of God came (and the scripture cannot be broken.) (John 10:34–35, NKJV)

Jesus was defending his claim as being the Son of God against the Jews who didn't believe that Jesus was the Son of God. This is a complicated argument, and I will not attempt to explain it in this book, but take notice of what John is writing as quoting Jesus. Jesus is referring to the men who wrote the Old Testament and is using the word *gods* to describe the writers. It was God speaking to these men who did the writing. These men are referred to as god's (a person with an anointing from God that would make him a little more than the average man of those days). I could go into the Hebrew language, but it would take an entire chapter to define the word *God's* when used with *men*. For simplicity, trust the two verses above to be true.

What I want to point out in these two verses is the use of the Word of God and Scriptures. These two titles are important to the authority of the Bible. When Jesus used the Word of God, he was referring to the Bible's origins coming not from man but from God. The entire Bible came from God through men; thus it is the Word of God, not the word of men. *Scripture* means "that which is written." Scriptures refer to all the written words of God compiled together.

Many other men had received all kinds of revelations about God and did not write them on parchment. If they did write them, God did not intend to use them for the sum total of the Bible. God was highly selective about what was to be put together as the scriptures in the Bible. The prophets spoke about things they were not allowed to write about. Even John—who wrote the above two scriptures— wrote Revelations and saw and heard things that he was commanded not to write. Melchizidek came to Abraham and knew all about God. He obviously had many revelations from God, yet none of his writings are in the Bible. He may or may not have written about any of his revelations. Methuselah walked with God and was taken to Paradise, not having died an earthly death, yet we have nothing written from him.

We can conclude that the Bible was written with God as the original author. The Word of God has the authority of God. God is the writer and owner of the Bible.

The main purpose, throughout the entire Bible, deals with one central theme. It deals with man's sinful state and how to be delivered from this sinful state back into a relationship with God. The Bible deals with the nature and consequences of sin and the way of deliverance from sin. It deals with God's desire that man be delivered from the penalty of sin in order to regain a relationship with him. In every book and every chapter of the Bible, this central theme is dealt with.

If he called them gods, to whom the Word of God came (and the scripture cannot be broken). (John 10:35, NKJV)

Notice the phrase "the scriptures cannot be broken." What does this phrase mean or refer to?

Another way to phrase this would be: "It is impossible to break the scriptures."

It is impossible for the scriptures to have one false fact. It is thus 100 percent true. If there is just one verse that is false or contrary to the rest of the canon of scripture, the scriptures would be broken. What is amazing is that every fact in the Bible is true. Many men and women have attempted to try to disprove many of the Bible's facts, and no one has succeeded. Many men and women have created false doctrines only to learn that these false doctrines don't work. Everyone who has ever studied the Bible and placed into practical application its true facts has learned that it indeed works. The scriptures have the authority of being totally true. I call this the tried-and-proved principle.

At Bible school, many students write notes in their Bibles. An older Christian woman at the Bible school I attended wrote TP next to several verses in various parts of her Bible. When asked what TP meant, she replied, "That means tried and proven." She explained that she would understand a truth and then put it into practice to see if it worked. She would write T next to that truth. T stood for *tried*. Once she witnessed that it worked, she would write P next to the T. The P was for *proven*. I use this example of tried and proven to many people I speak with. Try it for yourself! She had come to see that the Bible is tried and proven, which makes it the authority of God.

Here is an example of authority to what is written. If a king issued a certain edict for his kingdom, then that edict was written for all to read and be made aware of. It became law in the kingdom. The king had the power to enforce that edict. The edict carried the authority of the king. The edict was written by several scribes and was sent throughout the kingdom so everyone would know of the king's latest edict. People write the edict on parchment or paper. These writers were not the authors of the edict. They were just people writing what the king has commanded them to write.

If the edict was transgressed by one of the king's subjects, the king used his authority and issued the penalty described in the edict. Thus, the edict carried the authority of the king. The authority of the king upheld the edict. But if the king did not issue the penalty described in the new edict upon the king's subject, the edict became broken. It was not enforced by the king's authority.

If another of the king's subjects transgressed the king's edict, and the king enforced that edict through his authority, the remaining subjects would be in a state of confusion and would not know what to believe. The king's kingdom would become a broken state. Some edicts were enforced; at other times, they were not enforced. The population would become confused and enter into an attitude of chaos. All edicts would be challenged thus lawlessness and disregard for the king's authority would be sacrificed. The population would enter into an attitude of rebellion against all the edicts. Some would be pardoned, and others would be punished. The rebellion would be squelched, or the rebellion would triumph. If the entire populace rebelled, that king would lose all control of his subjects. That king would either flee or face the edicts of the new rebel government. This example describes what the word "broken" refers to.

What is exciting is for the believer in God, Jesus, the Holy Spirit, and the Bible is knowing that the Word of God is all completely true. All believers can place all their confidence upon the authority of God's written Word. God does and will uphold all of what he teaches and commands. This is the purpose of the Word of God having all authority. We believers can know that every truth and fact that we apply to our lives will work within our lives. The Word of God becomes a solid secure rock. The Word of God becomes a part of our foundation. One of the main reasons why God gave us his written Word is so that we could build a solid foundation.

Believers must begin building by reading the Word of God and applying the truths and facts of the Bible as God gives revelation to each of them. You will not get revelations about the Word of God if you don't read it and study it. When you get the revelation from God that the Bible is the Word of God and the Word of God is part God, part Jesus, part Holy Spirit—all woven together—you will have this part of your foundation intact.

The Bible is Written by God

> All scripture is given by inspiration of God, and is profitable for doctrine, for reproof, for correction, for instruction in righteousness, (2 Timothy 3:16, NKJV)

Notice the word *inspiration*. The exact interpretation should read: The exhaust breath of God. When you and I breathe, we suck in air and then exhaust that spent air from our lungs through our noses. When we speak, we are blowing the spent air from our lungs through our throats instead of our noses. The air passes over our vocal cords, and we produce sounds that we form into speech. In this verse, "the exhaust breath of God" indicates that God is speaking to the writers of the scriptures. Therefore, the way this verse should read in English should be:

> Every scripture is God-breathed, and profitable for teaching, for conviction, for setting aright, for instruction that is in righteousness. (2 Timothy 3:16, YLT)

Through this verse, we learn that God spoke to the writers of the Bible.

- Principle: God's written Word originates from God himself—not men or women.
- Principle: God is the author of the Bible.
- Principle: God designed the Bible for all his followers.
- Principle: The written Word of God is our instruction manual for developing a relationship with God.
- Principle: The Word of God has its own authority as well as God's authority.

How exactly did God speak to these writers?

Knowing this first, that no prophecy of scripture is of any private interpretation, for prophecy never came by the will of man, but holy men of God spoke as they were moved by the Holy Spirit. (2 Peter 1:20–21, NKJV)

Verse 21 explains exactly how God speaks to people. They hear the voice of God through the Holy Spirit, and they can either speak what God says or write what God says. These people are just repeating what the Holy Spirit is saying to them. They had to be careful to write or speak exactly what God was saying. Such people where trained and tested and proven long before God used them to write scripture or speak his words. God uses mature, responsible, tried men and women to speak through. These people are held accountable for speaking or writing God's words.

Nowhere in the Bible does God speak to immature people and command them to write what he has said.

Do not add to his words, lest he rebuke you, and you be found a liar. (Proverbs 30:6, NKJV)

The principle that I want you learn here is that God still works with everyone today just as he did in the Bible. You can hear the voice of God in your own life; you do not have to depend on another person to speak his words to you. The scriptures were breathed by God, and God can and will speak to us today. In the scriptures, we read that God requires every believer to learn to hear the voice of God through the Holy Spirit.

- Principle: God speaks to men and women through the Holy Spirit.
- Principle: God desires to speak to everyone who believes in him.
- Principle: God commands all his followers to hear his voice and spoken words.
- Principle: All believers are required to hear his voice.

But without faith it is impossible to please Him, for he who comes to God must believe that He is, and that He is a rewarder of those who diligently seek Him. (Hebrews 11:6, NKJV)

But He answered and said, "It is written, 'Man shall not live by bread alone, but by every word that proceeds from the mouth of God.'" (Matthew 4:4, NKJV)

Not everyone who says to Me, "Lord, Lord, shall enter the kingdom of heaven, but he who does the will of My Father in heaven." (Matthew 7:21, NKJV)

- Principle: you must know the will of God in your life and then do his will in order to enter the kingdom of God.
- Principle: God requires you to know his will for your life.

Later in this book, I will give more precise detail about how you can hear God speaking to you. For now, I want you to understand that one of your goals is developing a relationship with God in order to hear his voice. To get to a point where you can hear God's spoken words, you have to have a foundation laid within you. These facts that I presented come from God's written Word. I had to read the Word to learn these facts. I chose to believe that the Word of God is all true. I tested the Word of God and heard God's voice in my own life. I have since gone on to hear the voice of God on a continual basis. These verses of scripture are tried and proven in my life. This is how you build upon the foundation.

Let's move on with laying this foundation. But first I would like to address a few problems at this point. You will discover that there are many people who are opposed to God and refute the Bible as not being truly from God. The real truth of these people who oppose God is that they don't want to get to know God. But what makes matters really bad is that the church thinks that it is their calling to save these non-believing people. The church teaches that all Christians are to save every non-believing person. So the church teaches all kinds of strategies about how to accomplish bringing everyone to God. The church seeks to evangelize every soul upon the earth.

However, this is not how the church is designed to function, and the church is not called to be an evangelistic entity. The purpose of the church is to have you rooted and grounded in the written Word of God unto full maturity. From there, knowing God's will for each believer's life. God will go about evangelizing the world. God will deal with the people who refute the authority of the Bible and oppose Him. It is not for the believer to try to convince non-believers that the Bible is God's written authority. When the church attempts to do its own works for God, it does more damage than good.

Another major problem in today's modern church is that most churches don't bother with laying a foundation for the new believer. The purpose of this book is to lay a proper foundation in your life—no matter if you are new or old in God. I have seen that most modern-day believers are still wallowing in infancy. Few believers have moved on to maturity.

Forever, O LORD, Your word is settled in heaven. (Psalm 119:89, NKJV)

The entirety of Your word is truth, and every one of Your righteous judgments endures forever. (Psalm 119:160, NKJV)

Heaven and earth will pass away, but My words will by no means pass away. (Matthew 24:35, NKJV)

- Principle: The Word of God is established not just for life on earth but also for all eternity.
- Principle: All the principles established in God's written Word will be used throughout all eternity.

The entire Bible must be accepted as the absolute truth. A believer cannot pick and choose parts of the Bible as truth and reject the rest as not being true. For example, various churches are allowing gays to take part in their church services. The Bible spells out clearly that homosexuality is an act of sin. Instead of dealing with the sin of the gays, these churches are allowing sin to be practiced in the midst of believers. At present, a few of these churches are having the parts of the scriptures that spell out homosexuality deleted from the Bible. These Bibles are now in print with various verses deleted from the original texts. Because these church leaders have altered the scriptures, extreme judgments from God will follow. Don't tamper with God's written Word unless you want to receive severe and swift judgment.

> But there were also false prophets among the people, even as there will be false teachers among you, who will secretly bring in destructive heresies, even denying the Lord who bought them, and bring on themselves swift destruction. (2 Peter 2:1, NKJV)

- Principle: The entire Bible is the absolute truth about God.
- Principle: Besides the Bible, there is no other book that is the absolute truth of God.

- Principle: If you tamper or alter God's written Word, you will invoke swift and severe judgment from God, usually resulting in death.
- Principle: The entire Bible is totally true.

Covenant

The word testament means covenant. Covenant means agreement. It is an oath-bound promise whereby one party solemnly pledges to bless or serve another party in some specified way. Sometimes the keeping of the promise depends upon the meeting of certain conditions by the party to whom the promise is made. On other occasions, the promise is made unilaterally and unconditionally. The covenant concept is a central, unifying theme of scripture, establishing and defining God's relationship to man in all ages.

In the Old Testament, the Hebrew word for covenant is *berit*. The term probably derives from the verb *bara*, to bind. The noun *berit* originally denoted a binding relationship between two parties in which each pledged to perform some service for the other. The New Testament uniformly uses the Greek word *diatheke* for the covenant idea, avoiding the similar term *suntheke*, which would wrongly portray a covenant as a mutual contract or alliance rather than an oath-bound promise. This does not mean that a covenant may not, in some cases, take on characteristics common to a mutual agreement or contract, but the essence of the covenant concept is clearly that of a binding pledge. 1

The Old Covenant (Old Testament)

From the beginning of man, you will read in the Bible about God making covenants with man. In modern theological learning, we call these periods of time dispensations. You can later learn all about these dispensations in *God's Advanced Doctrines*. For now, all you need to know is that God makes covenants with men and women. Men and women do not make or create covenants with God. Each time God makes a covenant with mankind, it becomes more refined than the previous covenant. For the purpose of a foundation, I want to point out a few facts about the authority of the old and new covenants.[1]

The entirety of Your word is truth. (Psalm 119:160, NKJV)

Thy word is true from the beginning: (Psalm 119:160, KJV)

The first three words at the beginning of the Bible are "In the beginning." King David, who wrote the Psalms, was moved by God to write about the authority of the Bible from the very beginning. The Bible is true from the very first words. This is proof that the Old Testament has the authority of God.

- Principle: The Bible is true from the very first words.

---

1 Holman Illustrated Bible Dictionary (2003 Holman Bible Translator), covenant

Jesus's three confrontations with Satan reveal the authority of the old covenant.

> Then Jesus was led up by the Spirit into the wilderness to be tempted by the devil. And when He had fasted forty days and forty nights, afterward He was hungry. Now when the tempter came to Him, he said, "If you are the Son of God, command that these stones become bread." But He answered and said, "It is written, Man shall not live by bread alone, but by every word that proceeds from the mouth of God." Then the devil took Him up into the holy city, set Him on the pinnacle of the temple, and said to Him, "If you are the Son of God, throw Yourself down. For it is written: He shall give his angels charge over you, and, in their hands they shall bear you up, Lest you dash your foot against a stone." Jesus said to him, "It is written again, you shall not tempt the LORD your God." Again, the devil took Him up on an exceedingly high mountain, and showed Him all the kingdoms of the world and their glory. And he said to Him, "All these things I will give you if you will fall down and worship me." Then Jesus said to him, "Away with you, Satan! For it is written, you shall worship the LORD your God, and Him only you shall serve." Then the devil left Him, and behold, angels came and ministered to Him. (Matthew 4:1–11, NKJV)

Notice that each time Satan came to Jesus, Jesus's first three words were "It is written." Jesus quotes from the old covenant. Satan was attempting to get Jesus to deny his authority and denounce himself as being the Son of God. Jesus was using the authority of the old covenant, which Satan also has full knowledge of. After the third attempt from Satan, he leaves Jesus. Even Satan knows the authority of the old covenant! Satan doesn't try to misconstrue or alter the old covenant writings instead he lies about what is written. He did this with Eve and was successful. Satan backed away from Jesus without an argument. This passage proves that the Old Testament has the authority of God.

- Principle: Satan knows the authority of the Bible.
- Principle: Satan knows the authority of a mature believer.
- Principle: Satan knows who Jesus is—the Son of God—and his authority.
- Principle: Satan boldly approaches anyone, especially believers in God.
- Principle: Satan will attempt to steal believers from God through temptations and lies.

Do not think that I came to destroy the law or the prophets. I did not come to destroy but to fulfill. For assuredly, I say to you, till heaven and earth pass away, one jot or one tittle will by no means pass from the law till all is fulfilled. (Matthew 5:17–18, NKJV)

The law is a covenant given through Moses in the first five books of the Bible. The rest of the Old Testament is an extension of the law up to the new covenant. (Jots and tittles are parts of the Hebrew language writings. A jot is a small mark on top or below Hebrew letters, and tittles are the little curl added to the corners of many Hebrew letters.)

The prophets were men who God used to add new words from God to update the law covenant that was given through Moses. Note that God didn't use the priesthood of the law covenant to add more words; instead, he chose men who he raised up as prophets.

Jesus is in effect saying that the accuracy and authority of the Old Testament is so perfect that not even one tiny piece of it can be altered or removed until all events of humanity are complete. These verses from Jesus are proof that the Old Testament has the authority of God.

- Principle: Jesus submits to the authority of the Old Testament.
- Principle: Jesus relies upon the authority of the Old Testament.
- Principle: Jesus's entire being is intertwined with the Old Testament.

On two separate occasions, the Pharisees and Sadducees try to corner Jesus in an attempt to derail Jesus and his authority by testing him.

The Pharisees also came to Him, testing Him, and saying to Him, "Is it lawful for a man to divorce his wife for just any reason?" And He answered and said to them, "Have you not read that He who made them at the beginning made them male and female?" And said, "For this reason a man shall leave his father and mother and be joined to his wife, and the two shall become one flesh. So then, they are no longer two but one flesh. Therefore, what God has joined together, let not man separate." They said to Him, "Why then did Moses command to give a certificate of divorce, and to put her away?" He said to them, "Moses, because of the hardness of your hearts, permitted you to divorce your wives, but from the beginning it was not so. And I say to you, whoever divorces his wife, except for sexual immorality, and marries another, commits adultery; and whoever marries her who is divorced commits adultery." (Matthew 19:3–9, NKJV)

Jesus said, "Have you not read?" Jesus goes right to the Old Testament Word of God. Jesus even points to the beginning by saying, "At the beginning." Again they argue back with a cornering question about divorce and Jesus responds about true sin and refers to the beginning. He said, "But from the beginning." Jesus was using the authority of the Word of God and the authority of the Bible that was at the very beginning.

The same day the Sadducees, who say there is no resurrection, came to Him and asked Him, saying: Teacher, Moses said that if a man dies, having no children, his brother shall marry his wife and raise up offspring for his brother. Now there were with us seven brothers. The first died after he had married, and having no offspring, left his wife to his brother. Likewise the second also, and the third, even to the seventh. Last of all the woman died also. Therefore, in the resurrection, whose wife of the seven will she be? For they all had her. Jesus answered and said to them, you are mistaken, not knowing the Scriptures nor the power of God. For in the resurrection they neither marry nor are given in marriage, but are like angels of God in heaven. But concerning the resurrection of the dead, have you not read what was spoken to you by God, saying, I am the God of Abraham, the God of Isaac, and the God of Jacob? God is not the God of the dead, but of the living. (Matthew 22:23–32, NKJV)

Jesus said, "Not knowing the scriptures nor the power of God." He takes them to the Old Testament Word of God and reveals their inaccuracy of scriptures. He further attacks their false doctrine of the Old Testament by going to the Old Testament and revealing the truth of the Word of God. Again, Jesus is using the authority of the Word of God in the old covenant.

In both instances, the Pharisees and Sadducees back away from Jesus without further argument. Both groups respected the authority of the Word of God in the scriptures. They came to learn that Jesus knew the scriptures far better than they themselves did. This was a great embarrassment to both groups since Jesus corrected them in the midst of the common people.

Again these verses about Jesus and the two groups are proof that the Old Testament has the authority of God.

Let me introduce an argument that Derek Prince possesses. If the Old Testament scriptures are not absolutely accurate and an authoritative revelation from God, then Jesus was either deceived or was a deceiver. In other words, if the Old Testament scriptures are not 100 percent true, there is no absolute accuracy or authoritative revelation from God—and all of his claims to be the Son of God are false.

Let me introduce my argument. If the entire Bible was written by God, it has the full authority of God. If Jesus is the Messiah or the Son of God, then all that is predicted in the Bible about the Messiah will happen. Also, if the entire Bible is 100 percent true, and you choose to not accept it 100 percent, you will have doomed yourself to eternal hell. You cannot just accept parts of the Bible and reject the rest. God doesn't send you to hell or eternal damnation—you send yourself to hell.

If you want to be blessed in this life with eternal salvation from not going to hell, you had better build a foundation that you can build upon to ensure making it to heaven. This will include accepting the entire Bible at 100 percent whether or not you understand it.

The New Covenant (New Testament)

Notice that Jesus never wrote any words on parchment or paper. Jesus is one of the three Gods: the Father, the Son, and the Holy Spirit. None of these God's write down words on their own doing. Instead, they move upon humans to do this work.

And Jesus came and spoke to them, saying, "All authority has been given to Me in heaven and on earth. Go therefore and make disciples of all the nations, baptizing them in the name of the Father and of the Son and of the Holy Spirit, teaching them to observe all things that I have commanded you; and lo, I am with you always, even to the end of the age." (Matthew 28:18–20, NKJV)

Therefore, indeed, I send you prophets, wise men, and scribes: some of them you will kill and crucify, and some of them you will scourge in your synagogues and persecute from city to city. (Matthew 23:34, NKJV)

Jesus is now commanding the eleven disciples to go into all the nations, telling about him and teaching those who believe. The eleven disciples are to disciple these new believers and teach them to do all that he taught and commanded of the eleven. How is this done? Not just by discipling but also by instructing and teaching from the written Word of God.

Scribes are those who write words on parchment. A scribe usually recorded what was said while a king was speaking. Later in the life of some of the eleven disciples, God had them write on parchment just as God did with others in the Old Testament. Again, God is the author—not people. God's intention was to add to his words from the Old Testament. God wrote the new covenant in the first- and second-generation church. When the disciples went out and taught the written Word of God, all they had was the Old Testament scriptures. God added more information about the New Testament to the Old Testament. The New Testament does not do away with the Old Testament, but it is a fulfillment of the Old Testament.

These things I have spoken to you while being present with you. But the Helper, the Holy Spirit, whom the Father will send in My name, He will teach you all things, and bring to your remembrance all things that I said to you. (John 14:25–26, NKJV)

However, when He, the Spirit of truth, has come, He will guide you into all truth; for He will not speak on His own authority, but whatever He hears He will speak; and He will tell you things to come. (John 16:13, NKJV)

The working of the Holy Spirit moved people to write scriptures. Jesus revealed to the eleven disciples about how God will work in them and through them. Up till that moment in time, the disciples did not know when God intended to use them, let alone how to use them. So they were probably wondering what Jesus was talking about. After they received the Holy Spirit's baptism (recorded in Acts) they began to understand what Jesus was talking about in those verses.

For now, I want you to be concerned with the creation of the New Testament. It carries the same authority from God as the Old Testament does. You need to know that the Old Testament is not done away with. It still is alive and carries the full authority of God. The Old Testament is now being fulfilled since Christ's return to heaven. Today in the age of grace, both the New and Old Testament work together.

But you must continue in the things which you have learned and been assured of, knowing from whom you have learned them, and that from childhood you have known the Holy Scriptures, which are able to make you wise for salvation through faith which is in Christ Jesus. All Scripture is given by inspiration of God, and is profitable for doctrine, for reproof, for correction, for instruction in righteousness, that the man of God may be complete, thoroughly equipped for every good work. (2 Timothy 3:14–16, NKJV)

God has provide for man an entire manual about how to get to know him, how to be saved from your sins, and how to get to heaven in order to dwell with God eternally. Notice the phrase in verse 16: "All scripture *is* given by inspiration of God." Remember that inspiration is better translated as revelation. Also notice in verse 17 that the purpose of the scriptures is for us to become complete and equipped for what we are called to perform. Again, to accomplish all this, you have to have a foundation upon which to build in order to achieve all that God would have you do.

Beloved, I now write to you this second epistle (in both of which I stir up your pure minds by way of reminder), that you may be mindful of the words which were spoken before by the holy prophets, and of the commandment of us, the apostles of the Lord and Savior. (2 Peter 3:1–2, NKJV)

Peter is showing us that the Old Testament and the four disciples stories of Jesus are side by side and both have the authority of God. Peter is not just referring to the four gospels of the New Testament but also to the prophets in the Old Testament. Also notice that Peter is telling us that we must be mindful of what is written. We are being taught that we must continue to keep all that is written in the forefront of our minds. We are not to forget. To do this, we must re-read the scriptures on a continual basis. I personally have learned that it is sufficient to read one to three chapters daily. You can even miss a few days and still be fine. Many times because of the demands of work or busy schedules, it is not possible to have a daily devotion to reading a few chapters. Even I am not always able to keep to this devotion.

> And consider that the longsuffering of our Lord is salvation—as also our beloved brother Paul, according to the wisdom given to him, has written to you, as also in all his epistles, speaking in them of these things, in which are some things hard to understand, which untaught and unstable people twist to their own destruction, as they do also the rest of the Scriptures. (2 Peter 3:15–16, NKJV)

Peter is acknowledging that in his and Paul's lifetime, Peter is seeing that even in Paul's epistles, there is an authority from God. Neither man knew that God's plan was to use some of Paul and Peter's epistles as part of the New Testament. Take notice that Paul never knew Jesus when he was a Pharisee, but he may have seen and heard him. Paul had no teaching from Jesus as Peter had directly from Jesus. Yet the working of the Holy Spirit within Paul is obvious (as seen through his epistles). Paul had to depend upon the old covenant and the Holy Spirit for all the wisdom given to him from God.

These portions of New Testament scriptures are proofs that the New Testament has the authority of God and that God is the author of the New Testament.

The Old and New Testaments Combined

Summing up, the Old and New Testaments are the work of God. The New Testament provides us with a large amount of detail about how God works in and through humans with the Holy Spirit. Such knowledge was not given in the Old Testament. With all this detail provided in the New Testament, you and I can apply the same principles to our lives and get results. The Old Testament contains a few covenants from God while the New Testament contains just one covenant.

We also have learned that God wants us to come to full maturity in him in our spiritual lives. The truth is that coming to full maturity is a requirement for gaining admittance into heaven.

- Principle: To end up in heaven and avoid hell, you will have to grow to full maturity in Christ.
- Principle: You are required to receive revelations from God in the new covenant.
- Principle: To receive revelations from God, you must be maturing in Christ.

A covenant is an agreement from God to man. God's covenant has requirements that you must agree to do to obtain the blessings of that covenant. Today men and women teach that the New Testament provides less for men and women to do than the old covenant did. The truth is that the new covenant demands more from man than the old covenant did.

You have to accept that all scripture in the Bible is authority from God. This is because you are going to have to submit to every truth contained in the Bible. You can't obey part of the Word of God and ignore the rest. If you do, you will deceive yourself—and it will cost you eternity in hell. You are also going to have to know when others are creating false doctrines or lies to try to deceive you from the truth presented in the Bible. You are going to have to know the Bible to act as a guard to your relationship with God. Our biggest enemy is ourselves, and we are also going to have to guard our own lives by using the Bible. I can tell you that the reward of doing all this is well worth the work involved. In fact, it continues to get better and better as the years pass by. And don't worry about being limited to just this lifetime of sixty or eighty years—you have all eternity of rewards and blessings. But you are limited to an average of fifteen years of growing from infancy to full maturity in Christ. Growing to full maturity is one of the wills of God for every believer. Now having said all this, you can see that there is much that you will be involved with in the New Testament.

Remember that it becomes each and every believer's job to guard your faith. God will not do this for you. A pastor cannot do this for you. A believing spouse cannot do this for you. The Bible is rich in wisdom, but it will do you no good unless you read and apply all this wonderful wisdom. King Solomon was anointed with a special gift of wisdom, yet he failed to heed the wisdom that God gave him. As we mature in God, God is expecting us to learn and apply all the wisdom that he is going to be teaching each of us. It is God's desire that we all become wise men and women of God.

The Fruit that God's Words Produce within a Believer

> For the word of God is living and powerful, and sharper than any two-edged sword, piercing even to the division of soul and spirit, and of joints and marrow, and is a discerner of the thoughts and intents of the heart. (Hebrews 4:12, NKJV)

> It is the Spirit who gives life; the flesh profits nothing. The words that I speak to you are spirit, and they are life. (John 6:63, NKJV)

> For this reason we also thank God without ceasing, because when you received the word of God which you heard from us, you welcomed it not as the word of men, but as it is in truth, the word of God, which also effectively works in you who believe. (1 Thessalonians 2:13, NKJV)

> Therefore, lay aside all filthiness and overflow of wickedness, and receive with meekness the implanted word, which is able to save your souls. (James 1:21, NKJV)

> Good and upright is the LORD; therefore He teaches sinners in the way. The humble He guides in justice, and the humble He teaches his way. All

the paths of the LORD are mercy and truth, to such as keep His covenant and His testimonies. (Psalm 25:8–10, NKJV)

For the message of the cross is foolishness to those who are perishing, but to us who are being saved it is the power of God. (1 Corinthians 1:18, NKJV)

What good is your religion if it does nothing for your own personal welfare? Walking with God is all about change. You must be changed into God's requirement to end up in heaven. You must be changed from your old nature to God's nature. Life with God is a total transformation of your life. Being with God is living a holy life, not a worldly life. The word holy means to be separated. We have to learn and be changed into this holy life. Working with God and studying the Bible will produce major effects within your life – this spells change. The Bible can do a world of good within any person, but using the Bible along with God will produce profound changes within your life. If you're not interested in being changed, then walking with God is not for you.

Let's look at several fruits that the Bible will produce within each of us.

Faith

So then faith comes by hearing, and hearing by the word of God. (Romans 10:17, NKJV)

And now, O LORD, the word which You have spoken concerning Your servant and concerning his house, let it be established forever, and do as You have said. (1 Chronicles 17:23, NKJV)

Faith is the number one requirement for anything happening with God. The Bible gives all kinds of instructions and examples about how faith works with God. Without the Bible, we would never understand anything about how God works with men and women and their faith. We should always be reviewing all the examples of faith to serve as reminders to us and help us in our maturing with God. I will go into depth about faith in God in a later chapter.

New Birth

Having been born again, not of corruptible seed but incorruptible, through the word of God which lives and abides forever. (1 Peter 1:23, NKJV)

Whoever has been born of God does not sin, for His seed remains in him; and he cannot sin, because he has been born of God. (1 John 3:9, NKJV)

That you put off, concerning your former conduct, the old man which grows corrupt according to the deceitful lusts, and be renewed in the spirit of your mind, and that you put on the new man which was created according to God, in true righteousness and holiness. (Ephesians 4:22–24, NKJV)

The New Testament explains all about the new birth in Christ. This is the beginning of change toward being

holy unto God. The entire purpose of the New Testament
is to give much teaching to us so that we may maintain
our new birth and continue onward in God. The New
Testament is packed with practical guidelines that will
produce wonderful effects when applied to our lives.
Applying all of these principles will maintain our new
birth and ensure that each of us becomes all that God
intends for us.

Spiritual Food or Nourishment

As newborn babes, desire the pure milk of the word,
that you may grow thereby, (1 Peter 2:2, NKJV)

Now when the tempter came to Him, he said, "If
You are the Son of God, command that these stones
become bread." But He answered and said, "It is
written, Man shall not live by bread alone, but by
every word that proceeds from the mouth of God."
(Matthew 4:3–4, NKJV)

For though by this time you ought to be teachers,
you need someone to teach you again the first
principles of the oracles of God; and you have come
to need milk and not solid food. For everyone who
partakes only of milk is unskilled in the word of
righteousness, for he is a babe. But solid food belongs
to those who are of full age, that is, those who by
reason of use have their senses exercised to discern
both good and evil. (Hebrews 5:12–14, NKJV)

How do you explain spiritual food? As we begin to develop, we all need food just as an infant requires. Without food, we die. As we mature, our diets change. We no longer need just milk as an infant requires. An infant cannot eat whole foods. Once we mature, we can no longer survive on just milk. When growing, we need more whole foods. All the different food groups provide well-balanced nutrition. Because of our different activities, these require more nutrition than the normal amounts of whole foods. Alexander the Great and the Creaser's of the Roman Empire learned that they could march their armies for long distances by eating large quantities of certain types of foods. These armies would arrive at their destinations not being meager and depleted but strong and ready for battle. These well-fed men held a large advantage over those that were attacked. In most wars throughout history, almost all armies suffered greatly from lack of proper nourishment.

So it is in our spiritual lives that we need proper nourishment. Spiritual food is not physical food. Instead, it is faith and wisdom. We need to be helped along with encouragement. We need the wisdom and advice from others that know how to grow and mature. We need rebuking and admonishment. All these things are our spiritual food. Our spiritual food also comes from the Bible. The way we partake of the spiritual food from the Bible is to read it. As we do this consistently, we will develop unto maturity.

Physical Health and Healing

Fools, because of their transgression, and because of their iniquities, were afflicted. Their soul abhorred all manner of food, and they drew near to the gates of death. Then they cried out to the LORD in their trouble, and He saved them out of their distresses. He sent his word and healed them, and delivered them from their destructions. (Psalm 107:17–20, NKJV)

My son, give attention to my words; incline your ear to my sayings. Do not let them depart from your eyes; keep them in the midst of your heart; for they are life to those who find them, and health to all their flesh. (Proverbs 4:20–22, NKJV)

And behold, a woman of Canaan came from that region and cried out to Him, saying, "Have mercy on me, O Lord, Son of David! My daughter is severely demon-possessed." But He answered her not a word. And His disciples came and urged Him, saying, "Send her away, for she cries out after us." But He answered and said, "I was not sent except to the lost sheep of the house of Israel." Then she came and worshiped Him, saying, "Lord, help me!" But He answered and said, "It is not good to take the children's bread and throw it to the little dogs." And she said, "Yes, Lord, yet even the little dogs eat the crumbs which fall from their master's table." Then Jesus answered and said to her, "O woman, great is your faith! Let it be to you as you desire." And her daughter was healed from that very hour. (Matthew 15:22–28, NKJV)

God is very much interested in his believers being physically healthy. There are times we need healing from various problems that arise. I have learned that as we mature and feed on the spiritual food of the Bible, this also keeps us in physical health. It's quite amazing to be in great physical health just from reading the Bible. There are a lot of promises that deal with God protecting our bodies from all the diseases in the world. God will heal problems and keep us healthy. This is really a great health program that is free. I have been healed a few times from work-related accidents that would normally require surgery. God has taught me that there are certain vitamins that will help in the healing process and prevention. As a weightlifter, I've non-intentionally hurt myself a few times. God healed me, and he went on to show me how not to injure myself again. It's a great insurance policy.

God has also taught me how to maintain good health. I've changed my eating habits several times. I've never had a problem with obesity. As I've grown older, my eating habits have changed because the body requires different foods. My dad's hair grayed when he was in his forties. I'm now in my sixties and am just beginning to gray. People think that I'm still in my forties. As a mailman for the United States Postal Service, I was outside in the sun. I should be wrinkled up, but there is very little wrinkling while my co-workers are now wrinkled. A good and proper diet can go a long way, but I also believe that God works within the bodies of his believers to help in the aging process. I do my part, and God does his part.

Understanding

> The entrance of Your words gives light; it gives understanding to the simple. (Psalm 119:130, NKJV)

Notice the last word in this verse: simple. You don't have to be some kind of scholar to grasp the Bible's teachings. The Bible is written for anyone to gain an understanding about God.

Strength against Sin

> Your word I have hidden in my heart, that I might not sin against You! (Psalm 119:11, NKJV)

> Concerning the works of men, by the word of Your lips, I have kept away from the paths of the destroyer. (Psalm 17:4, NKJV)

> Do you not know that you are the temple of God and that the Spirit of God dwells in you? If anyone defiles the temple of God, God will destroy him. For the temple of God is holy, which temple you are. (1 Corinthians 3:16–17, NKJV)

> Or do you not know that your body is the temple of the Holy Spirit who is in you, whom you have from God, and you are not your own? For you were bought at a price; therefore glorify God in your body and in your spirit, which are God's. (1 Corinthians 16–20, NKJV)

Every time I get a revelation from God, I get really excited. With each revelation, I gain more insight and knowledge. Life becomes more and more enlightened. This truly is the meaning of life. Each revelation brings more questions. You understand more about the past up to the present. The future even becomes more insightful. The more you seek God, the more he is required by his promises to reveal more about himself and his kingdom. The more information you collect, the less confusing life is. When we are young in God, there are a lot of confusing ideas and truths. But when we mature, the more we understand—and life is no longer a long list of confusion. Life becomes more exciting as we mature.

With all this knowledge and understanding, our minds are more at peace with everyone and everything. We eventually learn that God has everything under total control. We no longer worry or fret. Our lives are more at peace than in the past. The more we gain, the more exciting life becomes. Excitement is what the world lusts after. But in a short time, there is no more excitement, and all becomes dull and boring. But with God, life is always on an incline, becoming much richer and more exciting. You become more and more like him. And as you do this, he opens up so much more of his wealth and riches. One undeniable fact is that you never get bored serving the Lord. Having a mind full of knowledge and understanding about God's kingdom through revelations is a utopia in and of itself.

Power over Satan

> In addition to all, taking up the shield of faith
> with which you will be able to extinguish all the
> flaming arrows of the evil one. And take the helmet
> of salvation, and the sword of the Spirit, which is the
> word of God. (Ephesians 6:16–17, NKJV)

Satan is alive on the earth. He has not been placed into the pit yet. He is still allowed to roam and attack anyone he chooses. Satan still has thousands of demons that are part of his kingdom. The only thing remaining for the demons on the earth is to attack man. Why are they still allowed to do this? This is explained in detail in *God's Advanced Doctrines*. For now, all you need to know is that all the demons are here to try to kill, steal, and destroy. God teaches in the Bible how we are to battle against these demons. It becomes our job to accomplish this. When we enter into the kingdom of God, we are plunged into a war zone. To survive, you must learn how to fight all these demons. The more we mature, the more insight we gain into Satan and the demon world. And the more insight we gain, the better we can battle against the demons and gain victory over them. The more we mature, the more we learn—and the more effective we become against these demons.

No church I've ever attended has taught about Satan's kingdom on earth. I never gained much information about Satan from any church. But as I matured, I had hundreds of encounters with the demon world. I had to learn firsthand about Satan. I lost a few battles because I didn't know how to battle and win. As a result, I suffered needlessly. Now that I have a lot of knowledge about Satan and the demons,

I can effectively defeat them in each and every encounter. I have the victory over Satan. I didn't use to have victory over the demon world, but as a result of the many battles, I eventually learned the hard way. I now find victory in every encounter with them. I'm no longer at Satan's mercy; instead, Satan now suffers me.

Cleansing and Sanctification

Who can say, I have made my heart clean, I am pure from my sin? (Proverbs 20:9, NKJV)

Husbands, love your wives, just as Christ also loved the church and gave Himself for her, that He might sanctify and cleanse her with the washing of water by the word, that He might present her to Himself a glorious church, not having spot or wrinkle or any such thing, but that she should be holy and without blemish. (Ephesians 5:25–27, NKJV)

You are already clean because of the word which I have spoken to you. (John 15:3, NKJV)

But we are bound to give thanks to God always for you, brethren beloved by the Lord, because God from the beginning chose you for salvation through sanctification by the Spirit and belief in the truth. (2 Thessalonians 2:13, NKJV)

Elect according to the foreknowledge of God the Father, in sanctification of the Spirit, for obedience and sprinkling of the blood of Jesus Christ: grace to you and peace be multiplied (1 Peter 1:2, NKJV)

Sanctify them by Your truth. Your word is truth. (John 17:17, NKJV)

To open their eyes, in order to turn them from darkness to light, and from the power of Satan to God, that they may receive forgiveness of sins and an inheritance among those who are sanctified by faith in Me. (Acts 26:18, NKJV)

For they indeed for a few days chastened us as seemed best to them, but He for our profit, that we may be partakers of His holiness. (Hebrews 12:10, NKJV)

But as He who called you is holy, you also be holy in all your conduct, because it is written, "Be holy, for I am holy." (1 Peter 1:15–16, NKJV)

I beseech you therefore, brethren, by the mercies of God, that you present your bodies a living sacrifice, holy, acceptable to God, which is your reasonable service. And do not be conformed to this world, but be transformed by the renewing of your mind, that you may prove what is that good and acceptable and perfect will of God. (Romans 12:1–2, NKJV)

For whom He foreknew, He also predestined to be conformed to the image of His Son, that He might be the firstborn among many brethren. (Romans 8:29, NKJV)

As His divine power has given to us all things that pertain to life and godliness, through the knowledge of Him who called us by glory and virtue, by which have been given to us exceedingly great and precious promises, that through these you may be partakers of the divine nature, having escaped the corruption that is in the world through lust. (2 Peter 1:3–4, NKJV)

Sanctification involves change. Sanctification means to be separated unto holiness; to be made pure from impurity, to be made more in the likeness of Jesus. The Word of God has this ability to change us and make us holy or sanctify us. It doesn't all happen at once, but it will happen over time. Reading the Bible is going to do a lot to sanctify you. Reading it on a continual basis is going to slowly transform you and make you more holy unto God. Holy means to be separated from something into something else. We lived in sin and wickedness, and now we are being changed unto being clean and pure. We become separated from sin and wickedness. Only Jesus can perform this cleansing for us. The Bible helps keep us separated from our evil natures. A great practical fruit from the Bible keeps us sanctified.

A Mirror

For if anyone is a hearer of the word and not a doer, he is like a man observing his natural face in a mirror; for he observes himself, goes away, and immediately forgets what kind of man he was. But he who looks into the perfect law of liberty and continues in it, and is not a forgetful hearer but a doer of the work, this one will be blessed in what he does. (James 1:23–25, NKJV)

But we all, with unveiled face, beholding as in a mirror the glory of the Lord, are being transformed into the same image from glory to glory, just as by the Spirit of the Lord. (2 Corinthians 3:18, NKJV)

I like this verse because the Bible is a mirror of seeing yourself and also seeing what you should be in God. The Bible works as checks and balances. You read it and are reminded about what you're not doing. The Bible reminds us of what we need to be doing in our lives. There is a lot to remember to do. As time passes, we forget certain things we should be doing. The Bible will remind us of all the things we are supposed to be doing. It serves to jog our memories about what we should be doing. It is an aid to remind us of our duties.

But the mercy of the Lord is from everlasting to everlasting on those who fear Him, and his righteousness to children's children, to such as keep His covenant, and to those who remember His commandments to do them. (Psalm 103:17–18, NKJV)

All these fruits are produced in us as we read the Bible. You must do your part to make these fruits occur within your life. You have to take time to read and study the Bible. Developing a daily habit to spend time reading a few chapters from the Bible will make a major change in your life. You *will* be changed—not *might* be changed. I can tell you from my own life that it does work. And to this day—after forty years of being born again from the Holy Spirit—it still works.

Another great benefit I've learned to do is to memorize certain Bible verses that carry truth and are meaningful to my life. I've learned that memorizing and reviewing verses goes a long way toward maturity. As I gain new revelations from God, there are always verses that describe each revelation. Memorizing these verses helps you in your maturity. These verses will help keep you excited and up to date. They are a great aid in helping to not forget.

CHAPTER 2

Being Saved from Sin

S alvation from sin is not included in the list of the six foundations found in Hebrews 6:1–2.

> Therefore, leaving the discussion of the elementary principles of Christ, let us go on to perfection, not laying again the foundation of repentance from dead works and of faith toward God, of the doctrine of baptisms, of laying on of hands, of resurrection of the dead, and of eternal judgment. (Hebrews 6:1–2, NKJV)

Salvation is not listed because it is taken for granted. Why would you write a letter to the Hebrew believers if they were not already believers having been saved? A few verses down, we read that "things that accompany salvation." This probably refers to the basic foundations and elementary principles of Christ found in the first verse.

But, beloved, we are confident of better things concerning you, yes, things that accompany salvation, though we speak in this manner. (Hebrews 6:9, NKJV)

Notice the phrase; 'things that accompany salvation.' Again salvation is not listed in Hebrews 6:1-2 because it is taken for granted. I decided to include salvation in this book as part of the foundation. Why would I do that since you are probably saved as the Hebrews where saved? Here's why. For the first-generation believers, there were no false doctrines concerning salvation. It wasn't till the second generation of the church that false doctrines began to appear. This letter to the Hebrews was written to the first or second-generation church. Two thousand years later, there are many false doctrines about salvation in today's church.

As I have come to know all about God in my lifetime, I have applied all the foundations and built a rock-solid life in God. While building my life in God, I have come to clearly see that today there are many false doctrines concerning salvation. If the believer is continually seeking God, the Holy Spirit is going to continually be leading him into more truth about God and the Bible. Proverbs 28:5 says, "Those who seek the Lord understand all things." Conversely, gaining more truth will also cause you to see what is false.

Part of this seeing and learning the truth involves God unraveling falsehoods. I had to go through this process. This becomes an involved process for the Holy Spirit. We shouldn't have to undergo being corrected of false doctrines. This becomes an extra burden for the Spirit. It also becomes an extra strain for the believer. If you're listening to and following the Holy Spirit, he will reveal what is false and what is true (John 16:13). All this takes time and working with the Holy Spirit. This is one of the roles of the Holy Spirit.

Another reason for including salvation in this book is few of the Christians I have met have obtained true salvation. Most Christians have only tasted salvation, but they don't know how to go on into total salvation. It's like they have put their foot into the swimming pool but have never dived into the pool. They don't know that there is a pool to dive into. I would like to show these believers that there is so much more to know about salvation. Only having tasted of salvation will cost you hell.

Another reason for teaching salvation in this book is that I have met thousands of people who think they are saved, but they haven't been saved. It's amazing to me how all the different churches twist the Bible and are able to convince people that they are saved. All this involves false doctrines about salvation.

Another reason is for those who don't know about salvation.

Many years ago, Jim Jones taught false doctrines about salvation. In the 1950s, Jim Jones formed a church in San Francisco called the People's Temple. In the 1970s, the People's Temple relocated to Jonestown, Guyana. On November 18, 1978, the 911 members of this church committed suicide. The church had become grossly indoctrinated with false doctrines about salvation.

Heaven's Gate was an American UFO religion doomsday cult based in San Diego, which was founded in the early 1970s by Marshall Applewhite (1931–1997) and Bonnie Nettles (1927–1985). On March 26, 1997, the group committed mass suicide in order to reach what they believed was an alien spacecraft following the Comet Hale–Bopp. Because of their false doctrines, they believed that the earth was about to be "recycled" (wiped clean), and the only way to survive was to commit suicide and join the alien spacecraft. Again, this church was grossly wrong about salvation.

The Bible clearly teaches us that we are not to murder and that starts with ourselves. These cults were teaching people that if they committed suicide, they would end up in heaven or go on to another place. People are willing to believe anything. God provides facts in the Bible that can be proven. Your salvation in God is based upon facts, but believing in doctrines that have no facts is foolishness. Yet thousands of people are out there doing just that. I can't make people see what is false or force people to believe what is true. All I can do is present the truth of the Bible. You're the one who must choose what to believe. You must determine what is true from what is false. Remember that the Holy Spirit will guide us into all the truth.

> However, when He, the Spirit of truth, has come, He will guide you into all truth; for He will not speak on His own *authority,* but whatever He hears He will speak; and He will tell you things to come. (John 16:13)

In this book, I'm going to reveal the many false doctrines that the church is teaching today. I have come to see what is true and false, and if I did not share these things, I would be lying to you. I will be writing about some things that most of you have never heard before. I will use the Bible to back up my insights. I will also be doing a lot of Bible study to help you understand what the scriptures are saying.

I'll begin by showing you what salvation is in the Bible. For those who already think you know what salvation is, try to keep an open mind with what I'm writing in this chapter. You are going to find it difficult to accept what I'm writing. I'm spelling out what the Bible is teaching, and this is going to go against much of what you've been taught. Remember that I'm only writing what the Bible is teaching and expounding upon what is written in the Bible. When you're done reading this chapter, it is your decision to accept what God has written in these verses—not what some man or woman taught you in the past.

God is your judge—not that man or woman who taught you false doctrines. In the end, it's just you and God facing each other on Judgment Day, and you will be judged for what you have chosen to believe. The things that people do in this life are based upon what they believe. Every person who has ever lived believes in something.

- Principle: What you do in life is based upon what you believe.
- Principle: It is impossible to not believe in something.

Salvation

Let's start looking into the Bible to learn what it is truly teaching about salvation.

If you love Me, keep My commandments. And I will pray the Father, and He will give you another

Helper, that He may abide with you forever—the Spirit of truth, whom the world cannot receive, because it neither sees Him nor knows Him; but you know Him, for He dwells with you and will be in you. (John 14:15–17, NKJV)

But the Helper, the Holy Spirit, whom the Father will send in My name, He will teach you all things, and bring to your remembrance all things that I said to you. (John 14:26, NKJV)

But when the Helper comes, whom I shall send to you from the Father, the Spirit of truth who proceeds from the Father, He will testify of Me. (John 15:26, NKJV)

However, when He, the Spirit of truth, has come, He will guide you into all truth; for He will not speak on his own authority, but whatever He hears He will speak; and He will tell you things to come. (John 16:13, NKJV)

Notice the Holy Spirit is referred to by Jesus as the "Spirit of truth" and the "Helper." If you keep the commandments of Jesus by doing what Jesus said to do, he will also give you the helper, the Holy Spirit, and the Spirit of truth as mentioned in John 14:15–17. In John 14:26, the Holy Spirit is intended to be our teacher. Notice that the Holy Spirit is to teach us all things, not some things. You could say that one of the desires of God is that we learn "all things." In John 16:13, the Holy Spirit's job is to guide us into all the truth—not some of the truth. Again God wants us to obtain all the truth. Also notice in John 14:17 that the Holy Spirit is to dwell inside our bodies.

Wow. At the very beginning, we learned that the Holy Spirit is intended to be our teacher; this comes directly from God. It is important to know that salvation involves the working of the Holy Spirit.

I would also like to interject a startling and profound truth about God. I'm not going to go into showing you throughout the entire Bible all the proofs to back up what I'm about to write because it would take an entire book to do this. In *God's Advanced Doctrines,* I go into much detail concerning this subject, but it is important to dive a little into this subject at this point.

God, Jesus, and the Holy Spirit are three separate beings. All three are called God because they have far more in their makeup than humans and angels have. A being who possesses more abilities than humans is considered to be a god. Just as an animal compared to a human, we would be gods over animals. As you read the Bible from cover to cover, you will see this to be true.

There is no such thing as the Trinity. The Trinity is a false doctrine. Knowing that there are three beings of God's will help you to understand many of the things I write about. It is important to understand that the Father, the Son, and the Holy Spirit are three separate individuals. Failure to get this correct will result in massive confusion, and you will never understand the roles of these beings in the Bible and in your personal life. I expound in more detail about this in *God's Advanced Doctrines.*

Then God said, "Let Us make man in Our image, according to Our likeness; (Gensis 1:26, NKJV)

Notice this verse is using the plural word Us. Who is us? It's not the angles but rather the Father, the Son, and the Holy Spirit. If God were three beings in one it would be more accurate to write *Let me make man in my image, according to my likeness.*

- False Doctrine: There is no such thing as God being three persons in one person.
- Bible Principle: The Father, Jesus, and the Holy Spirit are three separate beings.

The Holy Spirit has several roles to perform. One of the Holy Spirit's roles is to lead us into all the truth as seen in the above verses.

Nevertheless I tell you the truth. It is to your advantage that I go away; for if I do not go away, the Helper will not come to you; but if I depart, I will send Him to you. (John 16:7, NKJV)

Notice that the Holy Spirit is a separate being. Also notice that another role of the Holy Spirit is to be a helper to us. Also notice that Jesus is saying, "I tell you the truth." Is Jesus lying or speaking the truth? Also notice that this is a promise to all believers. With this, let's go on to read more about salvation.

- Principle: The Father, Jesus, and the Holy Spirit are three separate beings.
- Principle: Each of the three performs different roles, separate from each other.
- Principle: The Holy Spirit will guide each of us into all the truth.

- Principle: The Holy Spirit is to dwell inside of each believer.
- Principle: It is not the job of Jesus to guide us into all the truth.
- Principle: The Holy Spirit is a guide.
- False Doctrine: There is no such thing as the Trinity.
- False Doctrine: The Father, Jesus, and the Holy Spirit are not three in one person.

But seek first the kingdom of God and His righteousness, and all these things shall be added to you. (Matthew 6:33–34, NKJV)

This verse is really referring to God taking care of all your basic earthly needs during your life on earth, but it also is a universal principle that can be applied to all other areas of your life. When you are seeking God and his righteousness, God is going to be giving to you. This is a promise, but as with all promises, you are required to do your work.

Why do I begin with this verse? Because you have to be a seeker of God and his righteousness. His "righteousness" refers to being right and not being wrong. If you don't do the work of seeking, nothing is going to happen for you. I see millions of believers in the church, but few are seekers. There are believers, and there are seekers. There are very few seekers. The Bible teaches us that we are to be seekers and not just believers. To be a seeker, you must first become a believer.

- Principle: When you seek God's kingdom and his righteousness, he is going to be giving to you.
- Principle: We are to seek God's kingdom not just God himself.

- False Doctrine: All you have to do is believe in Jesus, and God will do the rest.
- False Doctrine: All you have to do is believe in Jesus and go around claiming things, and they will become yours.
- False Doctrine: Name it—and claim it.

Believers will never get to heaven. They think that all they have to do is believe. Only the seekers will end up in heaven (Matthew 7:21). Seekers find the will of God, not believers. You must seek the kingdom of God and his righteousness. You can't just seek one; both must be sought after. This must be your goal throughout your entire life. "God, I want more of your kingdom, and I want more of your righteousness. I hunger and thirst for your righteousness. I want to know more about your kingdom. I want to know what you would have me do in my lifetime on earth." Finding the personal will of God for your life is considered righteousness unto God. This is what this verse is teaching us. And when God shows us a little more, he amazingly fulfills the promise associated with the directions.

What is seeking the kingdom of God, and what is seeking his righteousness? Most people are taught by the church that all you have to do is seek God, and he will give you what your heart desires. When everyone tries this, they discover that it doesn't work. How profound! Something is wrong there—and God is not the one who is wrong. The church didn't teach you the truth. The church is wrong in what they taught.

- Principle: As you read the Word of God, learn to read it and not ignore parts of it!

- Principle: All promises are accompanied by directions to be carried out in deed.
- False Doctrine: All you have to do is just believe in God to be saved.

22But be doers of the word, and not hearers only, deceiving yourselves. 23For if anyone is a hearer of the word and not a doer, he is like a man observing his natural face in a mirror; 24for he observes himself, goes away, and immediately forgets what kind of man he was. 25But he who looks into the perfect law of liberty and continues in it, and is not a forgetful hearer but a doer of the work, this one will be blessed in what he does. 26If anyone among you thinks he is religious, and does not bridle his tongue but deceives his own heart, this one's religion is useless. 27Pure and undefiled religion before God and the Father is this: to visit orphans and widows in their trouble, and to keep oneself unspotted from the world. (James 1:22–27, NKJV)

Again, it is written that we are to be doers of the word of God. In verse 25, the doer looks into the perfect law of liberty. Notice the use of the word *liberty*. God is a god of freedom and liberty and desires us to live this way. If we continue looking or seeking and remain being doers, we will be blessed and free. In verse 27, we also read "and to keep oneself unspotted from the world." God wants us to remain in the truth and not venture into false teaching. Unspotted is referring to not accepting other false lies or false doctrines.

I think that you get the idea about what God is writing to his believers. God desires us to know all the truth. He gives us the Holy Spirit as a guide and teacher to gain all the truth. God wants us to seek him to find out what he would have us do in our lifetimes on earth. This brings us back to the subject of salvation.

Because of the work of the Holy Spirit in my life and my seeking God and maturing in God's kingdom, I have come to see a lot of false doctrines concerning salvation. These false doctrines prevent us from ever accomplishing anything with God.

The entire purpose of salvation is to be able to end up in heaven and not in hell. Most people who have accepted Jesus into their lives have done so for this very main purpose. The main purpose and goal of accepting Jesus into your heart remains the overall objective—to not be sent to hell and to end up in heaven! This main goal for all believers is right and proper. It is summed up as fearing God.

This chapter is all about how we get to heaven and how we find salvation from hell!

Studying The Bible

Before I get started, I would like to address a major problem our generation faces that the first generation of Christians didn't have. Once you see this dilemma, I think you'll agree that this problem needs to be understood before you begin to build on the foundation.

This major problem is false teachings. False teachings or false doctrines are in fact the biggest dilemma in our present-day church world. These false teachings will prevent people from ever getting to heaven. I'll soon show you this from the Bible.

Today, most people pay little attention to false doctrines. As a believer, you must give a lot of attention to what is true and false because if you don't, it will cost you heaven. Satan has introduced many false doctrines into the church to keep men and women from learning how to be saved unto heaven. Satan doesn't want anyone from God's creation to go to heaven. Satan's goal is to steal every one of us away from God so we also end up in hell with him. The very first thing that happened to Adam and Eve was Satan told lies or falsehood about God.

I'm going to attack a lot of these false doctrines and show you what the Bible really says about salvation unto heaven. You will probably find many of the subjects that I attack to be very offensive. Be assured that these reactions are quite normal. During your reading of this chapter and as you struggle with your reactions, keep strongly focused upon the Bible verses that I'm going to present to you. Remember that I'm attacking false doctrines, many of which the modern church has taught you. It is very difficult to come to realize that church pastors and leaders and priests have lied to you and taught false teachings about God. They do not know the truth.

I think that most of these church leaders mean well, but they really don't know what the truth is. Today, most ministers go to Bible School. Once they graduate, they are ordained as ministers and are supposed to be able to know the truth about God and the Bible. But what did they learn in Bible school? All of them learned what their Bible professors believed. If these professors don't know the truth, then they pass along only what they know, whether it is true or false.

When I was in Bible school, I only learned what the professors knew and believed. I accepted all that they taught. I thought that all the professors knew the truth about God so I never questioned what I was being taught. After all, they were the professors, and such a position must have meant they knew things. The professors even used Bible verses and Greek and Hebrew as they taught about biblical principles. But they only taught us what they wanted us to know.

I noticed in my last year of school that the professors never allowed us to challenge what they were teaching. I did challenge a few of them on occasion, but I was ignored or told that my concerns were not that major. Bible school was good in that I learned some wonderful things, but when it came to doctrinal issues, I had many unanswered questions.

I graduated from Bible school and knew the doctrines of what was taught at that school. As I matured in God, the Holy Spirit had to go back and untangle part of the mess that those professors had taught me. This took several years of working with the Holy Spirit. Had I been taught the correct truth about the Bible, I wouldn't have had to go through all this untangling. But praise be to God that he did perform all this work within my life through the working of the Holy Spirit. Going to a Bible school does not ensure that anyone will know all let alone much of the truth. Maturity in the Holy Spirit will ensure us of this. If anything, when much of what is taught is not the truth then this is proof that there is no maturity within that individual in God's kingdom.

The promise in James 1:22–27 is true. Now I have no more confusion. I can now perform the acts that God calls me to do with power. But best of all, I know that I'm going to heaven and not hell. The more truth you have about God, the clearer the Bible becomes, and the more assurance you have within your heart and mind that what you believe is truly correct. In fact, now that I have the truth, it becomes easy to see all the false doctrines and lies within the church.

This is how I'm going to introduce what the Bible teaches about salvation. I'm going to use many of the scriptures that deal with salvation. Some will be a little confusing, and I'll use Greek and Hebrew to help get what is being translated to our English version. Once you have all these verses of scripture, I'll bring them all together. At the same time, I'll expose many of today's false doctrines. You must read and reread these verses. Some of them you might even memorize. If you're using a laptop or tablet, you might use copy and paste to a word processor and then print them to be able to have them all together for convenience's sake.

Bad Bible Study Habits

I want to point out a common but dangerous practice of Bible Study that most people make including people from past history. Most men and women over the past centuries have used these bad study techniques including Martin Luther and John Calvin to name a few. Just about everyone I have ever studied—and what these church leaders believe— has a main flaw in approaching Bible study. They begin with one scripture that contains a principle, fact, or truth. At some point in their lives, they have come to understand this fact or principle. They begin to build all their experiences upon this one principle. They go searching through the Bible for other verses that support this principle. They draw conclusions or create theories. They begin to make theories about this principle and how it applies to other parts of their lives. They search for Bible verses to support these theories, and they find verses that can support their theories. In fact, you can make up any theory and find a verse in the Bible that will seemingly support your theory. But as church leaders do this, they must use that verse of scripture out of the context of what that entire subject in the Bible is dealing with.

I'll make up a false teaching here as an example using Bible verses to support my made-up doctrine so that you can get an idea of how easy it can be to make this blunder. John 11:35 says, "Jesus wept." That is a fact. I could then theorize that godly men and women must be able to weep. I could go on to say that all men and women of God must be able to weep or they are not men and women of God. I could pull out a scripture that says, "We are to be like Christ," (John 13:15) to support my theory. I could add that God will only use men and women who weep "now as He drew near, He saw the city and wept over it," (Luke 19:41). I could add to this theory that to be a Christian, you must be able to weep on occasion "So Peter went out and wept bitterly." (Luke 22:62). I could add more scripture to support this belief by finding other scriptures that deal with weeping. It could later be added that unless you have the ability to weep as Christ does, you will end up in hell because you are not like Christ.

To create this fictional theory, I had to take the first verse out of context with that portion of the Bible. Then I had to take the other verses out of their contexts to make them fit my fictional theory. The context of the first verse is that Jesus went to raise Lazarus from the dead. As he was with Mary, he saw her in great sorrow and weeping along with the other weeping Jews who came with her. Jesus wept as they all were walking to the grave.

And many of the Jews had joined the women around Martha and Mary, to comfort them concerning their brother. Then Martha, as soon as she heard that Jesus was coming, went and met Him, but Mary was sitting in the house. Then Martha said to Jesus, "Lord, if You had been here, my brother would not have died. But even now I know that whatever You ask of God, God will give You." Jesus said to her, "Your brother will rise again." Martha said to Him, "I know that he will rise again in the resurrection at the last day." Jesus said to her, "I am the resurrection and the life. He who believes in Me, though he may die, he shall live. And whoever lives and believes in Me shall never die. Do you believe this?" She said to Him, "Yes, Lord, I believe that You are the Christ, the Son of God, who is to come into the world." And when she had said these things, she went her way and secretly called Mary her sister, saying, "The Teacher has come and is calling for you." As soon as she heard that, she arose quickly and came to Him. Now Jesus had not yet come into the town, but was in the place where Martha met Him. Then the Jews who were with her in the house, and comforting her, when they saw that

Mary rose up quickly and went out, followed her, saying, "She is going to the tomb to weep there." Then, when Mary came where Jesus was, and saw Him, she fell down at his feet, saying to Him, "Lord, if you had been here, my brother would not have died." Therefore, when Jesus saw her weeping, and the Jews who came with her weeping, He groaned in the spirit and was troubled. And He said, "Where have you laid him?" They said to Him, "Lord, come and see." Jesus wept. Then the Jews said, "See how He loved him!" (John 11:19–36, NKJV)

This example of creating false doctrines shows how men and women of the past and present create false doctrines. They come into false beliefs by taking a verse or a few verses and then begin to build upon those verses. Those verses of scripture are most always taken out of context. Two other difficulties associated with false doctrines also arise. One is interpretation of the scripture, and the other is neglecting the other scriptures relating to that subject.

Here is another point about creating false doctrines. People think that God is a certain way or that God has certain characteristics. They take this idea about God and choose to believe it without any support. In order to prove that their idea is a truth about God, they go to the Bible to find scriptures to back up their ideas. To do this, they must take verses out of context of the subject. These people become so misaligned that they end up creating a whole new sect or cult of religion, such as John Calvin, Mormonism, Islam, Muslim, New Age, Jim Jones, the Comet People, Trinity believers etc. If these people have a following, they will then write a bible or Bible commentary of their own, including all their false ideas for their followers. Every book they write contradicts itself many times. The truth about these people is that they don't want to know the truth about God. They want to have a following because of pride and the desire to be heroes or be worshiped as leaders.

The method these false teachers use is always the same. They either have an idea and go about trying to prove an idea to be true through finding select Bible verses—or they begin putting verses together that seem to be suggesting or saying certain facts. This method is dangerous and will always lead you astray because in so doing they must ignore other verses of the Bible.

If you want to go to heaven and avoid going to hell, you're going to have to do things God's way, not your way. If you want to grow in God and learn about his kingdom, you're going to have to do a lot of reading, studying, and praying. You're going to have to go to work. God can't do this work for you. Just learning is not going to cause you to grow. Increasing your knowledge of God is not going to get you to heaven. To end up in heaven you are going to have to mature in God and in the truth.

Another common mistake that many people make is thinking they must understand the knowledge of God before they can apply it to their lives. Remember that the Holy Spirit guides us into all truth. When you see a fact in the Bible, your immediate response is to try to understand it and how it interrelates with how God operates in his kingdom. In truth, the way God works is that you see a truth and fact in the Bible—and then God waits for you to begin to practice that truth.

As you're practicing that truth or fact, God will bring the understanding of that truth and how it interrelates with his kingdom. This becomes a revelation from God. God works in a different way than humans do. Man thinks that he must understand what knowledge he has. God's way is that we gain some knowledge and put it to practice—and then he brings along the understanding. God designed the Bible to be studied alongside the workings of the Holy Spirit.

However, when He, the Spirit of truth has come, He will guide you into all truth; for He will not speak on His own authority, but whatever He hears He will speak; and He will tell you things to come. (John 16:13, NKJV)

What follows is what I have learned from the Holy Spirit about how to go about learning and building in God's kingdom. I want to go to heaven, and I want to do the right procedures so I don't get messed up believing false doctrines that will lead to more false doctrines and cut me off from going to heaven.

The way we learn the truth from God is to first start reading the Bible. As you do this, you will notice various facts in the Bible that will relate to your life. You will also notice other facts or stories that begin to standing out to you. Many times, you will not understand what is standing out to you or why. This is the Holy Spirit beginning to do his work. This is God working within you through the Holy Spirit. It doesn't make sense and is not logical. God wants you to begin practicing that truth or applying that truth to your life no matter how senseless it seems. Once you do this, and after a period of time of testing,

God will suddenly give you the understanding of that piece of knowledge through revelation from the Holy Spirit. This is how God works in each of our lives.

God's way is to introduce to you a few facts, let you practice them, and later give you total understanding. Man's way is to gain all the knowledge and then put it into practice. I call God's way the spiritual understanding and spiritual knowledge of God. It is also called revelation knowledge in the New Testament. Surprisingly, as this process happens within each of us, we learn what is wrong or false.

- Principle: God shows you what to practice and then gives the full knowledge and understanding later.
- Principle: As we gain in the spiritual knowledge and understanding of God, we also see what is false.

Let me make a note here about false doctrines. At Bible school, I was taught that false doctrines were not that big of a deal if you ended up innocently believing some of them. After all, you're innocent and didn't really know the truth. They also taught that once we all get to heaven, God will straighten out all our false ideas or doctrines, thus believing false doctrines is not that big of a deal.

I later discovered that it is more important to concentrate on making it to heaven. I have discovered that false doctrines are going to keep you from getting to heaven. Practicing and believing false doctrines will never bring you into a relationship with God. What they do is cause you to never gain a relationship with God or remove you from such a relationship with God.

God will not honor false ideas about himself. Believing false doctrines will send you to hell. False doctrines are to not be dealt with lightly. They all very serious falsehoods and need to be handled seriously. They are destructive for any believer. False doctrines are regarded as sin to God.

> But there were also false prophets among the people, even as there will be false teachers among you, who will secretly bring in destructive heresies, even denying the Lord who bought them, and bring on themselves swift destruction. And many will follow their destructive ways, because of whom the way of truth will be blasphemed. By covetousness they will exploit you with deceptive words; for a long time their judgment has not been idle, and their destruction does not slumber. For if God did not spare the angels who sinned, but cast them down to hell and delivered them into chains of darkness, to be reserved for judgment; and did not spare the ancient world, but saved Noah, one of eight people, a preacher of righteousness, bringing in the flood on the world of the ungodly; and turning the cities of Sodom and Gomorrah into ashes, condemned them to destruction, making them an example to those who afterward would live ungodly; and delivered righteous Lot, who was oppressed by the filthy conduct of the wicked (for that righteous man, dwelling among them, tormented his righteous soul from day to day by seeing and hearing their lawless deeds)—then the Lord knows how to deliver the godly out of temptations and to reserve the

unjust under punishment for the day of judgment. (2 Peter 2:1–9, NKJV)

- Principle: False doctrines will send you to hell.
- Principle: False doctrines are designed to keep you from going to heaven.

A heresy is a false teaching. Heresies will end up robbing believers of the truth that they know. Verse 1 says, "And bring on themselves swift destruction." Does this sound severe to you? It does to me. Verse 2 says, "And many will follow their destructive ways, because of whom the way of truth will be blasphemed."

False doctrines are all extremely destructive. And notice the final outcome of believing these false doctrines in verse 9. "Then the Lord knows how to deliver the godly out of temptations and to reserve the unjust under punishment for the Day of Judgment." These people end up going to hell, according to verse 9. In 2 Peter 2:12–20, we see what happens to followers of false teachings or false doctrines.

But these, like natural brute beasts made to be caught and destroyed, speak evil of the things they do not understand, and will utterly perish in their own corruption, and will receive the wages of unrighteousness, as those who count it pleasure to carouse in the daytime. They are spots and blemishes, carousing in their own deceptions while they feast with you, having eyes full of adultery and that cannot cease from sin, enticing unstable souls. They have a heart trained in covetous practices, and are accursed children. They have forsaken the right way and gone astray, following the way of Balaam the son of Beor, who loved the wages of unrighteousness; but he was rebuked for his iniquity: a dumb donkey speaking with a man's voice restrained the madness of the prophet. These are wells without water, clouds carried by a tempest, for whom is reserved the blackness of darkness forever. For when they speak great swelling words of emptiness, they allure through the lusts of the flesh, through lewdness, the ones who have actually escaped from those who live in error. While they promise them liberty, they themselves are slaves of corruption; for by whom a person is overcome, by him also he is brought into bondage. For if, after they have escaped the pollutions of the world through the knowledge of the Lord and Savior Jesus Christ, they are again entangled in them and overcome, the latter end is worse for them than the beginning. (2 Peter 2:12–20, NKJV)

In the end, the people who choose to believe in false doctrines end up in hell. Remember that the purpose of this book and chapter is for us to go to heaven and avoid hell. To gain heaven, we are going to have to understand the truth about salvation and are going to have to understand the false doctrines of salvation. A good way for this to happen is for me to spell it all out for you.

Seeing how people in the past have used the method of picking verses out of context leads into false doctrines is critical to Bible study. You don't want to fall into their same error and miss going to heaven. Don't be afraid of digging and studying the Bible for fear of ending up with a false doctrine. A good student will do a thorough job of researching. You will also have the aid of the Holy Spirit who will be giving lots of guidance along the way.

Making an Outline

Now that you have a basic understanding about how dangerous false doctrines and heresies are, we can proceed to dig out what the Bible is teaching us. As I do this, you will probably compare what the Bible teaches to what you have been taught in the past. I encourage you to go ahead and compare what you have been taught with what the Bible is actually teaching. Ideally, you will not have been taught a lot of falsehoods. Don't be surprised if you have a lot of false teachings. Once you see what the Bible is teaching, you must make the ultimate decision about what to believe.

I'll explain how I go about studying the Bible. This may serve as a model for you to employ in your own studies. I gather all the scriptures together that deal with a subject of interest in God's kingdom. This is what I'm going to do for you as we examine salvation. You must also include all the context of these scriptures and include the context into this gathering. When using context, you must stay focused on the context! You also include the scriptures that deal with the subject—even though you may not understand what the scripture is truly saying.

When all the scriptures are compiled, you begin your research and study. Once you have complied all the scriptures, begin to sort through them. Take notes and assemble an outline. You must be able to answer all eight of the thinking questions about this subject: who, what, where, when, why, how, is there one, are there many.

When you run into verses that don't make sense, it's usually a translation problem. That's when you go into Hebrew or Greek. (Hebrew was the original language of Israel. The Old Testament was written in Hebrew. Greek was the spoken language in the Roman Empire during the time of Jesus. Since everyone under Roman rule was required to speak Greek, the New Testament was written in Greek.)

Beginning the Outline

In my study of salvation, my outline will include:

- What is salvation?
- Who is salvation for?
- Where do I find this salvation?
- When does salvation begin?
- Why do I need salvation?
- How do I obtain salvation?

Another part of this study would include:

- How do I go to heaven?
- How do I avoid going to hell?

Another part of the outline is for definitions:

- What is eternal life?
- What is salvation?
  - Eternal life suggests living forever. Is this correct?
  - How do I get eternal life?

○ Salvation suggests being saved from something. What am I being saved from?

○ Being saved from what it is that I'm being saved from: Does this get me to heaven? If not, what is the requirement for heaven?

As you can see, I'm asking questions and using all the thinking words. As you are forming an outline, use common sense. As you go to work at your daily job and think about your outline, write down what you are thinking. Write down what comes to mind concerning more questions you may think of.

For example, a question we all ask—and few ever find the answer—is: how does a person go to heaven. Write down this question and add it to your outline when you get home. As you go about whatever your day requires of you, write down your thoughts and questions in a notebook. You never know when you're going to suddenly have a new question or a thought that will help you in your study or outline. When this happens, write it down. Most people go about creating a theory about answering this question – how does a person go to heaven? I think blah- blah- blah! Avoid making theories. Concentrate of on getting every bit of truth out of the scriptures. Think about what is written in the Bible and don't add more than what is written.

You want to give yourself much time because it's not going to all happen in one day. As the days pass, you keep adding to your outline, and surprisingly, you will begin to get answers to some of your questions. Many times, the Holy Spirit will begin answering your questions before you finish your outline.

Your outline doesn't have to be all-inclusive, but it should be thorough enough to be able to answer all the thinking words. And last, save all these notes because you will be able to go back and add more questions or thoughts that you learn about as you grow and build your life in God's kingdom.

During all this thinking, I'm aware that I want to know the truth about this subject I'm studying. I ask God several times a day to guide me to the correct answers in the scriptures, just short prayers as I go about work or daily duties. These prayers are only a few seconds in length and many times use the same words. For example, I'll say, "Lord, show me the answers to my questions. Guide me to the answers." These prayers are from an earnest heart. I'm not just saying them; I truly want and need answers. "I need to know the truth, Lord. I want to know the truth."

What you're doing is staying focused upon God and his kingdom. You are first seeking the kingdom of God and all his righteousness. You are working with God and allowing him to answer your questions. Sometimes I'll even fast for a few days. Fasting and praying for an answer really works. The fasting also forces you to stay focused on praying.

Again, the purpose of this study and this chapter is to reveal the false doctrines as well as the true doctrines so that we can end up in heaven. You are probably going to be in shock when you learn the church has lied to you. If you want to go to heaven, you must know the truth about how to get to heaven. What you have been taught about salvation is probably false. Salvation does not mean going to heaven. This is why I'm going to show the difference between the truth of salvation and God's requirements for getting to heaven. You will see all this as we examine the scriptures. I tell you this now so that you will be a little prepared. It's still going to be a shock when you see the truth in the scriptures. So here we go.

Here is our outline thus far:

- What is salvation?
- Salvation suggests that I'm being saved from something.
- What am I being saved from?
- Does this get me to heaven? If not, what is the requirement for heaven?
- Who is salvation for?
- Where do I find this salvation?
- When is salvation to begin?
- Why do I need salvation?
- How do I obtain salvation?
- How do I go to heaven?
- What is eternal life?
- Eternal life suggests living forever. Is this correct?
- How do I get eternal life?
- How do I avoid going to hell?

How Does a Person Go to Heaven?

With this study of salvation, I ask, "How do we go to heaven?" This is probably the most important question we will be asking. It's probably the question you're most interested in.

How does a person go to heaven? Is there one requirement? Are there several requirements?

I will list all the verses that deal with the subject of going to heaven.

There was a man of the Pharisees named Nicodemus, a ruler of the Jews. This man came to Jesus by night and said to Him, "Rabbi, we know that You are a teacher come from God; for no one can do these signs that You do unless God is with him." Jesus answered and said to him, "Most assuredly, I say to you, unless one is born again, he cannot see the kingdom of God." Nicodemus said to Him, "How can a man be born when he is old? Can he enter a second time into his mother's womb and be born?" Jesus answered, "Most assuredly, I say to you, unless one is born of water and the Spirit, he cannot enter the kingdom of God. That which is born of the flesh is flesh, and that which is born of the Spirit is spirit. Do not marvel that I said to you, "You must be born again." The wind blows where it wishes, and you hear the sound of it, but cannot tell where it comes from and where it goes. So is everyone who is born of the Spirit." Nicodemus answered and said to Him, "How can these things be?" Jesus answered and said to him, "Are you the teacher of Israel, and do not know these things? Most assuredly, I say to you, We speak what We know and testify what We have seen, and you do not receive Our witness. If I have told you earthly things and you do not believe, how will you believe if I tell you heavenly things? No one has ascended to heaven but He who came down from heaven, that is, the Son of Man who is in heaven. And as Moses lifted up the serpent in the wilderness, even so must the Son of Man be lifted up, that whoever believes in Him should not perish but have eternal life. For God so loved the world that He gave his only begotten Son, that whoever believes in Him should not perish but have everlasting life. For God did not send his Son into the world to condemn the world, but that the world through Him might be saved. He who believes in Him is not condemned; but He who does not believe is condemned already, because He has not believed in the name of the only begotten Son of God. (John 3:1–18, NKJV)

Now behold, one came and said to him, "Good Teacher, what good thing shall I do that I may have eternal life?" So He said to him, "Why do you call Me good? No one is good but One, that is, God. But if you want to enter into life, keep the commandments." He said to Him, "Which ones?" Jesus said, "You shall not murder," "You shall not commit adultery," "You shall not steal," "You shall not bear false witness," "Honor your father and your mother," and, "You shall love your neighbor as yourself." The young man said to Him, "All these things I have kept from my youth. What do I still lack?" Jesus said to him, "If you want to be perfect, go, sell what you have, and give to the poor, and you will have treasure in heaven; and come, follow Me." But when the young man heard that saying, he went away sorrowful, for he had great possessions. Then

Jesus said to His disciples, "Assuredly, I say to you that it is hard for a rich man to enter the kingdom of heaven. And again I say to you, it is easier for a camel to go through the eye of a needle than for a rich man to enter the kingdom of God." When His disciples heard it, they were greatly astonished, saying, "Who then can be saved?" But Jesus looked at them and said to them, "With men this is impossible, but with God all things are possible." Then Peter answered and said to Him, "See, we have left all and followed You. Therefore, what shall we have?" So Jesus said to them, "Assuredly I say to you, that in the regeneration, when the Son of Man sits on the throne of His glory, you who have followed Me will also sit on twelve thrones, judging the twelve tribes of Israel. And everyone who has left houses or brothers or sisters or father or mother or wife or children or lands, for My name's sake, shall receive a hundredfold, and inherit eternal life. (Matthew 19:16–29, NKJV)

For I say to you, that unless your righteousness exceeds the righteousness of the scribes and Pharisees, you will by no means enter the kingdom of heaven. (Matthew 5:20, NKJV)

Again, the kingdom of heaven is like a dragnet that was cast into the sea and gathered some of every kind, which, when it was full, they drew to shore; and they sat down and gathered the good into vessels, but threw the bad away. So it will be

at the end of the age. The angels will come forth,
separate the wicked from among the just, and cast
them into the furnace of fire. There will be wailing
and gnashing of teeth. (Matthew 13:47–50, NKJV)

But what do you think? A man had two sons,
and he came to the first and said, "Son, go, work
today in my vineyard." He answered and said, "I
will not," but afterward, he regretted it and went.
Then he came to the second and said likewise. And
he answered and said, "I go, sir," but he did not
go. "Which of the two did the will of his father?"
They said to Him, "The first." Jesus said to them,
"Assuredly, I say to you that tax collectors and
harlots enter the kingdom of God before you.
(Matthew 21:28–31, NKJV)

And when they had preached the gospel to that
city and made many disciples, they returned to
Lystra, Iconium, and Antioch, strengthening the
souls of the disciples, exhorting them to continue
in the faith, and saying, "We must through many
tribulations enter the kingdom of God." (Acts
14:21–22, NKJV)

Now as He was going out on the road, one came
running, knelt before Him, and asked Him, "Good
Teacher, what shall I do that I may inherit eternal
life?" So Jesus said to him, "Why do you call Me
good? No one is good but One, that is, God.
You know the commandments: "Do not commit
adultery," "Do not murder," "Do not steal," "Do

not bear false witness," "Do not defraud," "Honor your father and your mother." And he answered and said to Him, "Teacher, all these things I have kept from my youth." Then Jesus, looking at him, loved him, and said to him, "One thing you lack: Go your way, sell whatever you have and give to the poor, and you will have treasure in heaven; and come, take up the cross, and follow Me." But he was sad at this word, and went away sorrowful, for he had great possessions. Then Jesus looked around and said to His disciples, "How hard it is for those who have riches to enter the kingdom of God!" And the disciples were astonished at His words. But Jesus answered again and said to them, "Children, how hard it is for those who trust in riches to enter the kingdom of God! It is easier for a camel to go through the eye of a needle than for a rich man to enter the kingdom of God." And they were greatly astonished, saying among themselves, "Who then can be saved?" But Jesus looked at them and said, "With men it is impossible, but not with God; for with God all things are possible." Then Peter began to say to Him, "See, we have left all and followed You." So Jesus answered and said, "Assuredly, I say to you, there is no one who has left house or brothers or sisters or father or mother or wife or children or lands, for My sake and the gospel's, who shall not receive a hundredfold now in this time—houses and brothers and sisters and mothers and children and lands, with persecutions—and in the age to come, eternal life. (Mark 10:17–30, NKJV)

In using the outline, we see that there is very little mention of the use of the word *heaven* let alone the phrase of "go to heaven." What a shocker! We also notice that there is no such phrase in the Bible—go to heaven. This is even more shocking. You would naturally wonder why there is no mention of "going to heaven" in the Bible? This is a good question. Having no mention of "going to heaven" causes a difficulty in our study. There is the phrase *entering the kingdom of God*." Is this the same thing as going to heaven? Why does the Bible not include this phrase?

While still in shock, we will add this to our outline. And just what is *entering the kingdom of God*? So we also add this question to our outline. Also in our attempt to answer the first question, we noticed various other verses that seemed to mention *getting to heaven*. So we will make note of them as well and add them to the outline.

Jesus answered and said to him, "Most assuredly, I say to you, unless one is born again, he cannot see the kingdom of God." (John 3:3, NKJV)

Jesus answered, "Most assuredly, I say to you, unless one is born of water and the spirit, he cannot enter the kingdom of God. That which is born of the flesh is flesh, and that which is born of the Spirit is spirit. Do not marvel that I said to you, "You must be born again." The wind blows where it wishes, and you hear the sound of it, but cannot tell where it comes from and where it goes. So is everyone who is born of the Spirit. (John 3:5–8, NKJV)

Now behold, one came and said to Him, "Good teacher, what good thing shall I do that I may have eternal life?" (Matthew 19:16, NKJV)

Let's look at some of what we have read in these above verses and what we have observed. I added several observations to the outline.

- How does a person go to heaven?
- Is there one requirement?
- Are there several requirements?
- There is no mention of the phrase *go to heaven*. Why not?
- Where did the phrase *go to heaven* originate?
- What does the phrase *enter the kingdom of God* mean?
- What is born again?
- What does *unless one is born of water and the spirit* mean?
- What does *born of the Spirit is spirit* mean?
- What does *born of the spirit* mean?
- What is eternal life?
- What does *inherit eternal life* mean?
- What does *righteousness exceeds the righteousness* mean?
- What does *wicked from among the just* mean?
- What does *to continue in the faith* mean?

Our outline has increased! There are more questions that need answers. And we haven't even gotten any answers except that the phrase "go to heaven" is not in the Bible. We cannot just pick and choose what verses we like or will use;

we must consider all these scriptures. We have more work to do and more studying than first planned. So where do we start?

Why Is the Phrase Go To Heaven Not in the Bible?

This is a shocking discovery! I think it will help clear up some misconceptions that you may have. Then we can move on to investigate these other phrases we discovered and what they mean. Once finished with this, we can move back to the main outline. Remember I said sometimes Bible study takes a lot of work? We have a lot more digging to do.

Where did this phrase "go to heaven" come from? It's not in the Bible! The first place I heard about it was in the church when I was about eight years old. It was mainly taught as follows: If you believe in Jesus, you will go to heaven! When did the church introduce this phrase? Way back in church history. Why is this phrase used in the church? It's based on a false teaching. I know this because it's not in the Bible. Think a bit with me to answer the *why* question here.

Going to heaven is referring to us all dying and then going to heaven. The church teaches that you can't go to heaven till you die on earth. Therefore, we must all die and then find out if we will go to heaven or hell. Sometimes the church uses the phrase *eternal life* to mean that we go to heaven. Later we will see the falsehood in that teaching as well. So, is it true that we must die in order to go to heaven? The falsehood to this phrase is that we must first die on earth.

Amazingly, this is taught nowhere in the Bible. If you don't believe me, I challenge you to find it. There are some verses that seem to say this, but they are misread or misunderstood. When did this false doctrine or heresy show up in the church? I don't yet know the answer to that question. Who teaches this false doctrine - the church not the Bible. How is this doctrine taught - by misconstruing verses of scripture that seem to suggest this doctrine. When examining these verses, which we shall do, you will see that the verses don't even suggest this false doctrine.

In conclusion, I have answered one question that immediately clears up ideas that the church put in my thinking. You don't go to heaven after you die because there is no such thing taught in the Bible. This is such a shocking bit of knowledge. Remember that we have to take the Bible at what it says.

So what is the truth? How do people make it into heaven? Where do you go once you die on earth? What is the Bible really teaching us about heaven?

- False Doctrine: When you die, you either go to heaven or hell.

We add these questions to our outline:

- How do people make it into heaven? Or how do you end up in heaven?
- Where do you go once you die on earth?
- What is the Bible teaching us about heaven?

Instead of attempting to find answers to these three questions, let's finish what we have already noticed in the

---

verses that we found. Let's try to see if we can learn what the Bible is really teaching us in regards to making it into heaven.

I'm first going to study the phrase "enter into the kingdom of God" because that is mentioned several times, and it seems to deal somewhat with my original question. What is entering the kingdom of God?

> Jesus answered, "Most assuredly, I say to you, unless one is born of water and the Spirit, he cannot enter the kingdom of God." (John 3:5, NKJV)

I did a little research in the Greek to see if I could find anything dealing with this phrase. I did find that the more accurate translation is "to enter into the kingdom of God." In Greek, "enter into" means "to become partaker of; to go in and possess." The use of "enter into" is not future tense. It is present tense. *Enter into* is used in many other verses that describe that a person is entering into at the present. So it is telling us that we enter into the kingdom of God now in the present not in the future after we die.

With this bit of information, we learn that we can now enter into the kingdom of God. If we are waiting to die to enter into the kingdom of God as the church is telling us, then that becomes a false doctrine. The Bible is teaching us that we don't wait till we die to enter the kingdom of God. Instead, we can enter the kingdom of God during this lifetime. So now I will look at other scriptures to see if entering into God's kingdom is for the here and now.

> Now behold, one came and said to him, "Good teacher, what good thing shall I do that I may have

eternal life?" So He said to him, "Why do you call Me good? No one is good but One, that is, God. But if you want to enter into life, keep the commandments." He said to Him, "Which ones?" Jesus said, "You shall not murder," "You shall not commit adultery," "You shall not steal," "You shall not bear false witness," "Honor your father and your mother," and "You shall love your neighbor as yourself." The young man said to him, "All these things I have kept from my youth. What do I still lack?" Jesus said to him, "If you want to be perfect, go, sell what you have and give to the poor, and you will have treasure in heaven; and come, follow Me." But when the young man heard that saying, he went away sorrowful, for he had great possessions. Then Jesus said to his disciples, "Assuredly, I say to you that it is hard for a rich man to enter the kingdom of heaven. And again I say to you, it is easier for a camel to go through the eye of a needle than for a rich man to enter the kingdom of God." (Matthew 19:16–24, NKJV)

Jesus is telling the twelve disciples that it is difficult for a rich man to enter the kingdom of God, but it is not impossible. Jesus is telling the disciples that you must enter into the kingdom of heaven in this lifetime to have eternal life. If Jesus says this, then it is possible to enter the kingdom of God now. Notice also in verse 23 and 24 that there is the use of the kingdom of heaven and the kingdom of God. If the rich man is now being asked to give up his riches at that point, then it must also be true that he could enter into the kingdom of God at that point. The rich man couldn't do it because he didn't want to part from his present wealth. This man was rich at that moment in time. He was not rich in a future state somewhere in the future. We also see that eternal life is related to the subject of the kingdom of heaven.

> For they could not endure what was commanded: "And if so much as a beast touches the mountain, it shall be stoned or shot with an arrow." And so terrifying was the sight that Moses said, "I am exceedingly afraid and trembling." But you have come to Mount Zion and to the city of the living God, the heavenly Jerusalem, to an innumerable company of angels, to the general assembly and church of the firstborn who are registered in heaven, to God the judge of all, to the spirits of just men made perfect, to Jesus, the mediator of the new covenant, and to the blood of sprinkling that speaks better things than that of Abel. (Hebrews 12:20–24, NKJV)

This portion of scripture is a mouthful. In the days of Moses, God had all the Israelites gather at the base of Mount Zion. God revealed some of his power and presence to the Israelites at this gathering. The Israelites were not allowed to touch the mountain. Even if an animal were to touch the mountain, it was to be killed. The presence of God was so powerful that they were very much afraid, including Moses.

The writer of Hebrews was writing to the Christians that had already come to God through Jesus. And now being with God it is like, at that time, at Mount Zion. All the angels are there with God. The general assembly is all the followers of God from Adam and Eve up to when Jesus died and rose again. All these people are in the here and now as of the writing of this epistle. They are all not in the future tense. They are all part of the kingdom of God in the present tense. Verse 22 says, "Church of the firstborn *who are* registered in heaven." These are the "firstborn" believers at the time this epistle was written. Look at the phrase *registered in heaven*. Being registered means that you already are a member of heaven and thus have already entered into heaven! Again the point is that we enter into the kingdom of God now before we die.

> Therefore, since we are receiving a kingdom which cannot be shaken, let us have grace, by which we may serve God acceptably with reverence and godly fear. (Hebrews 12:28, NKJV)

Notice the use of *we are receiving a kingdom*. If we already have entered into the kingdom of God, then we are currently receiving a kingdom! To receive a kingdom suggests that we are being given the kingdom of God! How can you receive something if nothing is presently given or has been given or is being given? This is in the present tense use of this verse.

> But as many as received Him, to them He gave the right to become children of God to those who believe in His name. (John 1:12, NKJV)

Here, *children of God* is referring to those who are in God's family. Many times in the Bible, God refers to those who are in his covenant to be a part of his family or kingdom. Notice that we are given the right to become children of God. If does not say we will be given, but we are already given the right to become children of God. Again this is the present tense.

> For as many as are led by the Spirit of God, these are sons of God. For you did not receive the spirit of bondage again to fear, but you received the Spirit of adoption by whom we cry out, "Abba, Father." The Spirit Himself bears witness with our spirit that we are children of God, and if children, then heirs— heirs of God and joint heirs with Christ, if indeed we suffer with Him, that we may also be glorified together. (Romans 8:14–17, NKJV)

Notice the use of *adoption* and then the use of *heirs with Christ*. This verse is teaching that we are adopted into God's family. We become heirs with Christ. It does not say that we will become heirs with Christ. It also says with Christ. This is indicating that we who are in Christ are now with Christ. It does not say we will be with Christ. If we are suffering, it is now. This suffering has nothing to do with any future suffering. In fact, the Bible teaches us that in the future, there will be no suffering when the earth is done away with. Also, suffering with Christ is present tense. Also notice in verse 14 that for those who are led by the Spirit of God (the Holy Spirit) these people are already sons of God. It does not say *will be* sons of God. Again this is present tense.

> I will put My spirit within you and cause you to walk in My statutes, and you will keep My judgments and do them. (Ezekiel 36:27, NKJV)

This is not a direct verse of proving that we can enter the kingdom. It is an evidence of scripture of what will happen when we enter into the kingdom. The point here is that this all happens in this lifetime. It does not refer to a future event. This prophet foresaw that God would place the Holy Spirit within followers of God while still living on the earth.

> Giving thanks to the Father who has qualified us to be partakers of the inheritance of the saints in the light. He has delivered us from the power of darkness and conveyed us into the kingdom of the Son of His love. (Colossians 1:12–13, NKJV)

These two verses are teaching that we can enter into the kingdom of God in the present. They reveal to us that we are conveyed into the kingdom of the Jesus or the kingdom of God. We actually pass from the power of darkness and into the kingdom of God. It does not say that we will at some future time be conveyed into the kingdom. It does prove that this event happens in our lifetimes while on earth. The first verse teaches that we become partakers of the inheritance. It does not say that we *will become* partakers of the inheritance. To be qualified means that you already had to have approval; thus to be qualified is in the present tense.

> But when the kindness and the love of God our Savior toward man appeared, not by works of righteousness which we have done, but according to His mercy He saved us, through the washing of regeneration and renewing of the Holy Spirit, whom He poured out on us abundantly through Jesus

Christ our Savior, that having been justified by His grace we should become heirs according to the hope of eternal life. (Titus 3:4–7, NKJV)

A shortened version of these verses would read: *But when the kindness and the love of God our Savior (Jesus) toward man appeared… we should become heirs according to the hope of eternal life.*

In verses 6 and 7, the Bible is teaching us that we have undergone regeneration. This is past tense in which we have already experienced. In verse 6, "poured out through Jesus" is in the past tense. It already happened. In verse 7, "having been" is in past tense. It already occurred through Jesus. I'll get to eternal life a little later. This regeneration has already been mentioned in other scriptures. It is a past tense word. It means that we have been changed. The point of these verses is that if it is all past tense, then we have already partaken of God's kingdom. It proves that God's kingdom is now.

But you are not in the flesh but in the Spirit, if indeed the Spirit of God dwells in you. Now if anyone does not have the Spirit of Christ, he is not His. And if Christ is in you, the body is dead because of sin, but the Spirit is life because of righteousness. But if the Spirit of Him who raised Jesus from the dead dwells in you, He who raised Christ from the dead will also give life to your mortal bodies through His Spirit who dwells in you. (Romans 8:9–11, NKJV)

These verses are supporting verses that are written concerning entering into the kingdom. Notice the use of *dwells in you* and *Christ is in you*. Jesus taught that his kingdom will be with us. All these verses prove that Christ is to be within us. If Christ is in us, we also have his inheritance. These verses are evidence that the kingdom of God is now. "In us" does not mean *will be* in us. These are present tense scriptures.

> Do you not know that you are the temple of God and that the Spirit of God dwells in you? If anyone defiles the temple of God, God will destroy him. For the temple of God is holy, which temple you are. (1 Corinthians 3:16–17, NKJV)

In the Old Testament, God dwelled in the temple in Israel. He mentions several places in the Old Testament that he desires to dwell within humans. In the New Testament, we find God referring to men and women as being this temple. He refers to our bodies as being his temple. In verse 16, we are taught that the Spirit of God now dwells in us. This is evidence that we have entered into his kingdom, and one of the results is that his spirit dwells within us. Before we enter into the kingdom, this will not be evidence within us. These verses are supporting verses to being present tense in the kingdom of God.

> And what accord has Christ with Belial? Or what part has a believer with an unbeliever? And what agreement has the temple of God with idols? For you are the temple of the living God. As God has said: I will dwell in them and walk among them. I will be their God, and they shall be My people. (2 Corinthians 6:15–16, NKJV)

These verses again are evidence that we can now enter the kingdom of God. This has no reference to a future event; it is in the present.

> But if I cast out demons by the Spirit of God, surely the kingdom of God has come upon you. (Matthew 12:28, NKJV)

Jesus is revealing that through the Spirit of God, we can do extra ordinary events. These events are evidence that the kingdom of God is now in the present—not in some future time.

> From that time, Jesus began to preach and to say, "Repent, for the kingdom of heaven is at hand." (Matthew 4:17, NKJV)

Notice the phrase "is at hand." This is present tense. Notice the word "repent." If the kingdom is not in the presence, then repent (which is a verb) is absurd. Why should there be a call to repent if there is no reason for it? But the fact that Jesus is calling for repentance proves that the kingdom is now obtainable. Repentance is a requirement for entering the kingdom of heaven.

> Now we have received, not the spirit of the world, but the Spirit who is from God, that we might know the things that have been freely given to us by God. (1 Corinthians 2:12, NKJV)

Notice the phrase "freely given to us by God." This is evidence that God has suddenly made certain things available to man. These things are suddenly at the same point in time as Jesus referred to as the kingdom of heaven is at hand. Nowhere in the Bible's past up to this point in time is this statement made, but there are prophesies dealing with the coming of God's kingdom on earth and what God plans to do (Isaiah 44:22).

> 21Not everyone who says to me, Lord, Lord, shall enter the kingdom of heaven, but he who does the will of My Father in heaven. 22Many will say to Me in that day, Lord, Lord, have we not prophesied in Your name, cast out demons in Your name, and done many wonders in Your name? 23And then I will declare to them, I never knew you; depart from Me, you who practice lawlessness! (Matthew 7:21–23, NKJV)

In verse 21 Jesus is speaking to the disciples about how some people think they can enter into the kingdom of heaven at their present time of life on earth. In verses 22 and 23, Jesus is referring to Judgment Day when these same people will argue their cases before Jesus. In verse 23, the phrase "I never knew you" clearly reveals that it takes knowing Jesus personally as a requirement to enter into the kingdom of heaven.

All these verses reveal much about how to enter into God's kingdom. They are revealing how you can or cannot enter into God's kingdom. They also refer to doing extraordinary works that can only be accomplished by those in God's kingdom just as Jesus performed. These verses are clearly revealing people who are already within God's kingdom and still do not meet God's requirements. These verses are major proof that the kingdom of God is now obtainable. The point here is that the kingdom of God can already be accessed. It's not some future event. Also notice that those who do not do the will of God are not permitted to remain in the kingdom of heaven.

There are two points to take notice within these verses.

- There is mention of three different kingdoms. All the above verses mention the kingdom of heaven, the kingdom of God, and the kingdom of Christ.
- There is the mention of the will of God.

Keep these points in mind since I will refer to them later in this chapter. For now, know that there are possibly three separate kingdoms. How can there be three separate kingdoms? Are these three kingdoms really all just one kingdom? We'll have to add these questions to our outline.

What have we thus far learned from the above verses?

- Bible Truth: We can enter into God's kingdom at any time during our earthly lives.
- Bible Truth: The kingdom of God is obtainable now.
- Bible Truth: The kingdom of God is not something we strive to obtain in the future.
- Bible Truth: We can be rejected from the kingdom of heaven even though we have been in the kingdom of God.
- Bible Truth: We can only enter into the kingdom of God in our lifetimes.

We can now draw a few conclusions from our study by attempting to answer some of our questions, including how we end up in heaven.

We can only enter into the kingdom of God now in our present lifetime. In order to end up in heaven, we have to enter into the kingdom of God now. We also have to do certain things to maintain our position in the kingdom of God for it is clear that we can still not end up in heaven for all eternity.

Wow! Just this Bible study brought us many insights that most of you never knew before. Why doesn't the church teach us these truths? All they tell us is their own false doctrines. What a difference that our Bible study has just revealed to us. And we are not even halfway into our study to answering all our questions. Our study is beginning to reveal a lot of truths we didn't even know about. Our study is beginning to reveal how much is involved in getting to heaven. Our study is also revealing that we have never been taught any of these truths or principles by the church. Why have we not been taught these truths? Could it be that the church has never studied the Bible to learn all that is has to say? Apparently, this seems to be the answer. What more are we going to learn about getting to heaven?

Here is our outline thus far:

- How does a person get to heaven?
- Is there one requirement? **Answered**
- Are there several requirements?
- There is no mention of the phrase *go to heaven*. Why is the phrase *go to heaven* not included? **Answered**

- What does the phrase *enter into the kingdom of God* mean?
- What does *born again* mean?
- What does unless one is born of water and the spirit?
- What does *born of the Spirit* mean?
- What does *eternal life* mean?
- What does *inherit eternal life* mean?
- What does righteousness exceeds *the righteousness* mean?
- What does *wicked from among the just* mean?
- What does *to continue in the faith* mean?
- How do people make it into heaven? How do you end up in heaven?
- Where do you go once you die on earth?
- What does the Bible teach us about heaven?
- What is the difference between the kingdom of God, of Christ and of heaven?
- Are there three separate kingdoms or are they one in the same?

Which question should we tackle next? It doesn't matter which one we start with as long as we study all the answers to the questions.

What is the difference between the kingdom of God, Christ, and heaven?

We'll explore the three separate kingdoms—or are they the same? I'll also include what the church believes these phrases mean.

The Kingdom of Heaven

Here is a listing of all the verses that mention the phrase *the kingdom of heaven*. I use the Dake Topical Index to aid in my study. Dake wrote an annotated Bible that contains lots of notes and facts that is a great aid in studying the Bible and finding verses relating to subjects. (Matt. 3:2; 4:17; 5:3, 10, 19, 20; 7:21; 8:11; 10:7; 11:11–12; 13:11, 24, 31, 33, 44, 45, 47, 52; 16:19; 18:1, 3, 4, 23; 19:12, 14, 23; 20:1; 22:2; 23:13–14; 25:1).

These are all the passages in the Bible where this expression, *the kingdom of heaven*, is found. Notice that all these references are found in Matthew. The reason for this is that Matthew's gospel presents Christ as Jehovah's king. Mark's gospel presents Christ as Jehovah's servant. Luke presents Christ as Jehovah's man, and John presents Christ as Jehovah's anointed one, or the Divine One—Christ manifested in the flesh.

The Greek word for kingdom is *basileia*, meaning a realm or a region governed by a king. The word *heaven* in all the above passages is in the plural, thus the phrase *kingdom of heaven* literally means the kingdom from the heavens. It is a dispensational term that refers to the Messiah's kingdom on earth.

The kingdom of heaven is not now the literal reign of heaven over the earth, but is the sphere of profession, or the professing Christian world, as is clear in each of the parables dealt with below. This sphere of profession in the dispensation of grace covers that part of the world called Christendom. (The dispensation of grace is the covenant from God through Jesus till the end of Jesus's reign on earth.)

It now takes in good and bad, or anyone who professes to be a child of the future kingdom (Matthew 13).

So summing up thus far, we are taught from the Bible that Christ has set up his kingdom of heaven during our dispensation of grace. We can thus conclude that the kingdom of Christ is the same as the kingdom of heaven. Dake also provides some helpful thoughts. It appears that the kingdom of heaven is only for the time of the age of grace. The kingdom of heaven is not a material place. We are being built together to form the kingdom of God (Ephesians 2:22).

The kingdom of heaven is a sphere as Dake refers to it. I take the word sphere and use it this way: A sphere in the spiritual realm of the Holy Spirit. The kingdom of heaven is a literal kingdom, not consisting of a material place. The kingdom of heaven is a realm that is governed by Jesus. The kingdom of heaven is now being assembled. Assembled is gathering the entire royal subjects (Christians) and will continue until Christ ends his earthly reign. (1 Corinthians 15:24–28). All the rules, regulations, and provisions have been established. The kingdom of heaven consists of royal subjects who are all believers who have accepted Christ into their hearts. The kingdom of heaven is an organization of people.

I'll try to describe this heavenly realm with other examples. On earth, we live in a three-dimensional realm. This realm is our material realm. Within each of our bodies, our true being exists. This is called the spirit. Our spirit communicates with the three-dimensional realm through our body by use of the five senses. We communicate through touch, sight, hearing, smell, and taste. We call this experiencing.

The spirit is our true entity, not the body. The spirit is in a different realm that is not of the three-dimensional realm. The spirit can never suddenly stop existing because of the nature of our spirits. This is explained in the book *God's Advanced Doctrines*. Our bodies can suddenly stop When the body dies, the spirit continues to live, but it becomes separated from the body. The spirit does not require the body to live. I call this realm of existence the fourth dimension. The Bible refers to this realm as the heavens (Genesis 1:1). In all of Matthew's passages, *heaven* is in the plural, and *kingdom of heaven* literally means the kingdom from the heavens.

We could also call this realm the realm of the spiritual heavens. The use of the word *heaven* is not describing the physical or material. In Genesis, we find earth's atmosphere being called a heaven. We also find in Genesis that outer space is called a heaven. In both uses, these heavens are invisible realms. Photos from space vehicles reveal the earth's atmosphere—and that it can be seen. But while on earth, you can't see it. In outer space, you can't see this realm, but we know it's there because we have been there in space vehicles. Apparently there exists another realm in which our spirits are capable of existing, and Jesus calls this realm heaven. There is even a verse in 2 Corinthians 12:3 that calls this heaven the third heaven. I call this realm the realm of the spiritual heaven to help define exactly what I'm writing or speaking about. The former royal subjects of Jesus are now residing in the realm of the spiritual heaven.

> Now I saw a new heaven and a new earth, for the first heaven and the first earth had passed away. Also there was no more sea. (Revelation 21:1, NKJV)

I would like to add one more comment here about heavens. In all instances, each heaven is described as an expanse. It would be reasonable to call the third heaven an expanse. The third heaven or the realm of the spiritual heaven probably has various places that exist within this realm. Just as in the second heaven (outer space), there are celestial bodies (planets, suns, moons, etc.) that exist within that heaven. In the first heaven (earth's atmosphere), there exist clouds and gases. So it would be in harmony to conclude that the third heaven is also an expanse. When Paul writes about a person he knows who was caught up to the third heaven in 2 Corinthians 12:3, we must conclude that that person did in fact go to some place within the third heaven. In Revelations, John is allowed to see one of these places in the third heaven.

Now with this knowledge about heavens, we are able to begin answering our question about getting to heaven. The word *heaven* as used by the church is not a place; it is an expanse where there are places or just one place within that expanse. We know this because John saw one such place. So to say we are going to heaven when we die is to say, from the Bible's perspective, that we are going to the expanse of the third heaven. The third heaven is not a place; it is a realm or an expanse. It would be more accurate to phrase our question around what place we go to within the third heaven when we die. But remember that when we enter into God's kingdom we are already in the realm of the third heaven or the spiritual heaven. A great difficulty that believers in Christ have is learning to live in the kingdom of heaven while living on earth.

Dispensations are various times that God has established throughout kingdom of heaven. The New Testament or new covenant is the dispensation of grace, which we are currently living. The next dispensation will be the Millennium Reign. The Old Testament contained a few dispensations. It will be at the end of the Millennium Reign that the dispensation of grace will end. This Millennium Reign will become more of a material kingdom for the kingdom of heaven since Christ will rule and reign here on earth and not from the City of God where he presently resides. The Millennium Reign is the kingdom of heaven which is the kingdom foretold by the prophets for the purpose of re-establishing the kingdom of God over the rebellious part of the universe so that God may be all in all as in the beginning.

Since the return of the Israelites to Israel from the Babylonian captivity up to the present day, the Jews understand from the prophets that the Messiah is to establish Israel as a world nation as in the days of King David and Solomon. This is partly true but they misinterpret the prophets and believe that this must happen sometime on earth without a savior from sin. The prophets are referring to the Millennium Reign of Jesus (the Messiah.) Israel Rabbi's ignore the need for a savior from sin. Jewish Rabbi's don't understand the kingdom of heaven or the kingdom of God and the need for a Savior. They place their hope on the sacrifices in the temple to be built again on earth established in the old dispensation of Moses. The true Messiah is the savior of our sins and also is to establish the kingdom of heaven within each person's spirit that accepts the Messiah.

But now Christ is risen from the dead, *and* has become the firstfruits of those who have fallen asleep. For since by man *came* death, by Man also *came* the resurrection of the dead. For as in Adam all die, even so in Christ all shall be made alive. But each one in his own order: Christ the firstfruits, afterward those *who are* Christ's at His coming. Then *comes* the end, when He delivers the kingdom to God the Father, when He puts an end to all rule and all authority and power. For He must reign till He has put all enemies under His feet. The last enemy *that* will be destroyed *is* death. For *"He has put all things under His feet."* But when He says "all things are put under *Him,"* it is* evident that He who put all things under Him is excepted. Now when all things are made subject to Him, then the Son Himself will also be subject to Him who put all things under Him, that God may be all in all.

Otherwise, what will they do who are baptized for the dead, if the dead do not rise at all? Why then are they baptized for the dead? And why do we stand in jeopardy every hour? I affirm, by the boasting in you which I have in Christ Jesus our Lord, I die daily. If, in the manner of men, I have fought with beasts at Ephesus, what advantage *is it* to me? If *the* dead do not rise, *"Let us eat and drink, for tomorrow we die!"* Do not be deceived: "Evil company corrupts good habits." Awake to righteousness, and do not sin; for some do not have the knowledge of God. I speak *this* to your shame.

But someone will say, "How are the dead raised up? And with what body do they come?" Foolish one, what you sow is not made alive unless it dies. And what you sow, you do not sow that body that shall be, but mere grain--perhaps wheat or some other *grain*. But God gives it a body as He pleases, and to each seed its own body. All flesh *is* not the same flesh, but *there is* one *kind of* flesh of men, another flesh of animals, another of fish, *and* another of birds. *There are* also celestial bodies and terrestrial bodies; but the glory of the celestial *is* one, and the *glory* of the terrestrial *is* another. *There is* one glory of the sun, another glory of the moon, and another glory of the stars; for *one* star differs from *another* star in glory. So also *is* the resurrection of the dead. *The body* is sown in corruption, it is raised in incorruption. It is sown in dishonor, it is raised in glory. It is sown in weakness, it is raised in power. It is sown a natural body, it is raised a spiritual body. There is a natural body, and there is a spiritual body.

And so it is written, *"The first man Adam became a living being."* The last Adam *became* a life-giving spirit. However, the spiritual is not first, but the natural, and afterward the spiritual. The first man *was* of the earth, *made* of dust; the second Man *is* the Lord from heaven. As *was* the *man* of dust, so also *are* those *who are made* of dust; and as *is* the heavenly *Man,* so also *are* those *who are* heavenly. And as we have borne the image of the *man* of dust, we shall also bear the image of the heavenly *Man.* Now this I say, brethren, that flesh and blood cannot inherit the kingdom of God; nor does corruption inherit incorruption. (1 Corinthians 15: 20-50, NKJV).

As found in the Bible, at the beginning of the Millennium Reign of Christ on earth, all the royal subjects still live in the realm of the spiritual heaven and get to live back upon the earth along with Jesus as the king. We are given new bodies for our spirits to reside in. This dispensation will last a thousand years. At its end, the two heavens (the physical universe) will be done away with. The royal subjects of God through Jesus get to enter into a place in the heavenly realm where we will dwell for all future eternity.

The church teaches us that when we die we either go to heaven or hell; those who believe in God go to heaven and avoid going to hell. If you don't believe me concerning this teaching, just go to several churches and ask those church leaders if this is what is taught. The Bible teaches that heaven is quite different from what the church portrays. In fact, we understand from the Bible that the kingdom of heaven has nothing to do with a material place. We can say that there is no such thing that "when we die, we go to heaven."

- False Doctrine: For anyone who believes in God, when we die, we go to heaven.
- Bible Truth: There exists more than the kingdom of heaven.
- Bible Truth: There exists a realm where our spirits reside after our first death till Christ's return to earth.
- Bible Truth: We are currently living in the dispensation or age of grace.
- Bible Truth: When our bodies die, that is the last chance to become a royal subject in the kingdom of heaven.

- Bible Truth: In order to end up living with God for all future eternity, we must enter into the kingdom of heaven.

The Kingdom of God

Here is a list of all the scriptures that mention the phrase *the kingdom of God*: (Matt. 6:33; 12:28; 19:24; 21:31, 43; Mark 1:14, 15; 4:11, 22, 30; 9:1, 47; 10:14, 15, 23, 24, 25; 12:34; 14:25; 15:43; Luke 4:43; 6:20; 7:28; 8:1, 10; 9:2, 11, 27, 60, 62; 10:9, 11; 11:20; 12:31; 13:18, 20, 28, 29; 14:15; 16:16; 17:20, 21; 18:16, 17, 24, 25, 29; 19:11; 21:31; 22:31; 22:16, 18; 23:51; John 3:3, 5; Acts 1:3; 8:12; 14:22; 19:8; 20:25; 28:23, 31; Rom.14:17; 1 Cor. 6:20; 6:9, 10; 15:24, 50; Gal. 5:21; 1 Cor. 4:11; 2 Thess. 1:5; Rev 12:10. (Dake Topical Index).

This term *the kingdom of God* means the sovereignty of God over the universe and includes and embraces the kingdom of heaven and all other realms in the whole universe. It is moral and universal and has existed from the beginning and will know no end. The kingdom of God existed even before the creation of the earth. The angels and other spirit beings were in this kingdom when the earth was created (Job 38:4–7). The kingdom of heaven could not have existed then, for there was no earth for the kingdom from the heavens to rule. The term *kingdom of God* is used seventy-two times; the *kingdom of heaven* is used thirty-three times. (See also Matt. 13:43; 16:28; Col. 1:13; 2 Pet. 1:11; Rev. 11:15 (Dake Topical Index).

Even before the creation of the heavens and earth (Genesis 1:1), God was in existence. There was no need for the kingdom of heaven because Genesis 1:1 didn't happen before the fall of the angels. Yet the kingdom of God was at that time in existence because God was ruling and receiving praise from the angels and other beings. All these beings and the angels watched as the earth and heavens were created.

- Bible Truth: There are two kingdoms mentioned in the Bible that are from God.
- Bible Truth: The kingdom of God was in existence before the kingdom of heaven.
- Bible Truth: The kingdom of God is ruled by the Father.
- Bible Truth: The kingdom of God always existed in eternity past.
- Bible Truth: You can rebel against God in the kingdom of God and be expelled from the kingdom of God just as the fallen angels were expelled.
- Bible Truth: God does not tolerate any form of rebellion to his government.

Now with this information, let's do some deeper study to see the difference between these two kingdoms and how they work. What is their purpose? What are their differences? Why two distinct kingdoms?

I'm going to use Dake's Topical Bible because he is the only one who does a thorough job of thinking using the scriptures to show the difference between the two kingdoms. Remember that the entire purpose of this study is to find out how we are to end up with God the Father in eternity.

Comparing the kingdom of heaven (H) and the kingdom of God (G)

1. H. The Messiah is the king.
   G. God the Father is the king.
2. H. It is from the kingdom of God and lasts through the Millennium.
   G. It is eternal past and future.
3. H. It is limited in time.
   G. It is not limited in time.
4. H. It is Jewish, having been designed to be brought through the Jewish nation.
   G. It has always been established on God's character and being.
5. H. It is dispensational—grace and Millennium.
   G. It is eternal.
6. H. It has a beginning and an end.
   G. There is no beginning and end.
7. H. Men and women are not to seek the kingdom of heaven.
   G. Men and women are to seek the kingdom of God.

Here are some biblical principles that we have learned about both kingdoms:

- The kingdom of heaven is to introduce men and women into the kingdom of God.
- Men and women cannot enter into the physical heaven after the Millennium unless they are in the kingdom of God.
- Men and women cannot dwell with God in all eternity unless they are in the kingdom of God.

- Men and women cannot enter into the kingdom of God unless they have entered into the kingdom of heaven.
- You must learn the kingdom of God before you arrive in the third heaven.
- The kingdom of God is for those who forsake their will and submit to the will of God.
- You don't wait to get to the third heaven to be locked with God for all eternity.
- There is no such thing as eternal security (locked into heaven) once you have arrived in heaven.
- You can be removed from both kingdoms at any time.
- By failing to submit to God's will, you can be expelled from the kingdom of God. This happened to Satan and the fallen angels.
- The kingdom of God is for his royal subjects to obey the will of God.
- You have only this lifetime to enter into both kingdoms.
- If you don't enter into the kingdom of God in this present life, you will be condemned to hell.
- By failing to enter both kingdoms, you send yourself to hell because it is now your choice.
- You must enter into the kingdom of God in order to live in the Millennium Reign.
- You must prove your loyalty and faithfulness to God in the kingdom of God during the dispensation of grace and the Millennium Reign.

- The kingdom of God is designed for man to develop a relationship with God before we spend all eternity with him.
- The earth is the testing place for man to develop relationships with God.
- God needs to know who will serve him and who will rebel against him.
- The kingdom of God is for servants.

Notice that God didn't create humans in heaven or anywhere else. Why did God start man on earth? This question is discussed in *God's Advanced Doctrines*. We are interested in finding out about salvation and getting to heaven. We have now answered several of our questions by learning what the scriptures reveal to us about God's kingdom.

The kingdom of God is where we want to end up. The kingdom of heaven is where we get started. Once we appropriate all that is offered in the kingdom of heaven, we should move on into the kingdom of God. The kingdom of God consists of having an ongoing relationship with all three of the god beings: the Father, the Son, and the Holy Spirit. The kingdom of God is finding out what the Father's will is for your life and then doing his will. The kingdom of God consists of servants forsaking their own wills and doing the Father's will. The kingdom of God is for those who want to grow into full maturity.

Wow! Look what we have learned about both the kingdom of heaven and the kingdom of God! It's a lot different from what we have ever heard before. From what we can conclude thus far, we don't wait to get to heaven. Entering into the kingdom of God is being in heaven. We must enter into both kingdoms and become citizens of the kingdom of God now while we are in this lifetime. We only have this present lifetime to achieve this task. Once we are royal subjects, we are already in part of heaven!

We are already partaking of much that is in heaven here on earth. Everything that we will do in heaven is to already be practiced now. This involves serving God and doing his personal will for each of our lives. God is offering all people the opportunity to go ahead and begin our citizenship in heaven now. We are not to wait to get to heaven to begin all this. In truth, we must prove ourselves as worthy royal subjects (Matthew 7:21).

We have learned that we are to enter into the kingdom of God and partake of heaven without being there in the fourth physical dimension. With this, we will actually go the physical heaven at some point in the future. Is there a physical heaven? What is this physical heaven for? If we are already in the kingdom of heaven, why do we need a physical heaven? Where is this heaven? Let's look at this subject in case we discover anything more we need to know about going to heaven. I've already touched upon this question, but I'll look a little closer.

The kingdom of heaven is to introduce men and women into the kingdom of God. Men and women cannot enter the final place of heaven after the Millennium unless they are in the kingdom of God. Men and women cannot dwell with God in all eternity unless they are in the kingdom of God. Men and women cannot enter into the kingdom of God unless they have entered into the kingdom of heaven.

You must learn the kingdom of God before you arrive at the place for men and women in heaven. The kingdom of God is for those who forsake their own wills and submit to the will of God. You don't wait to get to the physical place in heaven to be locked with God for all eternity. There is no such thing as eternal security once you have arrived at the place in heaven. You can be removed from both kingdoms at any time.

By failure to submit to God's will, you can be expelled from the kingdom of God. The kingdom of God is for his royal subjects to obey the will of God. You have only this lifetime to enter into both kingdoms. If you don't enter into the kingdom of God in this present life, you will be condemned to hell. You must enter into the kingdom of God in order to live in the Millennium Reign. You must prove your loyalty and faithfulness to God in the kingdom of God during the dispensation of grace and Millennium Reign. The kingdom of God is for men and women to develop a relationship with God before we spend all eternity with him. The earth is the testing place for people to develop relationships with God. God needs to know who will serve him and who will rebel against him. Again, notice that God didn't create people in heaven or anywhere else. Why did God start man on earth?

There is a city in the third heaven. There may be other cities or places within the third heaven. This city that is mentioned is where the Father and the Son presently dwell.

And if anyone takes away from the words of the book of this prophecy, God shall take away his part from the Book of Life, from the holy city, and from the things which are written in this book. (Revelation 22:19, NKJV)

In this verse, the Bible speaks of a holy city in the third heaven. I call it the City of God because this is where the Father and Son dwell.

> And he showed me a pure river of water of life, clear as crystal, proceeding from the throne of God and of the Lamb. In the middle of its street, and on either side of the river, was the tree of life, which bore twelve fruits, each tree yielding its fruit every month. The leaves of the tree were for the healing of the nations. And there shall be no more curse, but the throne of God and of the Lamb shall be in it, and his servants shall serve him. (Revelation 22:1–3, NKJV)

Again this is a more detailed part of the City of God. Some of this may be symbolic, while it also may be what is truly there.

> Now I saw a new heaven and a new earth, for the first heaven and the first earth had passed away. Also there was no more sea. Then I, John, saw the holy city, New Jerusalem, coming down out of heaven from God, prepared as a bride adorned for her husband. And I heard a loud voice from heaven saying, "Behold, the tabernacle of God is with men, and He will dwell with them, and they shall be His people. God Himself will be with them and be their God. (Revelation 21:1–3, NKJV)

Here is a city that has been assembled in the expanse of the third heaven and is being brought down upon the new earth. This city is called the New Jerusalem. Notice that this city does not have to be built upon the new earth. It is placed upon the new earth and ready for occupation. This will be a very amazing event.

> Then one of the seven angels who had the seven bowls filled with the seven last plagues came to me and talked with me, saying, "Come, I will show you the bride, the Lamb's wife." And he carried me away in the Spirit to a great and high mountain, and showed me the great city, the holy Jerusalem, descending out of heaven from God, having the glory of God. Her light was like a most precious stone, like a jasper stone, clear as crystal. Also she had a great and high wall with twelve gates, and twelve angels at the gates, and names written on them, which are the names of the twelve tribes of the children of Israel: three gates on the east, three gates on the north, three gates on the south, and three gates on the west. Now the wall of the city had twelve foundations, and on them were the names of the twelve apostles of the Lamb. And he who talked with me had a gold reed to measure the city, its gates, and its wall. The city is laid out as a square; its length is as great as its breadth. And he measured the city with the reed: twelve thousand furlongs. Its length, breadth, and height are equal. Then he measured its wall: one hundred and forty-four cubits, according to the measure of a man, that is, of an angel. The construction of its wall was of jasper; and the city was pure gold, like clear glass. The foundations of the wall of the city were adorned

with all kinds of precious stones: the first foundation was jasper, the second sapphire, the third chalcedony, the fourth emerald, the fifth sardonyx, the sixth sardius, the seventh chrysolite, the eighth beryl, the ninth topaz, the tenth chrysoprase, the eleventh jacinth, and the twelfth amethyst. The twelve gates were twelve pearls: each individual gate was of one pearl. And the street of the city was pure gold, like transparent glass. But I saw no temple in it, for the Lord God Almighty and the Lamb are its temple. The city had no need of the sun or of the moon to shine in it, for the glory of God illuminated it. The Lamb is its light. And the nations of those who are saved shall walk in its light, and the kings of the earth bring their glory and honor into it. Its gates shall not be shut at all by day (there shall be no night there). (Revelation 21:9–25, NKJV)

This is the City where Christians will dwell upon the new earth.

The Third Heaven

The following verses are places in the Bible that refer to a third heaven.

I know a man in Christ who fourteen years ago— whether in the body I do not know, or whether out of the body I do not know, God knows—such a one was caught up to the third heaven. (2 Corinthians 12:2, NKJV)

We know that there is a third heaven.

> For in the resurrection they neither marry nor are given in marriage, but are like angels of God in heaven. (Matthew 22:30, NKJV)

Does this mean that the angels have a place of their own in heaven or does this mean that the angels are able to roam the expanse of the third heaven?

> He is the image of the invisible God, the firstborn over all creation. For by Him all things were created that are in heaven and that are on earth, visible and invisible, whether thrones or dominions or principalities or powers. All things were created through Him and for Him. (Colossians 1:15–16, NKJV)

I don't know which heaven is being referenced in verse 16. I don't know if all creation is from the beginning of the earth or the beginning of the angels. Colossians 1:9–23 discusses the earth and the work of Christ. In verse 23, there is mention of the first heaven (atmosphere) because the message is preached to everyone under heaven. *Under heaven* refers to those on the earth. Based upon the context, I assume that the mention of heaven in verse 16 refers to the third heaven because there is the distinction of *in heaven* and *on the earth*.

> After these things I heard a loud voice of a great multitude in heaven, saying, "Alleluia! Salvation and glory and honor and power belong to the Lord our God! (Revelation 19:1, NKJV)

I believe this is the third heaven. Notice the writer only hears the sound of the people who are somewhere in heaven. He does not see anything. The writer is granted to hear the praise of those who are somewhere in third heaven. This verse also reveals that there is a place somewhere in the third heaven where a multitude of people or angles are allowed to dwell. There is no reference about who consists of this multitude. It may have been the angels, the New Testament believers, the Old Testament believers, or all of these people. The point of this verse is that there is a third heaven.

> His eyes were like a flame of fire, and on His head were many crowns. He had a name written that no one knew except Himself. He was clothed with a robe dipped in blood, and His name is called the Word of God. And the armies in heaven, clothed in fine linen, white and clean, followed Him on white horses. (Revelation 19:12–14, NKJV)

The writer here sees heaven open, and Jesus and his army come from this open heaven on white horses. This is the return of Christ at the height of the Great Tribulation because the context of the rest of the chapter is dealing with the time of the Great Tribulation. I don't know which heaven this is referring too. Because Jesus is returning to earth, I'm assuming that it is the first heaven, but it very well may be the third heaven.

> Who has gone into heaven and is at the right hand of God, angels and authorities and powers having been made subject to Him. (1 Peter 3:22, NKJV)

This scripture clearly shows us that Christ and the Father are dwelling somewhere in the third heaven.

While the word was still in the king's mouth, a voice fell from heaven: "King Nebuchadnezzar, to you it is spoken: the kingdom has departed from you! And they shall drive you from men, and your dwelling shall be with the beasts of the field. They shall make you eat grass like oxen; and seven times shall pass over you, until you know that the Most High rules in the kingdom of men, and gives it to whomever He chooses." That very hour the word was fulfilled concerning Nebuchadnezzar; he was driven from men and ate grass like oxen; his body was wet with the dew of heaven till his hair had grown like eagle's feathers and his nails like birds' claws. And at the end of the time, I, Nebuchadnezzar, lifted my eyes to heaven, and my understanding returned to me; and I blessed the Most High and praised and honored Him who lives forever: For His dominion is an everlasting dominion, and His kingdom is from generation to generation. All the inhabitants of the earth are reputed as nothing; He does according to His will in the army of heaven and among the inhabitants of the earth. No one can restrain His hand or say to Him, "What have you done?" At the same time, my reason returned to me, and for the glory of my kingdom, my honor and splendor returned to me. My counselors and nobles resorted to me, I was restored to my kingdom, and excellent majesty was added to me. Now I, Nebuchadnezzar, praise and extol and honor the King of heaven, all of whose works are truth, and His ways justice. And those who walk in pride He is able to put down. (Daniel 4:31–37, NKJV)

King Nebuchadnezzar was exalting himself for his work of building a great empire. Then a voice spoke to him from heaven (probably Jesus). This was the third heaven. The entire context in Daniel 4 is dealing with a man who is exalting himself and how God intervenes in the king's exaltation. This is because God still intended to use Babylon for dealing with the Israelite exiles. From this chapter, we learn that God is able to reveal the third heaven to any man upon the earth.

In this manner, therefor, pray: Our Father in heaven, Hallowed be Your name. Your kingdom come. Your will be done on earth as it is in heaven. Give us this day our daily bread. And forgive us our debts, as we forgive our debtors. And do not lead us into temptation, but deliver us from the evil one. For Yours is the kingdom and the power and the glory forever. Amen. "For if you forgive men their trespasses, your heavenly Father will also forgive you. (Matthew 6:9-14, NKJV)

Jesus is giving an example of how to pray. In this example, we see that the Father dwells somewhere in the third heaven. Then in verse 14, there is the mention of the "heavenly father." Again this shows us that God the Father is dwelling someplace in the third heaven. We also learn that

God has the ability to hear all people's prayers. So no matter how great a distance there is from where the Father dwells in the third heaven, he has the ability to hear and observe all that we do on earth. This is a mystery to earth dwellers about how God can do this. It is proof that there is a fourth dimension that goes beyond the three-dimensional physical worlds that are governed by the laws of physics. The first and second heavens are of the three-dimensional physical existences as we humans can relate.

> At that time Jesus answered and said, "I thank You, Father, Lord of heaven and earth, that You have hidden these things from the wise and prudent and have revealed them to babes. **(Matthew 11:25, NKJV)**

I believe this verse refers to the third heaven since the Father is being praised for all existence.

> How you are fallen from heaven, O Lucifer, son of the morning! How you are cut down to the ground, You who weakened the nations! For you have said in your heart: "I will ascend into heaven, I will exalt my throne above the stars of God; I will also sit on the mount of the congregation on the farthest sides of the north; I will ascend above the heights of the clouds, I will be like the Most High." (Isaiah 14:12–14, NKJV)

In these scriptures, we learn how Satan (Lucifer) was removed from the third heaven. Satan's desire was to be like God and be the ruler. He truly believed that he could enter into heaven and rule in part of the third heaven. In other parts of the Bible, we learn that Satan's plan was to steal away all of the angels through deceptions and thereby rule over these deceived angels. We also know from the Bible that before Satan's fall, he was given much power—more than any other angel. No one knows how much power he was granted. Apparently Satan was granted quite a lot of power if he thought that he could be like God and could contend with God. To this day, Satan has many abilities and much power because of the three temptations when he encountered Jesus in the wilderness after Jesus was baptized by John the Baptist.

> Then Micaiah said, "Therefore, hear the word of the LORD: I saw the LORD sitting on his throne, and all the host of heaven standing by, on His right hand and on His left." (1 Kings 22:19, NKJV)

The prophet in this verse is granted the ability to see into the third heaven. He sees the Lord (Jesus) sitting on his throne and all the host of heaven standing on both sides of the throne. All those who are dwelling in heaven at this point are gathered at the throne of Jesus. Again we learn that God can somehow allow people on earth to view into the third heaven.

> And war broke out in heaven: Michael and his angels fought with the dragon; and the dragon and his angels fought, but they did not prevail, nor was a place found for them in heaven any longer. So the great dragon was cast out, that serpent of old, called the Devil and Satan, who deceives the whole world;

he was cast to the earth, and his angels were cast out with him. (Revelation 12:7–9, NKJV)

The entire chapter of Revelation 12 in my opinion is a quick history review of when Satan first rebelled and deceived one-third of the angels (stars) and was ultimately condemned to this earth. Satan's entire goal is to stop the Child (Jesus) and destroy him. We also see in verses 7–9 that Satan did attempt to take over heaven to become ruler. This war is not a future war as a lot of people and Bible scholars predict because in verses 10–11 we see the work of Christ that has occurred after this war.

10Then I heard a loud voice saying in heaven, "Now salvation, and strength, and the kingdom of our God, and the power of His Christ have come, for the accuser of our brethren, who accused them before our God day and night, has been cast down. 11And they overcame him by the blood of the Lamb and by the word of their testimony, and they did not love their lives to the death. 12Therefore rejoice, O heavens, and you who dwell in them! Woe to the inhabitants of the earth and the sea! For the devil has come down to you, having great wrath, because he knows that he has a short time."

13Now when the dragon saw that he had been cast to the earth, he persecuted the woman who gave birth to the male *Child.* 14But the woman was given two wings of a great eagle, that she might fly into the wilderness to her place, where she is nourished for a time and times and half a time, from the presence of the serpent. 15So the serpent spewed water out of his mouth like a flood after the woman, that he might cause her to be carried away by the flood. 16But the earth helped the woman, and the earth opened its mouth and swallowed up the flood which the dragon had spewed out of his mouth. 17And the dragon was enraged with the woman, and he went to make war with the rest of her offspring, who keep the commandments of God and have the testimony of Jesus Christ. (Revelation 12:10-17, NKJV)

At present in the earth's time scale, Satan's goal is to attack the believers in Christ as seen in verse 12. He has only a short time left before he is placed into the pit of hell. In verse 12, we read about what has been happening with Satan and all the believers since Adam and Eve. In verses 13–17, we read about what has been happening with Satan and all the believers since Jesus was born. We are literally involved in a war against Satan until he is placed into the pit. You will see this as you advance through this book.

What I want you to see in this chapter is that there is a third heaven, and all these events occurred in this heaven. We are not given what places these events occurred in the third heaven, and this remains a mystery to us. John is seeing events in verses 13–17 about the church and the war that Satan has unleashed upon the church. Today we see this war still happening.

Let not your heart be troubled; you believe in God, believe also in Me. In My Father's house are many mansions; if it were not so, I would have told you. I go to prepare a place for you. And if I go and prepare a place for you, I will come again and receive you to Myself; that where I am, there you may be also. (John 14:1–3, NKJV)

Jesus is describing a place in the third heaven. "My Father's house" is referring to the kingdom of God. Jesus is telling us that he will prepare mansions for those who believe and obey him. Apparently there is perhaps more than one neighborhood within the third heaven. We also learn that there is some kind of physical physics within the third heaven because we are to dwell in mansions. We can also assume that in the third heaven we will have some type of fourth dimension physical body because of having a mansion.

But now they desire a better, that is, a heavenly country. Therefore, God is not ashamed to be called their God, for He has prepared a city for them. (Hebrews 11:16, NKJV)

In this verse, we see that there is a third heaven. We also learn that there is a city to be prepared for the believers in Christ. This may be a separate city from the city that God dwells in, or it may be the same city that God resides in. I think that this verse is describing a separate city because this city is being prepared. This city is probably the New Jerusalem.

The City of God is already built and established. The City of God, as seen by John, already has boundaries and measurements and can't be expanded. There is a possibility that the City of God has much open expanse to accommodate more buildings. This would not be in harmony with natural laws of increasing. God doesn't know how many people will end up choosing to be with him in all eternity, and the numbers may be more than anticipated. Since there is only a fixed amount of space in the City of God, should there be more believers than anticipated, this entire multitude would not fit into the City of God. It would be more in harmony to have a separate city of believers that can be added to as needed.

> I know a man in Christ who fourteen years ago—whether in the body I do not know, or whether out of the body I do not know, God knows—such a one was caught up to the third heaven. And I know such a man—whether in the body or out of the body I do not know, God knows—how he was caught up into Paradise and heard inexpressible words, which it is not lawful for a man to utter. (2 Corinthians 12:2–4, NKJV)

I believe that Paul is talking about John and John's book of revelations. This is because Paul says this man heard and was not permitted to write or speak certain things that he heard. This is what happened to John. Also notice that this man was caught up to the third heaven. Also notice that he was taken to a place in heaven called *Paradise*. Is Paradise a place in the third heaven or is *Paradise* another word used in place of the City of God? Thus far in my walk with God, I think that paradise is a separate place from the City of God.

Then I saw an angel coming down from heaven,
having the key to the bottomless pit and a great
chain in his hand. (Revelation 20:1, NKJV)

In this verse, we see the third heaven. We also learn that
physical elements are able to come from the third heaven all
the way to the earth's surface. Apparently the physic makeup
of the fourth dimension can produce the physical substances
in our earthly third-dimensional elements.

Look down from Your holy habitation, from heaven,
and bless Your people Israel and the land, which You
have given us, just as You swore to our fathers, "a
land flowing with milk and honey." (Deuteronomy
26:15, NKJV)

Just as this verse acknowledges a third heaven, we also
see in all the other verses that the third heaven is past the
first heaven. The third heaven is always seen and described
as opening up. The third heaven is always witnessed as being
viewed by looking up into the first heaven (the atmosphere
of earth).

But you have come to Mount Zion and to the city
of the living God, the heavenly Jerusalem, to an
innumerable company of angels, to the general
assembly and church of the firstborn who are
registered in heaven, to God the Judge of all, to the
spirits of just men made perfect. (Hebrews 12:22–
23, NKJV)

This is an exciting verse that reveals that the angels of heaven are innumerable. That's a very large crowd of beings. God knows the exact number of angels, but to us, they appear innumerable. So where in the expanse of the third heavens do all these angels dwell? Do they have a separate city or multiple cities? This is a mystery to us humans.

For here, we have no continuing city, but we seek the one to come. (Hebrews 13:14, NKJV)

In this verse, we see again the mention of a city that is being prepared for the believers somewhere in the realm of the third heaven.

The LORD is in His holy temple, the LORD'S throne is in heaven; His eyes behold, His eyelids test the sons of men. (Psalm 11:4, NKJV)

This verse shows us that the Jesus does have a throne in the third heaven (the City of God).

Then I saw a great white throne and Him who sat on it, from whose face the earth and the heaven fled away. And there was found no place for them. And I saw the dead, small, and great standing before God, and books were opened. And another book was opened, which is the Book of Life. And the dead were judged according to their works, by the things that were written in the books. The sea gave up the dead who were in it, and Death and Hades delivered up the dead who were in them. And they were judged, each one according to his works. Then

Death and Hades were cast into the lake of fire. This is the second death. And anyone not found written in the Book of Life was cast into the lake of fire. (Revelation 20:11–15, NKJV)

This verse shows us that the throne of Jesus is a great white throne. This stood out to John so much that he mentioned the size of this throne.

All these verses are dealing with the third heaven. The writers saw the expanse of the third heaven. It's like you and I looking up at the expanse of the sky or how we can see the expanse of the second heaven (outer space) at night. They also saw certain places in this third expanse. From these verses, we learn that there is a third heaven, but it's not anything like what we've been told before.

I would like to explain a few facts about heaven. I will not dive much into this discussion since the purpose of this chapter is to reveal the truth about heaven and salvation. I think that you will find a little information regarding heaven to be fascinating and exciting. I cover this and other topics relating to heaven in this book.

Facts about Heaven

- No being with any kind of evil or selfishness can dwell in heaven.
- God will not tolerate wickedness or sin of any kind.
- All beings or residents must be pure and selfless.
- The nature of God and heaven involves purity and perfection of the heart.
- There can be no corruption in heaven.

- There is no decay in heaven, and there will never be any decay.
- The physical nature of heaven is materialistic but not having substance involving atoms as found in the existing universe. The material substance of heaven is of a different structure of elements which remains a mystery to man since we have no samples to make observations.

There are requirements to dwell in heaven. With this information, we can add this to why God would have us prove ourselves loyal servants to him here and now. We must learn about the kingdom of God and learn about God's character. Having this knowledge and understanding, you will understand God's requirements for all heaven's citizens.

Heaven is a place for those who want to dwell in perfection and purity. God, Jesus and the Holy Spirit dwell in an atmosphere of purity. They require all subjects to dwell in purity. There is no selfishness but rather self-preservation. All subjects are servants. God also desires to be intimate and wants to know each one of his royal subjects. To do this, we must always be pure and selfless because God is pure and selfless. God will not accept anything less than these rigid standards for his subjects. Any kind of selfishness will ultimately lead to wrongdoing and harm to yourself, and you thus will not be pure to yourself and in your devotion to God and his kingdom. Your heart will become wicked. All beings other than the three Gods are servants being selfless and remaining pure before the Father. In return for this attitude, God fellowships with all these beings, sharing all that he has. God created all beings for himself, Jesus, and the Holy Spirit so that they would not be lonely for eternity. For more information regarding heaven, refer to *God's Advanced Doctrines*. For the purposes of this book, I don't want to stray into other subjects, but touching upon these points is beneficial.

We have learned that even though there is a third heaven, it is nothing like we imagined. In Revelation 21 and 22, we find that there will be a new earth and a new city called New Jerusalem. This may be where all the servants of God, since Adam and Eve, are to dwell. There is no mention of the second heaven (outer space).

I also believe that the first heaven will be done away with. This is based upon some scriptures in Revelation. I believe this new earth may be a place somewhere in the third heaven. This is because there is no need for the light of a sun. There is no night. Therefore, the new earth has to be in another realm—that might be within the second heaven's realm being space.

God does place the New Jerusalem upon this new earth, but this is not the City of God. Therefore, God can come and go as he pleases. This new earth provides us with an answer to our main question. How does a person go to heaven? But there are still many mysteries that we have no answers to. Is this new earth where we former humans are to spend eternity? It would appear that this is where our final place is in eternity, somewhere in the third heaven's expanse.

The Bible gives no other details other than these two chapters in Revelation 21 and 22. Will we be able to visit other parts of the third heaven? I believe that we will because the City of God is a place designed for all the hosts of the third heaven to go worship God the Father. It would be out of harmony if we were not able to travel to the other places within the third heaven.

This third heaven opens up a lot of questions and mysteries. I would like to have a revelation concerning the third heaven because I'm curious and want to obtain more information about it. For anyone interested, it is not a bad or immoral thing to ask God to reveal more about this third heaven. You will never find God commanding us to not ask.

Here is our outline thus far.
What is Salvation?
> Salvation suggests that I'm being saved from something.
> -What are we being saved from?
> -Being saved from what I'm being saved from - does this get me into Heaven?
> -If not what are the requirements to get to Heaven?

Who is salvation for?
Where do I find this salvation?
When is salvation to begin?
Why do I need salvation?
How do I obtain salvation?
How do I go to Heaven?
> -Is there one requirement?
> -Are there several requirements?

What is eternal life?
> -Eternal life suggests living forever. Is this correct?
> -How do I get eternal life?

How do I avoid going to Hell?
There is no mention of the phrase, 'go to Heaven'
> -Why no phrase, 'go to Heaven'? **Answered**
> -Where did the phrase, 'go to Heaven' originate. **Answered**

What is the phrase 'enter into the kingdom of God'? **Answered**
What is 'born again'?
What is 'unless one is born of water and spirit'?
What is 'born of the Spirit is spirit'?
What is 'born of the Spirit"?
What is 'eternal life'?
What is 'inherit eternal life'?
What is 'righteousness exceeds the righteousness'?
What is 'wicked from among the just'?
What is 'to continue in 'the faith'?
How do people make it into Heaven?
Where do people go to once they die on earth?
What is the Bible teaching us about Heaven? **Answered**
Is it true that we must die to go to Heaven? **Answered**
What is the difference of the kingdom of God, Christ, and
    Heaven? **Answered**
Are there three separate kingdoms or are they one in the
    same? **Answered**
How do we enter into the kingdom of God to become
    partakers of Heaven?

Some of these questions have already been answered, but we want the rest answered. Having the Bible's view of the kingdom of God and heaven, we see that these doctrines are very different from what we thought. We have even learned some of the false doctrines that the church has taught about heaven. So now the big question arises: How do we enter into the kingdom of God to become partakers of heaven? I will add this question to our outline.

Salvation

I'm going to begin with the first question since most of our remaining questions stem from it. What is salvation?

The church teaches that if you accept Jesus into your heart, he will forgive you of your sins and you will go heaven. Jesus saves us from our sins, and we will go to heaven. Jesus is our savior if we accept him into our lives, and we will go to heaven. Just believe in Jesus, and you will be saved, have eternal life, and go to heaven.

Even the Bible School I attended taught these doctrines.

- False Doctrine: If you accept Jesus into your heart, he will forgive you of your sins and you will go to heaven.
- False Doctrine: If you confess with your mouth that Jesus is your savior, you will go to heaven.
- False Doctrine: Believe in Jesus, and you will be saved, have eternal life, and go to heaven.

Let's dive into the Bible and pull up scriptures that deal with salvation. There are so many verses that cover salvation that it would take several days to read them all. I'll list the different subjects and then dive into the main ones. Many of these scriptures are just saying the same thing. Salvation is a very broad topic because it is the main message of the Bible. We will also learn what salvation really is.

Salvation is an all-inclusive word of the Bible, gathering into itself all the redemptive acts and processes. It is used 119 times in the Old Testament. There are seven Hebrew and Greek words for salvation. They are used 388 times and are translated by twenty-three English words, some with various endings, which mean salvation, deliverance, save, health, help, welfare, safety, victory, savior, defend, avenge, rescue, and preserve.

In the Dake Topical Index, salvation is used as:

- deliverance from danger (Exodus 14)
- victory over enemies (1 Samuel 14)
- healing of the body (Acts 3:6; Acts 4:12)
- forgiveness of sin (Luke 19:9; Romans 10:9–10; Psalm 38:18–22; Psalm 51:1–13; Psalm 79:9)
- freedom from prison (Philippians 1:19)
- deliverance from captivity (Psalm 14)
- deliverance from wrath (1 Thessalonians. 5:9–10)

In the Dake Topical Index, salvation from sin comes through:

- confession (Romans 10:9; 1 John 1:9)
- grace through faith (Ephesians 2:8–9)
- sanctification of the Spirit and belief of the truth (2 Thessalonians 2:13)
- Godly sorrow (2 Corinthians 7:10)
- faith in Christ's blood (Romans 3:25)
- faith in Christ's name (Acts 4:12)

We are interested in deliverance from wrath. Wrath is God sending non-believers to hell. We don't want to end up in hell; we want to end up on our new earth in heaven.

For God did not appoint us to wrath, but to obtain salvation through our Lord Jesus Christ, who died for us, that whether we wake or sleep, we should live together with Him. (1 Thessalonians 5:9–10, NKJV)

Remember the difference between the kingdom of heaven and the kingdom of God? The kind of salvation we are interested in is what we need to enter into the kingdom of God. I'm going to start with the kingdom of heaven because we already understand that Jesus is the king of this kingdom. We also know that we must enter into the kingdom of heaven to be able to enter into the kingdom of God. Jesus died on the cross and was raised from the dead so that we could obtain forgiveness for our sins. I'll list many of the scriptures that deal with Jesus's work and the kingdom of heaven.

And she will bring forth a Son, and you shall call His name JESUS, for He will save His people from their sins. (Matthew 1:21, NKJV)

Jesus means *savior*. So what exactly does Jesus save us humans from?

This is a faithful saying and worthy of all acceptance, that Christ Jesus came into the world to save sinners, of whom I am chief. (1 Timothy 1:15, NKJV)

If we say that we have fellowship with Him, and walk in darkness, we lie and do not practice the truth. But if we walk in the light as He is in the light, we have fellowship with one another, and the blood of Jesus Christ His Son cleanses us from all sin. (1 John 1:6–7, NKJV)

By which also you are saved, if you hold fast that word which I preached to you—unless you believed in vain. For I delivered to you first of all that which I also received: that Christ died for our sins according to the Scriptures. (1 Corinthians 15:2–3, NKJV)

For when we were still without strength, in due time Christ died for the ungodly. For scarcely for a righteous man will one die; yet perhaps for a good man someone would even dare to die. But God demonstrates His own love toward us, in that while we were still sinners, Christ died for us. Much more then, having now been justified by His blood, we shall be saved from wrath through Him. For if when we were enemies we were reconciled to God through the death of His Son, much more, having been reconciled, we shall be saved by His life. (Romans 5:6–10, NKJV)

If we say that we have no sin, we deceive ourselves, and the truth is not in us. If we confess our sins, He is faithful and just to forgive us our sins and to cleanse us from all unrighteousness (1 John 1:8–9, NKJV)

For God did not appoint us to wrath, but to obtain salvation through our Lord Jesus Christ. (1 Thessalonians 5:9, NKJV)

So Christ was offered once to bear the sins of many. To those who eagerly wait for Him, He will appear a second time, apart from sin, for salvation. (Hebrews 9:28, NKJV)

For as by one man's disobedience many were made sinners, so also by one man's obedience, many will be made righteous. Moreover the law entered that the offense might abound. But where sin abounded, grace abounded much more, so that as sin reigned in death, even so grace might reign through righteousness to eternal life through Jesus Christ our Lord. (Romans 5:19–21, NKJV)

Notice the phrase *sin reigned in death* and the phrase *grace might reign through righteousness to eternal life through Jesus.*

And as Moses lifted up the serpent in the wilderness, even so must the Son of Man be lifted up, that whoever believes in Him should not perish but have eternal life. For God so loved the world that He gave His only begotten Son, that whoever believes in Him should not perish but have everlasting life. For God did not send His Son into the world to condemn the world, but that the world through Him might be saved. He who believes in Him is not condemned; but He who does not believe is condemned already, because he has not believed in the name of the only begotten Son of God. (John 3:14–18, NKJV)

For if when we were enemies we were reconciled to God through the death of His Son, much more, having been reconciled, we shall be saved by His life. And not only *that,* but we also rejoice in God through our Lord Jesus Christ, through whom we have now received the reconciliation. (Romans 5:10–11, NKJV)

And you know that He was manifested to take away our sins, and in Him there is no sin. (1 John 3:5, NKJV)

For the wages of sin is death, but the gift of God is eternal life in Christ Jesus our Lord. (Romans 6:23, NKJV)

Notice the use of the phrase *eternal life in Jesus* (Romans 6:23, NKJV).

Giving thanks to the Father who has qualified us to be partakers of the inheritance of the saints in the light. He has delivered us from the power of darkness and conveyed us into the kingdom of the Son of His love, in whom we have redemption through His blood, the forgiveness of sins. (Colossians 1:12–14, NKJV)

But now the righteousness of God apart from the law is revealed, being witnessed by the Law and the prophets, even the righteousness of God, through faith in Jesus Christ, to all and on all who believe. For there is no difference; for all have sinned and fall short of the glory of God, being justified freely by His grace through the redemption that is in Christ Jesus. (Romans 3:21–24, NKJV)

And from Jesus Christ, the faithful witness, the firstborn from the dead, and the ruler over the kings of the earth. To Him who loved us and washed us from our sins in His own blood. (Revelation 1:5, NKJV)

When Jesus heard it, He said to them, "Those who are well have no need of a physician, but those who are sick. I did not come to call the righteous, but sinners, to repentance." (Mark 2:17, NKJV)

Notice that Jesus is calling sinners to repentance.

Therefore, let it be known to you, brethren, that through this Man is preached to you the forgiveness of sins. (Acts 13:38, NKJV)

We can now see from the scriptures that Jesus's mission on earth was to die for all people's sins and to be raised from the dead so that we may obtain forgiveness of our sins in order to restore our relationship with the Father. For now, I want to focus on forgiveness of sins. Later, I will show you the other part of Jesus's work, which is restoring our life in the Father. Jesus's mission is twofold in obtaining salvation from wrath.

- Bible Principle: Jesus died and rose from the dead so that we may obtain forgiveness of sins.
- Bible Principle: Jesus arose from the dead that we may obtain eternal life.

Remember our original question: How do we enter into the kingdom of God to become partakers of the new earth in heaven? We have to obtain salvation from God's wrath against sin. We must also be restored to life from the death that was sentenced to all mankind starting with Adam's fall.

We have now learned that we must be forgiven for our sins and obtain eternal life. There are two requirements to enter the kingdom of God. I must first explain a few phrases or words before I explain the two requirements so that you understand what I'm writing.

So just what exactly is sin, and what is eternal life? We want to get the Bible's definition of these three words so that you have an exact understanding from God's point of view.

Most of us think that sins are our wrongdoings. This is partially true. We all choose to sin, and it is a choice, but there is more to the act of committing a wrong. Let's look at what the Bible teaches us about sin.

> For the wages of sin is death, but the gift of God is eternal life in Christ Jesus our Lord. (Romans 6:23, NKJV)

> There is therefore now no condemnation to those who are in Christ Jesus, who do not walk according to the flesh, but according to the Spirit. For the law of the Spirit of life in Christ Jesus has made me free from the law of sin and death. For what the law could not do in that it was weak through the flesh, God did by sending His own Son in the likeness of sinful flesh, on account of sin: He condemned sin in the flesh, that the righteous requirement of the law might be fulfilled in us who do not walk according to the flesh but according to the Spirit. For those who live according to the flesh set their

minds on the things of the flesh, but those who live according to the Spirit, the things of the Spirit. For to be carnally minded is death, but to be spiritually minded is life and peace. Because the carnal mind is enmity against God; for it is not subject to the law of God, nor indeed can be. So then, those who are in the flesh cannot please God. But you are not in the flesh but in the Spirit, if indeed the Spirit of God dwells in you. Now if anyone does not have the Spirit of Christ, he is not His. And if Christ is in you, the body is dead because of sin, but the Spirit is life because of righteousness. But if the Spirit of him who raised Jesus from the dead dwells in you, he who raised Christ from the dead will also give life to your mortal bodies through His Spirit who dwells in you. Therefore, brethren, we are debtors—not to the flesh, to live according to the flesh. For if you live according to the flesh you will die; but if by the Spirit you put to death the deeds of the body, you will live. (Romans 8:1–13, NKJV)

Knowing this, that our old man was crucified with Him, that the body of sin might be done away with, that we should no longer be slaves of sin. (Romans 6:6, NKJV)

For sin shall not have dominion over you, for you are not under law but under grace. (Romans 6:14, NKJV)

I say then: Walk in the Spirit, and you shall not fulfill the lust of the flesh. For the flesh lusts against the Spirit and the Spirit against the flesh; and these are contrary to one another, so that you do not do the things that you wish. But if you are led by the Spirit, you are not under the law. Now the works of the flesh are evident, which are: adultery, fornication, uncleanness, lewdness, idolatry, sorcery, hatred, contentions, jealousies, outbursts of wrath, selfish ambitions, dissensions, heresies, envy, murders, drunkenness, revelries, and the like; of which I tell you beforehand, just as I also told you in time past, that those who practice such things will not inherit the kingdom of God. But the fruit of the Spirit is love, joy, peace, longsuffering, kindness, goodness, faithfulness, gentleness, self-control. Against such there is no law. And those who are Christ's have crucified the flesh with its passions and desires. (Galatians 5:16–24, NKJV)

There are several points that are mentioned about sin. We see that following after the flesh is sin (Romans 8:1 and Galatians 5:16–17). What is following after the flesh?

Our bodies are made of flesh and blood. Our bodies have five senses that we use to communicate with our physical world—touch, smell, taste, sight, and hearing. The flesh also has cravings that accompany these senses. For example, when we are hungry, we have a craving for food, which is in conjunction with touch. But we can also crave other foods when we are not hungry that are in conjunction with taste. Our fleshly body is always craving.

The body also has a mind where we process thoughts. The mind is constantly processing the senses that the body is sensing and craving. The mind can also think and form ideas. The mind can read words and understand other people's ideas and thoughts through sight. The mind can hear words and ideas through speech. The mind is constantly sorting what the flesh is experiencing with all its sensors. The heart is connected to the mind and flesh in that it discerns what it loves or likes.

Men and women also have spirits. The spirit is the most mysterious part of people. The spirit has the capability to feel, but it can only feel or sense things that are spirit. This is also called the spiritual realm.

Some people have learned to become attuned to their spirits and have discovered that there really is a spiritual realm, but most of us don't know anything about the spirit. Yet everyone has encountered the spiritual realm several times. Almost everyone ignores these encounters because they don't know anything about their spirits. This is a short explanation of what men and women are made of. For more in-depth knowledge of this, see the book *God's Advanced Doctrines*. I want to stay focused upon the subject of this chapter without straying into other subjects.

In the verses above, the Bible is dealing with the flesh. The scriptures are revealing that to follow after the cravings of the flesh is considered sin. How can this be since we are made of flesh? How can we possible engage in daily life without having cravings of the flesh?

The cravings or desires of the flesh are separate from the necessities of the flesh. When our bodies need food, we get hungry and begin to crave food. It is a necessity to eat food in order to keep our bodies from dying of starvation. When we allow our bodies to crave sweets when we are not hungry, this is regarded like sin.

Our bodies have natures of their own. This "flesh nature" is what has made us sin. The flesh is always craving more than it needs, or it wants to engage in things that alter its natural state; an example is drunkenness. Everything humans do is for the gratification of the flesh or our physical bodies. God considers our flesh nature to be sinful. When humans allow the flesh nature to rise up and be uncontrolled, we enter into sin. It wasn't always like this. It all started with Adam and Eve. Let's look into the story of Adam and Eve to find out what really happened.

> And the LORD God formed man of the dust of the ground, and breathed into his nostrils the breath of life; and man became a living being. The LORD God planted a garden eastward in Eden, and there He put the man whom He had formed. And out of the ground, the LORD God made every tree grow that is pleasant to the sight and good for food. The tree of life was also in the midst of the garden, and the tree of the knowledge of good and evil. (Genesis 2:7–9, NKJV)

> Then the LORD God took the man and put him in the Garden of Eden to tend and keep it. And the LORD God commanded the man, saying, "Of every tree of the garden you may freely eat; but of the tree of the knowledge of good and evil you shall not eat, for in the day that you eat of it you shall surely die." And the LORD God said, "It is not good that man should be alone; I will make him a helper comparable to him." (Genesis 2:15–17, NKJV)

And the LORD God caused a deep sleep to fall on Adam, and he slept; and He took one of his ribs, and closed up the flesh in its place. Then the rib which the LORD God had taken from man he made into a woman, and He brought her to the man. And Adam said, "This is now bone of my bones and flesh of my flesh; she shall be called woman because she was taken out of man." Therefore, a man shall leave his father and mother and be joined to his wife, and they shall become one flesh. And they were both naked, the man and his wife, and were not ashamed. (Genesis 2:21–25, NKJV)

Now the serpent was more cunning than any beast of the field which the LORD God had made. And he said to the woman, "Has God indeed said, 'You shall not eat of every tree of the garden?'" And the woman said to the serpent, "We may eat the fruit of the trees of the garden; but of the fruit of the tree which is in the midst of the garden, God has said, 'You shall not eat it, nor shall you touch it, lest you die.'" Then the serpent said to the woman, "'You will not surely die. For God knows that in the day you eat of it your eyes will be opened, and you will be like God, knowing good and evil.'" So when the woman saw that the tree was good for food, that it was pleasant to the eyes, and a tree desirable to make one wise, she took of its fruit and ate. She also gave to her husband with her, and he ate. Then the eyes of both of them were opened, and they knew that they were naked; and they sewed fig leaves together and made themselves coverings. And they heard the sound of the LORD God walking in the garden in the cool of the day, and Adam and his wife hid themselves from the presence of the LORD God among the trees of the garden. Then the LORD God called to Adam and said to him, "Where are you?" So he said, "I heard your voice in the garden, and I was afraid because I was naked; and I hid myself." And He said, "Who told you that you were naked? Have you eaten from the tree of which I commanded you that you should not eat?" Then the man said, "The woman whom You gave to be with me, she gave me of the tree, and I ate." And the LORD God said to the woman, "What is this you have done?" The woman said, "The serpent deceived me, and I ate." (Genesis 3:1–13, NKJV)

Then to Adam He said, "Because you have heeded the voice of your wife, and have eaten from the tree of which I commanded you, saying, "You shall not eat of it. Cursed is the ground for your sake; in toil you shall eat of it all the days of your life. Both thorns and thistles it shall bring forth for you, and you shall eat the herb of the field. In the sweat of your face you shall eat bread till you return to the ground, for out of it you were taken; for dust you are, and to dust you shall return." (Genesis 3:17–19, NKJV)

Then the LORD God said, "Behold, the man has become like one of Us, to know good and evil. And now, lest he put out his hand and take also of the tree of life, and eat, and live forever." (Genesis 3:22, NKJV)

From reading this account, we find that God made Adam and placed him in a garden. In the garden, God also placed two trees. One was the tree of life. For the tree of life, there was no command concerning it. The other tree was the tree of the knowledge of good and evil. Of this tree, God gave a command to not touch or eat of its fruit. Along with the command was the warning of what type of judgment would occur if the command was disobeyed (death).

Satan came along and tempted Eve. In Genesis 3:6, Eve turned her attention to the tree and saw that the fruit did look good to eat and was pleasant to the eyes. Eve at this point began to crave the fruit of the tree. She was also wondering what knowing good from evil meant. She was craving the experience. Satan was attempting to get the woman to follow the lusts of her flesh.

Satan also knew what kind of death God was talking about to Adam (even though Adam probably didn't know) which is separation of God from man. Adam and Eve probably only understood *lest you die* meant to die physically.

Why was Satan trying to tempt Eve to disobey God? Because of Satan's past experience with God, Satan wants to destroy anything God does.

If Satan can get man to disobey God, then God loses man. Satan knows that God is pure, and any form of rebellion from any creation of God is not allowed to dwell in heaven. Satan attempts to ruin any plans that God makes.

Satan was attacking Eve's mind. Eve thought, *Why should God know about knowing good from evil and not me? Is it fair for God to know more than me?* Eve caved into the desires of her flesh. Adam found Eve, not wanting to lose her and be alone again, and he also ate the fruit. Their understanding suddenly opened, and they knew that they were naked, which was now an evil thing. They both suddenly gained an innate knowledge of good and evil.

After God's judgments, we no longer see God fellowshipping with man. Man had lost his purity, and God could no longer fellowship with man. God separated himself from man because man was not pure. This separation is the death that God was telling Adam about in (Genesis 2:17.) Man chose to follow the desires of the mind and flesh instead of following one simple command from God. Man's fleshly nature became corrupt and this corrupt nature is regarded as sin.

Because of Adams rebellion the nature of the flesh is regarded as wicked and sinful. The mind has followed after the cravings of the flesh.

The death that God was telling Adam about in garden concerning the tree of the knowledge of good and evil was a separation of God from humans for all eternity. The word *death* means something was alive and is now dead. The word death is describing a separation. This is eternal death.

The Holy Spirit was dwelling within Adam and Eve. God removed his Holy Spirit from man. This removal of the Holy Spirit was the death God was speaking about. This death was not only for Adam; it spread to the entire human race that was to follow. The spirit of man became dead as it was separated from God. It is like an electric device that is plugged into an electrical current from a wall socket. As long as the electricity is flowing into the device to make the device function, it has life. But if you pull the plug, that device will stop working. It is now a dead device. Though the device is still there, it is no longer functional unless you plug it back into the socket. We all have spirits, but they are dead unto God—and the only way a dead spirit can be made alive is from God. There is no other way for your spirit to be made alive. So when a person is born they are born with a dead spirit unto God. Adams first two sons (Cane and Able) where born with dead spirits. And so death is passed on to all humanity.

It's interesting to note that Adam and Eve didn't ask God to explain in more detail what the trees were all about. Eve didn't even consider who Satan was. She never even questioned him. Most of us would have first wondered who was speaking to us. *Why is this being telling me that God has lied to me?*

> Therefore, just as through one man sin entered the world, and death through sin, and thus death spread to all men, because all sinned—(For until the law sin was in the world, but sin is not imputed when there is no law. Nevertheless, death reigned from Adam to Moses, even over those who had not sinned according to the likeness of the transgression of Adam, who is a type of Him who was to come. But the free gift is not like the offense. For if by the one man's offense many died, much more the grace

of God and the gift by the grace of the one man, Jesus Christ, abounded too many. And the gift is not like that which came through the one who sinned. For the judgment which came from one offense resulted in condemnation, but the free gift which came from many offenses resulted in justification. For if by the one man's offense, death reigned through the one, much more those who receive abundance of grace and of the gift of righteousness will reign in life through the One, Jesus Christ.) Therefore, as through one man's offense, judgment came to all men, resulting in condemnation, even so through one Man's righteous act the free gift came to all men, resulting in justification of life. For as by one man's disobedience many were made sinners, so also by one Man's obedience, many will be made righteous. Moreover, the law entered that the offense might abound. But where sin abounded, grace abounded much more, so that as sin reigned in death, even so grace might reign through righteousness to eternal life through Jesus Christ our Lord. (Romans 5:12–21, NKJV)

Sin is that which is not pure. Sin reigns in death. Sin becomes the ruler to man's now fallen nature—the flesh. This all means that there is nothing man can do to stop sinning on his own volitions. From Adam, we are now born with a corruptible, sinful nature. We are born separated from God. We are born with dead spirits. Even if just one man is ever able to live without committing a sin, he will still be condemned to hell because of his fallen nature or impure nature. In order to get out of this condemnation to hell, we must be restored back to a relationship with God. We must be made pure. Our spirit must be made alive again. Proverbs 20:9 asks, "Who can say I have cleansed my heart; I am pure from my sin"?

A little later in Genesis, we find that some people want to return to having a relationship with God.

> And as for Seth, to him also a son was born; and he named him Enoch. Then men began to call on the name of the LORD. (Genesis 4:26, NKJV)

> Enoch lived sixty-five years, and begot Methuselah. After he begot Methuselah, Enoch walked with God three hundred years, and had sons and daughters. So all the days of Enoch were 365 years. And Enoch walked with God; and he was not, for God took him. (Genesis 5:21–24, NKJV)

We are not given any details about how God interacted with people before Noah's flood. We can only assume that these people tried to not follow after the cravings of the flesh. They probably also had some revelation knowledge of God and were able to use faith, which rendered them as righteousness before God.

As time passed, in the end, man's fallen nature won over mankind. All people had given themselves to their fleshly cravings, and the entire earth had become corrupt. Satan succeeded in stealing away from God all that he made upon the earth, except Noah.

Then the LORD saw that the wickedness of man was great in the earth, and that every intent of the thoughts of his heart was only evil continually. And the LORD was sorry that he had made man on the earth, and He was grieved in His heart. So the LORD said, "I will destroy man whom I have created from the face of the earth, both man and beast, creeping thing and birds of the air, for I am sorry that I have made them." But Noah found grace in the eyes of the LORD. This is the genealogy of Noah. Noah was a just man, perfect in his generations. Noah walked with God. And Noah begot three sons: Shem, Ham, and Japheth. The earth also was corrupt before God, and the earth was filled with violence. So God looked upon the earth, and indeed it was corrupt; for all flesh had corrupted their way on the earth. And God said to Noah, "The end of all flesh has come before Me, for the earth is filled with violence through them; and behold, I will destroy them with the earth. (Genesis 6:5–13, NKJV)

God was having a discussion with Noah, the only remaining man who had not given over to the flesh. The only solution was for God to start anew or end it all. Why didn't God just put an end to it all? Why didn't God wait for Noah to die off and for all people become evil? Instead, he tried again. But this time, he made a covenant with Noah and future mankind. Since some people did desire to walk with God, he opted to make a second try with humans in hopes of gaining more royal servants with whom he could share his eternal future.

God knew that humans' flesh was weak and in a fallen nature, and he placed limitations on Satan's fallen race. He also made a covenant with mankind. This time, it was different because we were starting out with Noah who walked with God. Noah also understood the past and saw how human's fallen flesh nature can rise to power within.

Noah also knew how to have a relationship with God. Would this give people a better beginning point? As time passed, most people caved in to their fleshly natures. But there were still many more people who served God. Many people born after Noah really wanted to walk with God. They didn't want to end up in hell; they would rather end up in heaven.

As nations began to develop, God created a nation for himself through whom he could bring about his Son who would die and rise from the dead, offering a direct relationship with him. Through Jesus, people could be pardoned for their sins and gain the power of the Holy Spirit to help keep their fleshly natures in check and to gain back life from Adams death.

God would be able to gain more servants to have relationships with. Through this covenant of the kingdom of heaven, people's fallen state is dealt with. God is now providing extra power through the Holy Spirit to help those who wish to overcome their fleshly cravings to indulge in sin. God cannot remove the original disobedience of Adam and Eve and the judgment that is given to all mankind following Adam, which is death or separation from God. Through Christ God now provides a way out from this death that is caused by sin. This became the work of the Christ. Jesus saves us from our sins. Through Jesus we can obtain the indwelling of the Holy Spirit thus be made alive unto God.

God might not have gained every man or woman that was born on earth, but he did gain a vast number. This was better than gaining nothing. God made a few more mid-course covenants with people, and the latest one is what we call the dispensation of grace. This is the present covenant that mankind is under. This covenant of grace is what is referred to as salvation from sins in a general term. We are saved from the wrath of God that is caused by sin. Apart from being cleansed from sin we must also be made alive unto God which is a separate work. These two actions must occur to be saved from the wrath of God. I discuss this in more detail later in this book.

Thus far we have seen the difference of the kingdom of heaven and the kingdom of God. The kingdom of heaven is Christ's work to save humanity from their sins. The kingdom of God is for those in the kingdom of heaven to have their spirit returned to a relationship with God the Father.

The Covenant of Grace

What is the covenant of grace? We'll add this to our outline. Again, the purpose of this study and this chapter is to reveal the false doctrines that we are all taught and believe in our modern society so that we can know the truth. Also, we want to learn the truth about what is written in the scriptures. You are probably going to be in shock that you've been lied to by the church. If you want to go to heaven, you must know the truth about how to get to heaven. What you have been taught about salvation is false; salvation does not mean going to heaven. This is why I'm going to show the difference between the truth of salvation and what God's requirement to get to heaven. You will see all this as we examine the scriptures. I tell you this now so that you will be a little prepared. It's still going to be a shock to you when you see the truth in the scriptures.

Here is our outline thus far:

What is Salvation?

Salvation suggests that I'm being saved from something.

-What are we being saved from? **Answered**

-Being saved from what I'm being saved from - does this get me into Heaven?

-If not what are the requirements to get to Heaven?

Who is salvation for? **Answered**

Where do I find this salvation? **Answered**

When is salvation to begin?

Why do I need salvation? **Answered**

How do I obtain salvation?

How do I go to Heaven?

-Is there one requirement?

-Are there several requirements?

What is eternal life?

-Eternal life suggests live forever. Is this correct?

-How do I get eternal life?

How do I avoid going to Hell?

There is no mention of the phrase, 'go to Heaven'

-Why no phrase, 'go to Heaven?' **Answered**

-Where did the phrase, 'go to Heaven' originate? **Answered**

What is the phrase 'enter into the kingdom of God?' **Answered**

What is 'born again?'

What is 'unless one is born of water and spirit?'

What is 'born of the Spirit is spirit?'

What is 'born of the Spirit?"

What is 'eternal life?'

What is 'inherit eternal life?'

What is 'righteousness exceeds the righteousness'

What is 'wicked from among the just?'

What is 'to continue in 'the faith'

How do people make it into Heaven?

Where do people go to once they die on earth? **Answered**

What is the Bible teaching us about Heaven? **Answered**

What is the difference of the kingdom of God, Christ, and Heaven? **Answered**

Are there three separate kingdoms or are they one in the same? **Answered**

What is the covenant of Grace?

So is it true that we must die in order to learn if we go to Heaven? **Answered**

Is entering the kingdom of God the same thing as going to Heaven? **Answered**

How do you end up in Heaven?

Where do you go once you die on Earth? **Answered**

What is the Bible teaching us about Heaven? **Answered**

Wow. We are learning a lot by digging into the Bible, and we are beginning to get a basic idea of what Jesus and the kingdom of heaven and the kingdom of God are all about. We are also beginning to see that we have not been taught very much truth about God or what really is taught in the Bible. We are seeing a lot of false doctrines that the church has been teaching us.

So what is this age or covenant of grace all about? How does it work? What are the new requirements from God? What are God's expectations with this covenant of grace? When does it come to an end? How do we appropriate all that is offered to gain salvation from death or separation from God? Can we be removed from the original death that has spread to all mankind from Adam's fall?

After we review most of the verses that deal with salvation from death caused by sin, we can begin to answer many of these questions.

The Bible deals a lot with these questions and the subject of salvation because this is the main reason why it was written. All that I have written up to this point is to provide you with a basic foundation to explain man's condition since Adam and Eve. This information also is to educate you about what exists as we know it. This provides you with the proper knowledge for understanding what God offers everyone. As far as salvation from death goes, you can draw a conclusion about how we end up in heaven, but be warned that there are a lot of scriptures to read through because the main theme of the Bible is salvation from death or sin.

From our scripture search, we know that there is the kingdom of God and the kingdom of heaven. We are now in the age of grace. The Bible teaches us that we enter into the kingdom of God during the age of grace. Men and women must enter into the kingdom of heaven and then into the kingdom of God to obtain salvation from sin's death. This is a very simple thing to do. You must be called by God to enter the kingdom of heaven. You can't enter into the kingdom of heaven unless you are called by God. You can't do it on your own.

> No one can come to Me unless the Father who sent Me draws him; and I will raise him up at the last day. (John 6:44, NKJV)

You have to have the Father literally draw you to Jesus, and this is how God draws people to Jesus. You must hear or read the message about Jesus and what he has done for you. An example of this would be reading this chapter. Once you read it, God may begin to draw or call you to accept Jesus into your life. You will probably hear the message of Jesus several times. It usually doesn't happen in just a onetime hearing. In a short amount of time, you will encounter this message several times. God will place in your path various people who will tell you the same message. And after you hear the message of Jesus a few times, there will be a gentle tugging in your heart each time you hear the message about Jesus. You will know in your spirit that God is doing this tugging or drawing because no one else can do this. You will know that there is an extra exertion taking place in your spirit.

God calls or draws many people to his Son, but few ever really respond. Once it becomes clear to you that this is God tugging at your heart, you can respond and accept Jesus into your heart or you can rebel against it by ignoring it. God will only tug for a select amount of time. If you remain stubborn and refuse to respond, he will suddenly stop drawing you to Jesus.

Most of the time, the drawing begins when you hear the message and show some interest in it—even though you don't understand much of it. What if you don't hear the gospel message, but you want to know God? There is another way that people can get the Father to draw them to Jesus. If you see what Christ has done for you by reading a book like this and you truly want to get to know God, start asking him to draw you to Jesus. If you keep asking, God will see your heart's desire in wanting to get to know Him. If your heart is of a right motive and not for selfish gain, He will begin to draw you to Jesus, and Jesus will lead you to the Father. God will send you one of his servants and help you accept Jesus into your heart.

I'm going to assume that you have already had this experience with Jesus because this book is written mainly for those who have already accepted Jesus into their hearts but don't understand how to gain a deeper life with God. Accepting Jesus into your heart is entering into the kingdom of heaven.

For most of you who read this book, this is where things get difficult because this is where the church has introduced a lot of false doctrines that you have accepted. This is where I have to attack these false doctrines, and you are going to have to do some careful studying of the scriptures to follow what I'm saying. You're going to have to think and pray about what I've written. A lot of you will have to read this chapter several times before you understand it. Once you see all that I'm presenting to you then it's up to you to make decisions. So here goes.

Remember the last false doctrine I pointed out? The church teaches us that if you accept Jesus into your heart, he will forgive you of your sins and you will go heaven. Jesus saves us from our sins, and you will go to heaven. Jesus is our Savior if we accept him into our lives, and we will go to heaven. Just believe in Jesus, and you will be saved, have eternal life, and go to heaven. Every one of these statements is false. They are all false doctrines.

Before you get upset—as most people do—give me a chance to show you the truth. Once you see what the Bible is truly teaching, you can decide if these are false doctrines. Before I proceed, I want you to understand a principle about Satan.

- Bible Principle: It is Satan's goal to keep you from entering into God's kingdom.

It is Satan's goal to kill, steal, and destroy you. He's not going to think about it, but he is going to do these things to you. Satan doesn't want you to hear the truth; instead, he lies about God. Satan wants you to spend eternity in hell, suffering the same condemnation that he will suffer.

Over the years (two thousand), Satan has done a lot of work to introduce false doctrines into the church. Satan is a master at lying. He is so good that he has succeeded in deceiving almost all of mankind. He accomplished a total deception of all mankind in Noah's time. How do you think that he would accomplish this today?

Satan won't walk up to you and say, "Hi! I'm Satan, and I'm going to lie to you." Satan is not stupid, but he is the master of deception. He is the best of the best! Instead, over the past two thousand years, Satan has been working to deceive the church through false doctrines. As a result, we have a lot of false doctrines today.

If you accept these false doctrines, you will miss out on making it to heaven. You will end up in hell. Satan will have deceived you. It is your job to discern what the truth is, but you have to know what the truth is. It is your job to tell others the truth when you discover we've been lied to.

- Bible Truth: Believing false doctrines will send you to hell!

Making It into Heaven

There are two requirements for us to meet in order to end up in heaven. The first requirement is to enter back into the life of God. You must be born again. The second is obeying God's personal will. This is entering into the kingdom of God.

Before I list a bunch of scriptures, I'll give an illustration about death and life in God. This will help you to better understand some of the following Bible scriptures.

I'm going to use an illustration that will help you see what true salvation from death into eternal life is. Remember the number line from school? This is what I will use as an illustration.

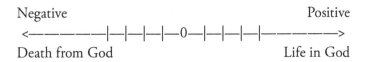

Negative   Positive

<—————|—|—|—|—0—|—|—|—|—————>

Death from God   Life in God

When we are not in the kingdom of heaven, we are in death. We are literally dead to God. We are on our way to hell. No matter what we do, we are living in the negative of the number line. The negative on the number line are those who are dead to God. There is nothing any of us can do just to get back to zero. Zero is having been cleansed and made pure so that we can enter back into a relationship with God, which will be the positive on the number line.

When you enter back into a relationship with God, you pass from death back into life in God. So long as we are in the negative, we are in death. And as long as we are at zero, we are still in death. Being cleansed of our sins does not give us life. This is where most Christians get this doctrine all messed up. Being cleansed of sin is not obtaining the life of God. You have to be in the positive to be in the life of God.

Below are a lot of verses that I compiled so that you can see what the requirements are in order to end up in heaven. This is not an inclusive list, but these show the two requirements.

Who can say, "I have made my heart clean, I am pure from my sin"? (Proverbs 20:9, NKJV)

This has to be done for us. Jesus does this work for us. We accept Jesus, and we are purified. We are now at zero. We have yet to move into the positive. Being forgiven for our sins and cleansed does not place us in the positive. Being at zero does not take us from death into life.

The church teaches us that all we have to do is accept Jesus into our hearts and we will go to heaven. The church also teaches us that if we accept Jesus into our hearts, we are made alive in God. So the majority of us (90 percent of all Christians) are still sitting at zero. We are taught that we are growing and progressing with God. We are taught that all we have to do is read the Bible and do a little praying to be in the positive. That is as false as a lead balloon.

- False Teaching: All we have to do to go to heaven is accept Jesus into our hearts.
- False Teaching: If we accept Jesus into our hearts, we are made alive in God.

Think with me. Just because you are zeroed out—forgiven for your sins and made pure—doesn't mean we have eternal life or anything more. All it means is that we are made pure and are ready to advance with God. You can't move on with God unless you are purified of your sins. This is the first requirement of God.

Being purified involves repenting of all your sins—not most of them and hanging onto your pet sins. To be purified, you must turn from all your sins. You must accept Jesus into your heart so that he can purify you. Every one of us who has accepted Jesus into our hearts has experienced that purifying. That is not eternal life.

Accepting Jesus into your heart is just being purified. Being made pure from Jesus is not eternal life. It is only being forgiven for your sins—nothing more. Once you have become zero or pure, you are eligible to advance with God into the kingdom of heaven. And most of us haven't done this because we are not taught this as the next step. In order to advance with God, you must be made zero or pure. Once you are purified, you need to move on to the next requirement.

Here is the truth. Once you accept Jesus into your heart, you are made clean or purified. You literally experience this within your spirit. You can feel the purity of Christ, but you are still dead. You are still separated from God. Just because you felt the cleansing power of Jesus does not make you alive unto God. In order to move on to the next requirement, you must be purified from your sins. When you are purified you have entered into the kingdom of heaven.

When you begin to move into the positive, you will gain the life of the Holy Spirit and become born again of the Holy Spirit. Jesus's work is now finished. Now it becomes the job of the Holy Spirit to make you alive unto God. When this happens, you become born again. You must become born of the Holy Spirit. Jesus cannot make you born again or born anew. Being purified is not being born again. Jesus can only forgive you for your sins and purify you through his blood. In order to become born again of the Holy Spirit, you must be made zero or purified. The Holy Spirit is not going to dwell with someone who is not purified.

- False Doctrine: When you accept Jesus into your heart, you are born again.
- False Doctrine: When you accept Jesus into your heart, you also receive the Holy Spirit.

The bringing you into life from death involves the working of the Holy Spirit not Jesus. You must have the nature of God dwelling within you, which is the work of the Holy Spirit. The power of the Holy Spirit enables us to override our flesh nature and keep it at bay. Through the Holy Spirit, we can become born again. Once we become born again, we pass from the kingdom of heaven into the kingdom of God. Look closely at the following scriptures. Notice the difference in the working of the Holy Spirit and the work of Jesus.

> There was a man of the Pharisees named Nicodemus, a ruler of the Jews. This man came to Jesus by night and said to Him, "Rabbi, we know that You are a teacher come from God; for no one can do these signs that You do unless God is with him." Jesus answered and said to him, "Most assuredly, I say to you, unless one is born again, he cannot see the kingdom of God." Nicodemus said to Him, "How can a man be born when he is old? Can he enter a second time into his mother's womb and be born?" Jesus answered, "Most assuredly, I say to you, unless one is born of water and the Spirit, he cannot enter the kingdom of God. That which is born of the flesh is flesh, and that which is born of the Spirit is spirit. Do not marvel that I said to you, "You must be born again." The wind blows where it wishes, and you hear the sound of it, but cannot tell where it comes from and where it goes. So is everyone who is born of the spirit." (John 3:1–8, NKJV)

Notice that the scripture does not say: *born of Jesus*; instead, it says *born of the Spirit*, which is the Holy Spirit. Jesus is telling Nicodemus that you have to be born of flesh and then be born of the Holy Spirit. You must have two births. Being born of water is being born in your fleshly life from your mother's womb. You also need to be born of the Holy Spirit.

> For if you live according to the flesh you will die; but if (you live) by the Spirit you put to death the deeds of the body, you will live. (Romans 8:13, NKJV)

Notice *if you live by the spirit*. It does not say if you live by Jesus. The deeds of the body or the flesh are what cause sin.

> Or do you not know that as many of us as were baptized into Christ Jesus were baptized into His death? Therefore, we were buried with Him through baptism into death, that just as Christ was raised from the dead by the glory of the Father, even so we also should walk in newness of life. For if we have been united together in the likeness of His death, certainly we also shall be in the likeness of His resurrection, knowing this, that our old man was crucified with Him, that the body of sin might be done away with, that we should no longer be slaves of sin. (Romans 6:3–6, NKJV)

Notice *we should walk in the newness of life*. The use of the word newness is describing a new type of life. That doesn't mean that we are doing this. The use of *should walk* describes that we have a choice. This is speaking about the second requirement. It is a choice that we have to make.

Notice *we also shall be in the likeness of his resurrection*. Shall be does not mean will be. Shall be is assuming that we will go ahead had accept the Holy Spirit. Shall be is future tense. Notice in verse 6, *our old man (of flesh) was crucified with Him and our body of sin might be done away with so that we are no longer slaves of sin*. It doesn't say that our body is done away with. When we gain the Holy Spirit, we gain power to keep the sinful flesh at bay. Being born of the Spirit gives us new life, and we are no longer slaves of sin and flesh.

> There is therefore now no condemnation to those who are in Christ Jesus, who do not walk according to the flesh, but according to the Spirit. For the law of the Spirit of life in Christ Jesus has made me free from the law of sin and death. For what the law could not do in that it was weak through the flesh, God did by sending His own Son in the likeness of sinful flesh, on account of sin: He condemned sin in the flesh. (Romans 8:1–3, NKJV)

Notice that we are to walk according to the Spirit, not according to Jesus. Notice in verse 2 the *law of the Spirit of life in Christ Jesus*; this is referring to the Holy Spirit (not Jesus). The Holy Spirit is in Jesus. In verse 3, we see that the work of Jesus is overriding the power of sin by providing forgiveness. The Holy Spirit gives us life (not Jesus) in verse 2. Jesus provides forgiveness in verse 3 so we may obtain life in the Holy Spirit in verse 1. Without the work of Jesus, you can't have the Holy Spirit and life.

> And those who are Christ's have crucified the flesh with its passions and desires. If we live in the spirit, let us also walk in the Spirit. (Galatians 5:24–25, NKJV)

Notice in verse 24 that those who are Christ's do the crucifying. The flesh with its passions and desires must be overcome by another power. Acts 1:8 says, "You shall receive power when the Holy Spirit has come upon you." Jesus doesn't provide any power.

Jesus only provides salvation from sin. The Holy Spirit provides the power. Notice the word *if* in verse 25. It suggests that there are people who have moved on to receive the Holy Spirit, and there are people who have not received the Holy Spirit. Notice also in verse 25 that it is our responsibility to maintain a relationship with the Holy Spirit. It's not a onetime experience.

> Not by works of righteousness which we have done, but according to His mercy He saved us, through the washing of regeneration and renewing of the Holy Spirit. (Titus 3:5, NKJV)

Notice that *we are saved by washing of regeneration and renewing of the Holy Spirit*. This is a two-step process. Notice how regeneration is Jesus's work, and renewing is the work of the Holy Spirit. Regeneration is the gaining of purity. Renewing is being changed. Salvation here is not just from sin; it is being made anew. Salvation in this verse is referring to being saved from sin and death.

> If we say that we have fellowship with Him, and walk in darkness, we lie and do not practice the truth. But if we walk in the light as He is in the light, we have fellowship with one another, and the blood of Jesus Christ His Son cleanses us from all sin. If we say that we have no sin, we deceive

ourselves, and the truth is not in us. If we confess our sins, He is faithful and just to forgive us *our* sins and to cleanse us from all unrighteousness. (1 John 1:6–9, NKJV)

Notice that the only work that Jesus does is to cleanse us from our sins and from all unrighteousness. Darkness is referring to death from God. Light is being alive in God.

For this is My blood of the new covenant, which is shed for many for the remission of sins. (Matthew 26:28, NKJV)

Notice that the only work of Jesus is for the forgiveness of sins. This work required the shedding of his blood.

And He is before all things, and in Him all things consist. And He is the head of the body, the church, Who is the beginning, the firstborn from the dead, that in all things He may have the preeminence. For it pleased the Father that in Him all the fullness should dwell, and by Him to reconcile all things to Himself, by Him, whether things on earth or things in heaven, having made peace through the blood of his cross. And you, who once were alienated and enemies in your mind by wicked works, yet now He has reconciled in the body of His flesh through death, to present you holy, and blameless, and above reproach in His sight. (Colossians 1:17–22, NKJV)

Notice that only the work of Jesus consists of forgiveness of sin. Being reconciled is to pay a purchase price for you to come back into a relationship with God. The price is the blood of Jesus. Jesus purifies us. Once pure, we can be presented holy, blameless, and above reproach—in other words, being made pure. Having been purified, we can move on in God. Being made pure is a requirement for being able to move on in God. To have life in God, you have to be made pure. To be made pure, you have to have your sins removed. You can only have your sins removed by going through an act of redemption, which is to be forgiven from God's wrath against your sins. No one can remove your sins and the penalties incurred against your sins. Only a judge can grant a pardon by forgiving. In this case with people, Jesus is the judge.

> That having been justified by His grace, we should become heirs according to the hope of eternal life. (Titus 3:7, NKJV)

Notice that *having been made pure we should become heirs*. It does not say we will automatically become heirs. *Should become* suggests that God wants us to move on into his kingdom.

> Being justified freely by His grace through the redemption that is in Christ Jesus, whom God set forth as a propitiation by His blood, through faith, to demonstrate His righteousness, because in His forbearance God had passed over the sins that were previously committed, to demonstrate at the present time His righteousness, that He might be just and the justifier of the one who has faith in Jesus. (Romans 3:24–26, NKJV)

Notice that it would be too easy to just simply say that all has been done for us. But this is not so because at the end of verse 26, it only works for the *one who has faith in Jesus.* You must have a correct definition of faith, which is discussed later in this book. For now, all you need to understand about faith is that it is something you must perform. Having said this, you must do your work to appropriate the justification of Jesus redemption.

> In whom we have redemption through His blood, the forgiveness of sins. He is the image of the invisible God, the firstborn over all creation. For by Him all things were created that are in heaven and that are on earth, visible and invisible, whether thrones or dominions or principalities or powers. All things were created through Him and for Him. And He is before all things, and in Him all things consist. And He is the head of the body, the church, who is the beginning, the firstborn from the dead, that in all things He may have the preeminence. For it pleased the Father that in Him all the fullness should dwell, and by Him to reconcile all things to Himself, by Him, whether things on earth or things in heaven, having made peace through the blood of His cross. And you, who once were alienated and enemies in your mind by wicked works, yet now He has reconciled in the body of His flesh through death, to present you holy, and blameless, and above reproach in His sight. (Colossians 1:14–22, NKJV)

> Therefore, having been justified by faith, we have peace with God through our Lord Jesus Christ

through whom also we have access by faith into this grace in which we stand, and rejoice in hope of the glory of God. And not only that, but we also glory in tribulations, knowing that tribulation produces perseverance; and perseverance, character; and character, hope. Now hope does not disappoint because the love of God has been poured out in our hearts by the Holy Spirit who was given to us. For when we were still without strength, in due time, Christ died for the ungodly. For scarcely for a righteous man will one die; yet perhaps for a good man someone would even dare to die. But God demonstrates His own love toward us, in that while we were still sinners, Christ died for us. Much more then, having now been justified by His blood, we shall be saved from wrath through Him. For if when we were enemies, we were reconciled to God through the death of His Son, much more, having been reconciled, we shall be saved by His life. And not only that, but we also rejoice in God through our Lord Jesus Christ, through whom we have now received the reconciliation. (Romans 5:1–11, NKJV)

Notice in both of these portions of scripture that we are enemies to God. It was not by choice that we are enemies, but we were born into this world as enemies to God because of the sin of Adam that has passed on to all mankind. We are all born into the negative on the number line. Thanks a lot, Adam!

In this age of grace, God has made a way for all who want to be reconciled back to him and thus pass from death from God to life in God. This would be on the positive end of the number line, but it will only work for those who appropriate it. God has made this available to all mankind, but each of us must decide if we want it. It is not automatic for all humanity. In Romans 5:1, notice *justified by faith*. Faith is an act that you must perform. Also notice that this entire context is written to people who already are in the kingdom of God.

> To Him all the prophets witness that, through His name, whoever believes in Him will receive remission of sins. (Acts 10:43, NKJV)

All who believe in Jesus will receive forgiveness of sins. This is the work of Jesus. Jesus does not give us the Holy Spirit when we receive forgiveness of our sins.

> If we confess our sins, He is faithful and just to forgive us our sins and to cleanse us from all unrighteousness. (1 John 1:9, NKJV)

Part of being forgiven for your sins is to confess your sins. This will be covered in another chapter. Only Jesus can cleanse and purify. There is no other being in existence that can accomplish this.

> Then Jesus called a little child to Him, set him in the midst of them, and said, "Assuredly, I say to you, unless you are converted and become as little children, you will by no means enter the kingdom of heaven." (Matthew 18:2–3, NKJV)

First, we are converted from sin to righteousness. Notice that *we are to be like little children*. Jesus is referring to beginning life over again by being born again as he explained to Nicodemus. (John 3:1–8)

> Then Peter said to them, "Repent, and let every one of you be baptized in the name of Jesus Christ for the remission of sins; and you shall receive the gift of the Holy Spirit. (Acts 2:38, NKJV)

Notice that you must do the work of repentance from sin and be baptized for remission of sins. Once you have done this, you are placed back to zero on the number line. Then you can go on to receive the Holy Spirit. These are three separate experiences. The first two are required in order to be eligible to receive the third experience. Notice that receiving the Holy Spirit is the main goal in this verse.

God wants you to move on to having the Holy Spirit. A common mistake with this verse is that it is assumed that we automatically receive the Holy Spirit. It is promising that you will receive the Holy Spirit if you want it. When you receive the Holy Spirit, your spirit is made alive. It's like being plugged back into the wall socket and receiving electricity for the electronic device to function. If you receive the Holy Spirit, you begin to move into the positive on the number line. This is life in God.

> Repent therefore and be converted, that your sins may be blotted out, so that times of refreshing may come from the presence of the Lord. (Acts 3:19, NKJV)

Times of refreshing is one of the benefits of the Holy Spirit. Notice that you will need to be at zero in order to experience the times when the Holy Spirit will move within you. Once you obtain the Holy Spirit, you can experience the wonderful power of the Spirit. Every time the Spirit moves within my body, it is very much refreshing.

> By which have been given to us exceedingly great and precious promises, that through these you may be partakers of the divine nature, having escaped the corruption that is in the world through lust. But also for this very reason, giving all diligence, add to your faith virtue, to virtue knowledge, to knowledge self-control, to self-control perseverance, to perseverance godliness, to godliness brotherly kindness, and to brotherly kindness love. For if these things are yours and abound, you will be neither barren nor unfruitful in the knowledge of our Lord Jesus Christ. For he who lacks these things is shortsighted, even to blindness, and has forgotten that he was cleansed from his old sins. Therefore, brethren, be even more diligent to make your call and election sure, for if you do these things you will never stumble; for so an entrance will be supplied to you abundantly into the everlasting kingdom of our Lord and Savior Jesus Christ. (2 Peter 1:4–11, NKJV)

These verses provide us with a list of things that we must be doing as servants of God. Verse 4 says, "You may be partakers of the divine nature." This is the Holy Spirit. Verse 10 says, "If you do these things, you will never stumble." You can lose your salvation by falling back into sin and death.

Therefore, if anyone is in Christ, he is a new creation; old things have passed away; behold, all things have become new. (2 Corinthians 5:17, NKJV)

Notice that we can gain all these promises through the work of Christ. Notice also in 2 Peter 1:4 that you may be partakers. *You may* is a choice you make. Having the divine nature of the Holy Spirit will provide the escape of the corruption from sin that comes through the lusts of the flesh. In 2 Corinthians 5:17, we see the totality of all that we obtain from Christ. As a result, everything becomes new. This being born again is an entirely new life.

But as many as received Him, to them He gave the right to become children of God, to those who believe in His name. (John 1:12, NKJV)

Believing in his name is referring to his authorship. A common mistake in this verse is just to believe in the name of Jesus. Notice *as many as received him.* These are people who have chosen to accept Christ; it is a choice and is not automatic with all mankind.

For God so loved the world that He gave His only begotten Son, that whoever believes in Him should not perish but have everlasting life. For God did not send His Son into the world to condemn the world, but that the world through Him might be saved. He who believes in Him is not condemned; but he who does not believe is condemned already, because he has not believed in the name of the only begotten Son of God. And this is the condemnation, that the light has come into the world, and men loved darkness rather than light, because their deeds were evil. (John 3:16–19, NKJV)

Believing in Jesus is not just acknowledging that Jesus died and rose from the dead. The act of believing is not like the English form of belief. In the Greek, believing has a very different meaning. I go into this in the chapter about faith. A common mistake with these verses is to misuse the word *believe*. Believing in Jesus is accepting the totality of all that God is providing through Jesus, which also includes being born again from the Holy Spirit. Notice in verse16 that this life we gain through the Holy Spirit is also called *everlasting life*. As long as we are servants obeying the Father, the new life we have lasts forever.

He who sins is of the devil, for the devil has sinned from the beginning. For this purpose the Son of God was manifested, that He might destroy the works of the devil. Whoever has been born of God does not sin, for His seed remains in him; and he cannot sin, because he has been born of God. In this the children of God and the children of the devil are manifest: Whoever does not practice righteousness is not of God, nor is he who does not love his brother. (1 John 3:8–10, NKJV)

Notice in John 3:16 that *whoever believes*. This is for those who make the choice to accept Jesus. You must make a choice; it is not done for you. Also notice that it is God's desire that all people come to him so God has made this salvation available to all not just a select amount. There are false doctrines that teach that only a select portion of people will be saved. Notice in 1 John 3:9 how there is mention of *being born of God*. Also notice in verse 10 that the children of God are those who have *been born of God*. Again we see the use of being born.

Also notice that people are either referred to as a child of God or a child of the devil. I'll also add here that hell was created for the devil and all who follow Satan. Mankind was created much later—after Satan and the fallen angels were condemned to the earth.

Once man was created, anyone who chose's to follow Satan's ways is condemned to hell. To avoid going to hell, you must come out of Satan's realm and enter into God's realm. Sin is how Satan keeps us dead to God. Having God's nature within us is what keeps sin dead or at bay. Having the Holy Spirit within us gives us the power to keep sin dead within our lives (Acts 1:8). Being forgiven for your sins does not provide power against the lusts of your flesh. The Holy Spirit provides this power.

> And this is the testimony: that God has given us eternal life, and this life is in His Son. He who has the Son has life; he who does not have the Son of God does not have life. These things I have written to you who believe in the name of the Son of God, that you may know that you have eternal life, and that you may continue to believe in the name of the Son of God. (1 John 5:11–13, NKJV)

These verses are a little difficult to explain. A common mistake is to assume that if you just believe in Jesus, you will have eternal life. Many people think that they will have eternal life just by accepting Jesus into their lives. Notice in verse 13 that *these things I have written to you who believe.* John is writing to those who already have accepted Jesus and have received the Holy Spirit. Also notice that it is our job to continue to believe. It is not a onetime act on our part.

> In Him we have redemption through His blood, the forgiveness of sins, according to the riches of His grace. (Ephesians 1:7, NKJV)

Again we find that the work of Jesus is to purchase us back to God. Redemption suggests that we (mankind) were once with God. (Adam and Eve). To get back we have to be forgiven.

> And of His fullness we have all received, and grace for grace. For the law was given through Moses, but grace and truth came through Jesus Christ. (John 1:16–17, NKJV)

Notice that grace and truth came through Jesus. Jesus gave us the dispensation of grace. He also provides us with the gift of the Holy Spirit. The Holy Spirit's main job in all believers is to guide us into all the truth.

> And you He made alive, who were dead in trespasses and sins, in which you once walked according to the course of this world, according to the prince of the power of the air, the Spirit who now works in the sons of disobedience, among whom also we all once conducted ourselves in the lusts of our flesh,

fulfilling the desires of the flesh and of the mind, and were by nature children of wrath, just as the others. But God, who is rich in mercy, because of His great love with which He loved us, even when we were dead in trespasses, made us alive together with Christ (by grace you have been saved), and raised us up together, and made us sit together in the heavenly places in Christ Jesus, that in the ages to come He might show the exceeding riches of His grace in His kindness toward us in Christ Jesus. For by grace you have been saved through faith, and that not of yourselves; it is the gift of God, not of works, lest anyone should boast. (Ephesians 2:1–9, NKJV)

In these above verses, we see that God can make us alive. All people are dead, but only those who have accepted Jesus and the Holy Spirit have come out of this death. Notice in verse 8 that *God offers us a gift.* A gift must be received. Notice in verse 9 that none of these things can be obtained through our own abilities and *works.* There are millions of people involved in all kinds of religions who are just doing *works.* None of them will achieve one thread from God because they are doing their own works to try to end up in heaven. How sad it will be for all those people engaged in religious works to appease God who will learn, after they die, that none of their efforts will gain them access into heaven. Your heart must be purified, and then you must enter into the kingdom of God in God's way. You must take on God's nature through the Holy Spirit and put to bay the nature of the flesh and sin.

For the grace of God that brings salvation has appeared to all men, teaching us that, denying ungodliness and worldly lusts, we should live soberly, righteously, and godly in the present age, looking for the blessed hope and glorious appearing of our great God and Savior Jesus Christ, who gave Himself for us, that He might redeem us from every lawless deed and purify for Himself His own special people, zealous for good works. (Titus 2:11–14, NKJV)

These verses seem to contradict the ones right above them. Here, we read about doing good works. *Good* works and *religious* works are very different. Religious works are all the requirements that a religion would have you do in order to be accepted by God. Good works in Jesus are all the things we must do to maintain our salvation from death. Good works are to keep believers in Christ alive.

If you're not in Christ, then any kind of work to please God is religious work. Those who are in the negative or at zero on the number line are still dead. Anything they do is a religious work and will not help them in any way. But those in the positive side of the number line do good works because God requires this to maintain eternal life. All those who have accepted Jesus into their lives and don't have the Holy Spirit are still in the zero and are still dead. So all the works they do in the Bible are religious works. Their works are worthless to God.

Whoever commits sin also commits lawlessness, and sin is lawlessness. And you know that He was manifested to take away our sins, and in Him there is no sin. (1, NKJV)

Here again, we see that the purpose of Christ is to cleanse us of our sins. Notice that a definition of sin is given in verse 4. How do we know what is lawlessness? This information is provided to us in the covenant of the law given through Moses in the Old Testament. The law was given so that man would know what lawlessness is. Obeying the law cannot make you righteous and pure. It can only tell you that you are not righteous and pure.

> And for this reason He is the Mediator of the new covenant, by means of death, for the redemption of the transgressions under the first covenant, that those who are called may receive the promise of the eternal inheritance. (Hebrews 9:15, NKJV)

Again, Jesus in the only one who can provide redemption from our sins that are spelled out in the Old Testament. Notice the phrase *those who are called.*" You must be called by God in order to be able to come to Jesus. No one can come to Jesus on his or her own volition. God must draw you to himself or call you to himself.

> I say then: Walk in the Spirit, and you shall not fulfill the lust of the flesh. For the flesh lusts against the Spirit, and the Spirit against the flesh; and these are contrary to one another, so that you do not do the things that you wish. But if you are led by the Spirit, you are not under the law. Now the works of the flesh are evident, which are: adultery, fornication, uncleanness, lewdness, idolatry, sorcery, hatred, contentions, jealousies, outbursts of wrath, selfish ambitions, dissensions, heresies, envy, murders,

drunkenness, revelries, and the like; of which I tell you beforehand, just as I also told you in time past, that those who practice such things will not inherit the kingdom of God. But the fruit of the Spirit is love, joy, peace, longsuffering, kindness, goodness, faithfulness, gentleness, self-control. Against such there is no law. And those who are Christ's have crucified the flesh with its passions and desires. If we live in the Spirit, let us also walk in the Spirit. Let us not become conceited, provoking one another, envying one another. (Galatians 5:16–26, NKJV)

Notice in verse 16 and 26 that we are to walk *in the spirit*. It does not say we are to walk in Jesus. Verse 25 says, "If we live in the spirit." New life is in the spirit—not in Jesus. The use of the word *if* also reveals that it is our choice to accept the Holy Spirit. Notice in verse 17 that the flesh is against the Spirit—and the Spirit is against the flesh. The Holy Spirit is our power against the flesh, not Jesus.

It is the Spirit who gives life; the flesh profits nothing. The words that I speak to you are spirit, and they are life. (John 6:63, NKJV)

These words come from Jesus. Jesus is telling us that the Spirit gives us life—not Jesus. Jesus is talking about another being, the Holy Spirit. It is the Holy Spirit's job to make you born again. With the Holy Spirit, you move into the positive end of the number line.

As You have given Him authority over all flesh, that He should give eternal life to as many as You have given Him. And this is eternal life, that they may know You, the only true God, and Jesus Christ whom You have sent. (John 17:2–3, NKJV)

Knowing God is having a relationship with the Father. An ongoing relationship is what the Father considers to be eternal life. This is because it is what believers will be doing throughout all eternity. Notice that verse 3 is talking about a relationship with the Father. Eternal life is living in God—here and now—and having the Holy Spirit's life in you. The same things that we will do in eternity are done here and now. We commune or fellowship with God, and this is eternal life. Eternal life begins when we begin a relationship with the Father through the Holy Spirit.

For our citizenship is in heaven, from which we also eagerly wait for the Savior, the Lord Jesus Christ, who will transform our lowly body that it may be conformed to His glorious body, according to the working by which He is able even to subdue all things to Himself. (Philippians 3:20–21, NKJV)

If we are walking in the Spirit or living in the Spirit, we are already citizens of heaven. These verses do not say *will become* citizens. We don't have to wait to get to heaven. With the return of Christ, we get to have our bodies undergo transformations. This becomes another bonus for having life in God.

But has now been revealed by the appearing of our Savior Jesus Christ, who has abolished death and brought life and immortality to light through the gospel. (2 Timothy 1:10, NKJV)

Through Jesus's work, we can obtain life and immortality through the working of the Holy Spirit. This immortality is eternal life.

Blessed be the God and Father of our Lord Jesus Christ, who according to His abundant mercy has begotten us again to a living hope through the resurrection of Jesus Christ from the dead, to an inheritance incorruptible and undefiled and that does not fade away, reserved in heaven for you, who are kept by the power of God through faith for salvation ready to be revealed in the last time. In this you greatly rejoice, though now for a little while, if need be, you have been grieved by various trials, that the genuineness of your faith, being much more precious than gold that perishes, though it is tested by fire, may be found to praise, honor, and glory at the revelation of Jesus Christ, whom having not seen you love. Though now you do not see Him, yet believing, you rejoice with joy inexpressible and full of glory, receiving the end of your faith—the salvation of your souls. Of this salvation the prophets have inquired and searched carefully, who prophesied of the grace that would come to you, searching what, or what manner of time, the Spirit of Christ who was in them was indicating when He testified beforehand the sufferings of Christ and the glories that would follow. (1 Peter 1:3–11, NKJV)

Notice in verse 4 that all this is reserved in heaven for you. We are in the age or dispensation of grace. Through Christ, we can obtain the Holy Spirit who gives us life back into God. It's this same eternal life that we will have in heaven. We already gain what is in future heaven right here and now in this age of grace.

We have heaven in us which is knowing God as explained in John 17:3. When you finally arrive in physical heaven, there will be very little difference in what you already know about the Father through life in the Holy Spirit. The major difference is that you will be in a different environment and will have a different body (not being of corruptible flesh). We believers will always be getting to know more and more about God.

> For this reason I, Paul, the prisoner of Christ Jesus for you Gentiles—if indeed you have heard of the dispensation of the grace of God which was given to me for you, how that by revelation He made known to me the mystery (as I have briefly written already, by which, when you read, you may understand my knowledge in the mystery of Christ), which in other ages was not made known to the sons of men, as it has now been revealed by the Spirit to His holy apostles and prophets: that the Gentiles should be fellow heirs, of the same body, and partakers of His promise in Christ through the gospel, of which I became a minister according to the gift of the grace of God given to me by the effective working of his power. To me, who am less than the least of all the saints, this grace was given, that I should

preach among the Gentiles the unsearchable riches of Christ, and to make all see what is the fellowship of the mystery, which from the beginning of the ages has been hidden in God who created all things through Jesus Christ; to the intent that now the manifold wisdom of God might be made known by the church to the principalities and powers in the heavenly places, according to the eternal purpose which He accomplished in Christ Jesus our Lord. (Ephesians 3:1–11, NKJV)

Notice verse 2 mentions the *dispensation of grace of God*. Notice verse 11 mentions the *eternal purpose*. There is more to come and to be involved with once we get to physical heaven. But the biggest and most glorious of all experiences is to know God, and this will always be first and foremost in heaven. We now have access to what we will be doing first and foremost in heaven throughout all eternity. The Father is not a boring being. He is always an incredibly exciting being just to be with. You will never know of what I just wrote here until you enter into the life of the Holy Spirit or move into the positive end of the number line.

Notice also that Paul received the Holy Spirit several days after he accepted Christ into his heart. This is another proof that the Holy Spirit is a separate experience. Also in these verses, Paul speaks about receiving revelations from God and the dispensation of grace. This didn't happen till after he had received the Holy Spirit.

Whew! That was a lot of Bible verses that dealt with the subject of salvation from sin and gaining back life in God. And many more verses throughout the Bible deal with these two subjects. I hope you have gained a grasp of what the Bible is teaching about salvation. I hope you have seen that there are two requirements for entering into the kingdom of God.

Let's look at our outline again.

What is Salvation? **Answered**
Salvation suggests that I'm being saved from something.
    -What are we being saved from? **Answered**
    -Being saved from what I'm being saved from - does this get me into Heaven? **Answered**
    -If not what are the requirements to get to Heaven? **Answered**
Who is salvation for? **Answered**
Where do I find this salvation? **Answered**
When is salvation to begin? **Answered**
Why do I need salvation? **Answered**
How do I obtain salvation? **Answered**
How do I go to Heaven? **Answered**
    -Is there one requirement? **Answered**
    -Are there several requirements? **Answered**
What is eternal life? **Answered**
    -Eternal life suggests live forever. Is this correct? **Answered**
    -How do I get eternal life? **Answered**
How do I avoid going to Hell? **Answered**
There is no mention of the phrase, 'go to Heaven'
    -Why no phrase 'go to Heaven' **Answered**
Where did the phrase, 'go to Heaven' originate? **Answered**
What is the phrase 'enter into the kingdom of God?' **Answered**

What is 'born again?' **Answered**

What is 'unless one is born of water and spirit?' **Answered**

What is 'born of the Spirit is spirit?' **Answered**

What is 'born of the Spirit?" **Answered**

What is 'eternal life?' **Answered**

What is 'inherit eternal life?' **Answered**

What is 'righteousness exceeds the righteousness? **Answered**

What is 'wicked from among the just?' **Answered**

What is 'to continue in 'the faith?' **Answered**

How do people make it into Heaven? **Answered**

Where do people go to once they die on earth? **Answered**

What is the Bible teaching us about Heaven? **Answered**

What is the difference of the kingdom of God, Christ, and Heaven? **Answered**

Are there three separate kingdoms or are they one in the same? **Answered**

What is the covenant of Grace? **Answered**

So is it true that we must die in order to learn if we go to Heaven? **Answered**

Is entering the kingdom of God the same thing as going to Heaven? **Answered**

How do you end up in Heaven? **Answered**

Where do you go once you die on Earth? **Answered**

What is the Bible teaching us about Heaven? **Answered**

Now we have answered all the questions in the outline save one. We have even gained insight to heaven that we didn't know before, such as how knowing God is eternal life. We have come to see that there are three separate beings that all have the same nature: the Father, the Son, and the Holy Spirit. We have also come to see that the Holy Spirit has a much different role than Jesus does. Jesus died and was raised from the dead so that we may be forgiven for our sins and made pure. Now we can partake of all that the Holy Spirit has to offer which is life in God.

The question of how to get to the physical fourth dimension of heaven in the end is only partially answered. At the beginning of the number line, I mentioned that there are two requirements for ending up in heaven. What I write now is startling but ever so true. This second requirement is what most believers fail to achieve.

Obeying God's Personal Will

Let me explain this title. The Bible contains the general commands of God that we believers are to obey and required to do to maintain a relationship with him.

One of these general commands is to determine God's specific, detailed will for your life. We obey God's general will, but then we are also to learn exactly what we are to do in our lifetime on earth as servants. Most people don't know that this is something we are responsible for—let alone that there is such a thing.

For instance, are you supposed to be a businessman, an attorney, a preacher, or perhaps a doctor or nurse? Maybe you are supposed to have a specialized field in technology? A lot of people are in the wrong field of work, such as being a pastor when you're really supposed to be a veterinarian.

Almost everyone who reads this book and wants to learn what God would have you personally do will be shocked to find out they are not in God's will. I knew that I was to work for the Post Office as a letter carrier after I graduated from Bible school. I had to refuse three ministry positions that were offered to me. I fasted and prayed to learn what I was supposed to do, and the Holy Spirit revealed for me to go back home to Colorado. I spent that summer praying and fasting, and in the third month, the Holy Spirit revealed that I was to work for the Post Office. I was not to go to college to get a degree in electrical or computer engineering as I was planning.

God used that job to train me for my calling in the ministry. I meet people who were able to contribute to my calling that I would have never met anywhere else. Those key people were from all walks of life and God used them to train me for my calling. I never thought that God could do such a thing while I was a letter carrier. I took the time to seek God for his personal will for my life.

Most of the mighty men and women of God in the Old Testament and the New Testament had all kinds of different jobs and careers before they entered the ministry. Most of them received a calling during or before these careers but had to wait for the set time that God had for them. This even happened to Jesus. Some of them kept their careers and were able to perform their calling simultaneously.

Not every person who God used in the Bible had a full-time position in the ministry. Even Jesus started his career as a carpenter. In Jesus's day, a carpenter was usually a businessman. He didn't just make wooden items. He would go get the wood, which was a difficult undertaking. It required carts and oxen. They needed a place to store the wood and a shop to break the logs down into smaller items of workable wood. That required equipment. They had to house the oxen and feed them. They had to have other employees to help with all the work. They had to have the skills for making wooden items.

Most carpenters also built roofs, doors, and windows for homes. Being a carpenter entailed having a lot of skills, employees, equipment, housing, and animals. This was Jesus's career before he went into the ministry. The apostle Paul was a tent maker for the Roman soldiers while he would be involved in ministry in various towns or cities. It is not uncommon to have a secular job while being in the ministry for God.

Let's look at what is written in the Bible about God's personal will for each of us.

> But He answered and said, "It is written, 'Man shall not live by bread alone, but by every word that proceeds from the mouth of God.'" (Matthew 4:4, NKJV)

Notice that we are to live by what God speaks to us. This is not reading the Bible. It is literally having God speak to you personally. It does not say that we are to live by what we read in the Bible.

> Then Jesus said to him, "Away with you, Satan! For it is written, 'You shall worship the LORD your God, and Him only you shall serve.'" (Matthew 4:10, NKJV)

Notice that we are to serve the Father. This suggests that in order to be a servant, you have to do what God would reveal you to do. Servants are people who do what they are told to do. A servant has to receive commands or instructions from the master.

> I am the true vine, and My Father is the vinedresser. Every branch in Me that does not bear fruit He takes away; and every branch that bears fruit He prunes, that it may bear more fruit. You are already clean because of the word which I have spoken to you. Abide in Me, and I in you. As the branch cannot bear fruit of itself, unless it abides in the vine, neither can you, unless you abide in Me. I am the vine; you *are* the branches. He who abides in Me, and I in him, bears much fruit; for without Me you can do nothing. If anyone does not abide in Me, he is cast out as a branch and is withered; and they gather them and throw them into the fire, and they are burned. If you abide in Me, and My words abide in you, you will ask what you desire, and it shall be done for you. By this My Father is glorified, that you bear much fruit; so you will be My disciples. (John 15:1–8, NKJV)

In verse 2, we see that we are to bear fruit. A lot of people misuse this verse to mean the fruit of the Holy Spirit. The fruit here is the fruit of your deeds. Notice how verse 7 uses *and my words*. This phrase uses the word *rhema* for word. *Rhema* means spoken words (not written words). Having Jesus's words is having Jesus speak to you personally.

We are required to have Jesus speak to us personally if we want this promise to take effect. The deeds we perform are the works that God assigns to each of us. By doing God's will, we do these deeds. These deeds are the fruit we bear. If a person does not have God's personal will, he or she cannot bear the fruit that God wants. They are bearing different fruit, which is that of their own wills.

Also, do not become confused by this promise. It's not referring to asking God for anything you desire, which is how most people misuse this verse. The way the promise works is that a person already has the personal will of God and is serving God by performing his personal will. At different times during this service, problems, difficulties, hindrances, sickness, or situations arise that prevent the person from performing the service. Asking for God's help to clear up or provide deliverance from any of these issues will be performed (as promised) so that you can continue in your service to doing God's will.

> But without faith it is impossible to please Him, for he who comes to God must believe that He is, and that He is a rewarder of those who diligently seek Him. (Hebrews 11:6, NKJV)

Again, the second requirement is obeying what God would personally have you do. I'll go in depth in another chapter about faith, but for now, I'll use a short definition of faith. Faith is having God personally talk to you as is mentioned in Matthew 4:4. In Mathew 4:10, notice the last phrase Jesus uses in response to Satan (*and him only you shall serve*).

You cannot serve anyone unless they issue a command or request (such as the job environment or marriage) and this includes yourself. Notice in John15:2 that you must bear fruit. What kind of fruit is Jesus referring to? The context of John 15 is having the words of God abide in you. These words are God's personal spoken words. These words also include the Commandments laid forth in the Old Testament and the New Testament. Bearing fruit is having God give personal guidance and you obeying that guidance. Not obeying his personal guidance is failing to produce the fruit of his will.

Hearing the voice of God directly is the main goal of the covenant of grace. There are no other mediators as with the priesthood in the Old Testament. Jesus is our mediator in the dispensation of grace. Along with the age of grace, we also obtain a relationship with God by entering into the kingdom of God. This relationship requires that we hear the voice of God.

You can't have a relationship unless you have someone you can converse with. We need to get personal guidance from God about what he would have us do with our lives. For example, throughout our entire lives on earth, we will always be making decisions. God knows the better decisions to make versus the bad decisions. He wants us to make the better decisions. If we take these decisions to God, he will give us answers. Another example is dangerous situations that can harm or even cause death. A person who is hearing God's voice can avoid these dangerous conditions because God will warn you to avoid wherever you are headed. I have experienced this a number of times and know a lot of people who experience these warnings from God.

God is a rewarder for those who diligently seek him. In the written word, we learn that it is our job to seek God.

The reward we receive is usually hearing his spoken words. To please someone, you have to know what he or she wants.

"Not everyone who says to Me, 'Lord, Lord,' shall enter the kingdom of heaven, but He who does the will of My Father in heaven. Many will say to Me in that day, 'Lord, Lord, have we not prophesied in Your name, cast out demons in Your name, and done many wonders in Your name?'" And then I will declare to them, "I never knew you; depart from Me, you who practice lawlessness!" (Matthew 7:21–23, NKJV)

In verse 21, we learn that we must do the will of the Father who is in heaven. This will of God is not just practicing the commands of the Bible. Verse 23 says, "I never knew you; depart from me." God views those, who do not learn what his personal will is for them, to be lawless or unrighteous. We can also say that the righteous are those who are doing the personal will of God. Also notice in verse 23 that those who do not learn what God's personal will is for them will cost them eternity in hell. That's a major judgment! Also notice that this passage is referring to people who are Spirit Filled and flowing in the gifts of the Spirit but are not doing the personal will of God. These people are already in the kingdom of God. Therefore you can be full of the Holy Spirit and flow in the power of the Holy Spirit and still end up in hell because you didn't do the personal will of God.

We learned in the previous part of this chapter that eternal life is to know God the Father. In verse 21, we learn that we must do the will of the Father. These are two separate requirements. It is a requirement to know what God's will is in your personal life. In verse 22, Jesus says that there are many people who did many good tasks, but these same people were not doing God's personal will. Notice that these people who Jesus is talking about are those who are in the kingdom of heaven or the kingdom of God. These same people are rejected in verse 23. Part of getting to know God is learning his personal will and doing it.

This second requirement is the most difficult thing I have ever had to do in my fifty years of walking with God. Everyone I have met who has learned God's will for them has told me the same thing. Finding out God's will for your life is a difficult task. You must first learn to hear his voice. That in of its self is difficult and takes a lot of trial and error. Hearing God's voice takes time to learn requiring maturity in the Holy Spirit. It requires being alive in the Holy Spirit.

If you want to be a servant, you are going to have to find God's will for your life. This will become the major task for the rest of your life. If you want to end up in heaven, you are going to have to be a servant and learn what God would have you do. You will have to sacrifice all your life's plans and do what God would have you do. I wanted to enter the Air Force Academy to fly aircraft for a career, but God wanted me in the Post Office.

The entire goal of Christianity is to find out what God would have you do in your lifetime. In fact, this will always be your goal throughout all eternity, which is to serve God and do as he directs. This is what it is like to live in heaven. You will have to decide if you want to be a servant. Only servants will end up in the fourth dimension heaven. And when we servants arrive in heaven, we don't stop serving God. We continue to serve throughout eternity. There are many benefits to being a servant for God.

Getting God to talk to you is difficult. Most people who attempt this give up once they see how much work is involved in getting God to speak. Very few ever go on to do all the work that is required just to have God talk to you.

Because narrow is the gate and difficult is the way which leads to life, and there are few who find it. (Matthew 7:14, NKJV)

I can tell you from my own experience that if you ever go on to learn God's will for your life, you will receive a great amount of blessings. You will also undergo sufferings, which are designed to prune you and teach you wisdom. In the end, you will always be mightily blessed. You will get to experience things most people only dream of.

I have always wanted to see the entire world and photograph it. I had planned to do this through flying aircraft in the Air Force, but God had a different plan. Later I became a professional fine arts photographer in my spare time for that specific purpose. I knew that one day I would be traveling all over the world, doing work for God because at an early age, I learned how to hear the voice of God. I will be able to see the entire world, photograph it, and share all these images with others who only dream about seeing the world.

God has given me one of my heart's desires just as he promised. But I'm first a servant and do his work. While doing his work, I get to take photographs. But an even greater blessing is added to all this traveling, which is meeting so many wonderful people all around the earth. I have friends all over the earth and am continually making more.

Wow! God has given me far more riches in this life than I ever thought possible. This all came from me learning to first hear God's voice and then later learning how to get God to show me what he would have me do. Much of this is discussed in the chapter on faith. I was willing to give up everything just to learn all about God, and I did just that. In return, he has given everything I gave up back to me. Only now, there are extra blessings added to what I wanted to do. God is in the blessing business, but you must do things his way to obtain the blessing. That requires being a servant, not just a believer. You must first become a blessing to God.

To sum up this subject of salvation, we have learned a lot about the false doctrines that the church teaches about salvation. We have learned what the Bible teaches us about salvation and a few types of salvation. Most importantly, we have come to learn just how we can end up in heaven and avoid ending up in hell. This chapter only deals with salvation unto heaven and from sin.

There are a few other subjects that God requires for this heavenly salvation. The remainder of this book covers these subjects. I hope that you can see that including this chapter about salvation was necessary for understanding the rest of the book. I know that many readers are not going to accept this chapter because they are rebelling against the truth. False doctrines are always an attempt at a quick fix and avoiding a lot of work.

CHAPTER 3

Repentance

T hough this is the third chapter in this book, it is the beginning of the six basic Bible teachings or six beginning doctrines in the Christian faith. The past two chapters provided information that the writer of the book of Hebrews was taking for granted (as mentioned in Hebrews 6:1–2). The author of Hebrews was writing to the Hebrew believers and was assuming that those believers had already entered into the kingdom of god. In truth there are really 8 basic doctrines in the Christian faith.

> Therefore, leaving the discussion of the elementary principles of Christ, let us go on to perfection, not laying again the foundation of repentance from dead works and of faith toward God, of the doctrine of baptisms, of laying on of hands, of resurrection of the dead, and of eternal judgment. (Hebrews 6:1–2, NKJV)

The scripture above is showing us that there are six beginning doctrines for us to know and practice. Notice that we are to understand these six beginning doctrines before we can go on to perfection. I have explained that we are to build upon a foundation in order to mature in God. The six elementary doctrines are what remain for the foundation. The New American Standard Bible translation for verse 1 is:

Therefore, leaving the elementary teaching about Christ, let us press on to maturity. (Hebrews 6:1, NASB)

Notice in both versions how we see the request to move on to maturity in God. It's more accurate to *press on to maturity.* This reveals that we can reach a higher level of maturity. Those of us who have received the Holy Spirit as mentioned in John 3:5–6 undergo growth and development in the new, born again life. For this to happen, you have to understand and practice the six basic principles or doctrines taught here in Hebrews 6:1–2. We are to grow up in full maturity of the Holy Spirit. We are not to remain in babyhood the rest of our lives. We also are to push ourselves or press on to full maturity. This pushing or pressing also shows us that if we don't move on to maturity we will just remain babies.

Once you read through the rest of this book, you will see how we literally build our new lives by working with the Holy Spirit. God is not going to do all this building for anyone. Notice how Hebrews 6:1 mentions *let us press on to maturity.* If you don't build, you will not mature. Also notice that **we** are to *press on.* There is no mention that God is going to do this for us.

But, beloved, we are confident of better things concerning you, yes, things that accompany salvation, though we speak in this manner. (Hebrews 6:9, NKJV)

And we desire that each one of you show the same diligence to the full assurance of hope until the end, that you do not become sluggish, but imitate those who through faith and patience inherit the promises. (Hebrews 6:11–12, NKJV)

Verse 9 mentions *things that accompany salvation.* Verse 12 says, "Through faith and patience inherit the promises." To obtain these things, we must move on to full maturity. Likewise, if we never move on to maturity, then we will not obtain these promises. There are a lot of things to learn.

Also notice that it is the responsibility of each believer to move on to maturity. God is not going to do it all for us (as the church teaches). You have to work with God. The first works that you are to do are the six basic doctrines.

A new outline for repentance:
What is the definition of the word repentance?
What is dead works?

In English, repent is a verb. This is an action we are to do. In Greek, the word for repent is *metaneion*. This Greek word is also a verb. Its definition is "to change one's mind." This is not an emotion but instead a sober decision. To repent is not based upon any feelings; it is a decision. It's important to know that you may undergo many emotions when experiencing Christ, but to repent is strictly a decision.

Many churches teach that we are to perform penance, which are special religious rites or acts or ordinances. This has nothing to do with repentance. Repentance is to change your mind.

In the Hebrew language of the Old Testament, repent means to turn or to turn back. The use comes from someone moving or walking along and suddenly turning around and going in the opposite direction. This process in the Old Testament involves making a decision. You can't turn and go the opposite way unless you decide to do so.

In the Old Testament and New Testament, repenting involves a decision and then turning around and moving in that direction. Remember that repentance is act that each of us is to perform. God does not repent you or force you to change your mind.

> Likewise, I say to you, there is joy in the presence of the angels of God over one sinner who repents. Then He said: "A certain man had two sons. And the younger of them said to his father, "Father, give me the portion of goods that falls to me." So he divided to them his livelihood. And not many days after, the younger son gathered all together, journeyed to a far country, and there wasted his possessions with prodigal living. But when he had spent all, there arose a severe famine in that land, and he began to be in want. Then he went and joined himself to a citizen of that country, and he sent him into his fields to feed swine. And he would gladly have filled his stomach with the pods that the swine ate, and no one gave him anything. But

when he came to himself, he said, "How many of my father's hired servants have bread enough and to spare, and I perish with hunger! I will arise and go to my father, and will say to him, 'Father, I have sinned against heaven and before you, and I am no longer worthy to be called your son. Make me like one of your hired servants.'" And he arose and came to his father. But when he was still a great way off, his father saw him and had compassion, and ran and fell on his neck and kissed him. And the son said to him, "Father, I have sinned against heaven and in your sight, and am no longer worthy to be called your son." But the father said to his servants, "Bring out the best robe and put it on him, and put a ring on his hand and sandals on his feet. And bring the fatted calf here and kill it, and let us eat and be merry; for this my son was dead and is alive again; he was lost and is found." And they began to be merry. Now his older son was in the field. And as he came and drew near to the house, he heard music and dancing. So he called one of the servants and asked what these things meant. And he said to him, "Your brother has come, and because he has received him safe and sound, your father has killed the fatted calf." But he was angry and would not go in. Therefore, his father came out and pleaded with him. So he answered and said to his father, "Lo, these many years I have been serving you; I never transgressed your commandment at any time; and yet you never gave me a young goat, that I might make merry with my friends. But as soon as this son of yours came, who has devoured your livelihood with harlots, you killed the fatted calf for him." And he said to him, "Son, you are always with me, and all that I have is yours. It was right that we should make merry and be glad, for your brother was dead and is alive again, and was lost and is found." (Luke 15:10–32, NKJV)

Here is an example in the New Testament about repentance. This is a parable that Jesus is using to explain or teach what repentance is. In verse 18, we read that the prodigal makes a decision. In verse 20, he makes the action to return. Then he came to his father. This is repentance. You make a decision, take action, and carry out your decision.

In each of our own sinful lives, we are moving away from God. We are living in the negative on the number line described in chapter two. There is absolutely nothing that any man can do to get back to zero. In truth, you must have God first reveal to you that you are in the negative on the number line. You must have a revelation from God in order to see that you need his help. God has to first get your attention to your dead state of being.

No one can come to Me unless the Father who sent Me draws him. (John 6:44, NKJV)

- Principle: No man comes to the Father unless he is called or drawn by God.

John the Baptist

The entire New Testament begins with the message of repentance. The New Testament begins with John the Baptist. His message is that of repentance in order to receive the Messiah.

> The beginning of the gospel of Jesus Christ, the Son of God. As it is written in the Prophets: "Behold, I send My messenger before your face, Who will prepare your way before you." The voice of one crying in the wilderness: "Prepare the way of the LORD; make His paths straight." John came baptizing in the wilderness and preaching a baptism of repentance for the remission of sins. (Mark 1:1–4, NKJV)

John's work was to prepare the way of the Lord. This requires repentance from sin. You can't receive forgiveness from sin until you first repent from sinning and accept Jesus's forgiveness. John's ministry was to show all people that they were full of sin.

We all need to repent from our sins to turn away from our sins if we want to be with God. Up to this point in man's time scale, we don't find anyone preaching about repenting from sin. People would go to John and confess their sins. John would baptize them in water as a sign that they were stopping from doing any more sinning.

The water baptism was the action of showing others that you were serious with yourself and your life. The baptism was an outward act that you had changed your mind. But the problem was that the change did not bring forgiveness of sin within these people. John was making it very clear to those who heard him that the Lord was coming and would bring forgiveness of sins. John was showing and teaching people about repentance being a requirement to receive forgiveness when the Lord arrives. John's ministry was never taught by the priests of Israel. This was a totally new message to the Israelites. John made it clear that the Messiah was about to appear at that point in time, and the people were all excited and getting ready for the Messiah.

In those days, John the Baptist came preaching in the wilderness of Judea, and saying, "Repent, for the kingdom of heaven is at hand!" For this is he who was spoken of by the prophet Isaiah, saying: "The voice of one crying in the wilderness: 'Prepare the way of the LORD; Make His paths straight.'" And John himself was clothed in camel's hair, with a leather belt around his waist; and his food was locusts and wild honey. Then Jerusalem, all Judea, and all the region around the Jordan went out to him and were baptized by him in the Jordan, confessing their sins. But when he saw many of the Pharisees and Sadducees coming to his baptism, he said to them, "Brood of vipers! Who warned you to flee from the wrath to come? Therefore, bear fruits worthy of repentance, and do not think to say to yourselves, "We have Abraham as our father." For I say to you that God is able to raise up children to Abraham from these stones. And even now the ax is laid to the root of the trees. Therefore, every tree which does not bear good fruit is cut down and thrown into the fire. I indeed baptize you with water unto repentance, but He who is coming after me is mightier than I, whose sandals I am not worthy to carry. He will baptize you with the Holy Spirit and fire. His winnowing fan is in His hand, and He will thoroughly clean out His threshing floor, and gather His wheat into the barn; but He will burn up the chaff with unquenchable fire." (Matthew 3:1–12, NKJV)

Verse 11 mentions *he who is coming after me.* John already knows that Jesus will be coming along and is preparing the way of repentance.

- Principle: You can't receive forgiveness from sin until you first repent from sinning and then begin to believe in Jesus.

Repentance from Sin

Now after John was put in prison, Jesus came to Galilee, preaching the gospel of the kingdom of God, and saying, "The time is fulfilled, and the kingdom of God is at hand. Repent, and believe in the gospel." (Mark 1:14–15, NKJV)

Notice that the first command that Jesus is issuing is to repent and believe in him. You must repent and also believe in Christ. You can't just repent; you must also believe in Christ.

Then He said to them, "Thus it is written, and thus it was necessary for the Christ to suffer and to rise from the dead the third day, and that repentance and remission of sins should be preached in his name to all nations, beginning at Jerusalem. (Luke 24:46–47, NKJV)

After Christ's death and resurrection before returning to heaven, Jesus gave the disciples their commission to go into all the world. Their first message was to preach repentance and forgiveness (remission) of sin. Again this is the first of the six basic doctrines.

"Therefore, let all the house of Israel know assuredly that God has made this Jesus, whom you crucified, both Lord and Christ." Now when they heard this, they were cut to the heart, and said to Peter and the rest of the apostles, "Men and brethren, what shall we do?" Then Peter said to them, "Repent, and let every one of you be baptized in the name of Jesus Christ for the remission of sins; and you shall receive the gift of the Holy Spirit. (Acts 2:36–38, NKJV)

After their commission, the disciples were waiting in Jerusalem for the promised Holy Spirit. This event occurred fifty days after Jesus was raised from the dead. After the non-believers witnessed this outpouring of God, they wanted to know more about what had happened. This outpouring of the power from God had never happened before.

Peter preached about the Holy Spirit. Inverse 37, they asked, "What shall we do?" The first instructions were to repent and believe in Jesus for the forgiveness of sins.

Be baptized in Christ, and then you can receive the Holy Spirit. Again the first of the six basic doctrines is to repent and believe in Jesus.

How I kept back nothing that was helpful, but proclaimed it to you, and taught you publicly and from house to house, testifying to Jews, and also to Greeks, repentance toward God and faith toward our Lord Jesus Christ. (Acts 20:20–21, NKJV)

Apostle Paul was preparing to leave the region of Miletus and Ephesus to return to Jerusalem. In verse 24 and 25, Paul told everyone that he had done his commission or ministry in those regions. He taught all about the kingdom of God. In verse 21, we read about "repentance toward God and faith toward our Lord Jesus Christ." Again, the very first doctrine to be taught was repentance and believing in Christ.

Repentance from sin is the very first action that all humans are required to do, and then we believe in Jesus to forgive us our sins. None of us can do anything with God till we are cleansed from our sins. We must first be made zero on the number line.

- False Doctrine: Believing in Jesus is all you have to do.

The message of John the Baptist, Jesus, the disciples, and Apostle Paul and Peter is to repent and believe in Jesus for the forgiveness of sins.

But now commands all men everywhere to repent. (Acts 17:30, NKJV)

This is the general edict of God in this age of grace. All people are to repent from their sins if they want to end up with God and in heaven.

Repentance from Dead Works

Our second question in the above outline asked about dead works. I'll tackle this question first by explaining *works*.

Works are all activities and acts of all people that are not based upon repentance and faith in God. These works are referred to those who are attempting to please God without repentance. These people are anyone who is trying to do good things for God. These people are usually those who are involved with the religions of the earth. Such people are involved with acts in the name of religious piousness or morality. Charity, prayers, church attendance, every kind of religious rite and ordinance are works. Even placing a bumper sticker on your auto that states, "God bless America" is a religious work. Thus, any action that you are doing in an attempt to please God without repentance from sin is *works*.

Remember the number line from chapter two?

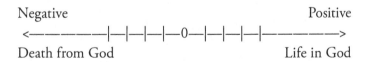

Negative   Positive

<———————|—|—|—|—0—|—|—|—|—————>

Death from God   Life in God

The word dead is referring to those who are still dead to God. On the number line in chapter two, copied above, I describe the word *dead* in more detail. As long as you have not moved into the positive from zero, you are still dead to God. Even if you are at zero, having received forgiveness of sins, you are still dead to God. You have to be in the positive to be alive in God. These dead people include "professing Christians" from many of today's churches. Unless you are born of the Holy Spirit, you are still a dead man to God. There are millions of these kinds of "professing Christians" in today's world. Being forgiven for your sins does not make you alive to God.

Combining the two words, we see that dead works involve people who are still in a dead state of being to God but are trying to do acts of good to appease or please God.

What is the author in Hebrews really saying in Hebrews 6:1 (*repentance from dead works*)? He is telling the readers that they must be alive in God and not dead to God. They must have the Holy Spirit, which makes us alive in God. The writer is saying that your attempts to do all these good works are worthless. You have to stop doing these dead works. You have to repent from doing dead works. Only works that are done to God coming from being alive in God are of any credit or value. The only works that God will have you do come from obeying the written Word of God and obeying God's personal guidance for your life. This will be covered in the chapter on faith.

For example, you may have been attending a dead denominational church or another church. You get called from God to accept Christ into your heart and repent from your sins. It doesn't matter whether or not the call came from that church or another person separate from that church. You follow through with this calling, repent for your sins, and are forgiven for your sins. You go on to receive the baptism of the Holy Spirit and become alive in God. You have passed from death into life in God.

You are now on the positive side of the number line, but you are still in the church you are attending. If you're truly alive, it will shortly become very clear to you that that dead church is practicing a lot of dead works. Those of us who are alive in the Holy Spirit refer to these churches as "dead churches." Upon seeing these things, the Holy Spirit will begin telling you to leave that church. You can't mature in God if you are among the dead. If you decide to remain in that dead church, you will continue to practice dead works. You will need to repent from dead works if you ever want to mature in God. You will never mature or grow up in God in such an environment. The dead cannot teach you anything about being alive because they are dead. Only those who are alive can teach you about life in God.

- Principle: Those who remain or dwell with others will take on those other people's habits.
- Principle: In order to mature in the Holy Spirit, you must be with others who are maturing and growing in the life of God.

I'm going to do little preaching here. I'm amazed by how many people began a work of repentance and then decided to keep a few "pet sins." I see this constantly. When you are called to accept Jesus, God is commanding you to repent from your sins. He is not asking you to repent from some or most your sins. He is commanding you to repent from all your sins. He didn't say to repent from most of them and then revert back to a few of them. Repentance is forever.

I constantly have people asking me why they never go on to mature and partake in the promises of God. They tell me that they never get healed from sickness. They tell me it's as though they are still part of the curse of death. Things still go wrong in their lives, and they have no blessings from God. I have people tell me that they never can get God to communicate with them. The lists go on and on. For most of these people, the answer is because they never totally repented from their sins. They kept a few pet sins.

Repentance for many people can be a difficult task. For those who have major addictions, this becomes even more difficult. It is not impossible to repent from all your sins. I've witnessed many times where God literally helped people repent in certain situations, such as drug, tobacco, and alcohol abuse.

God is in the freedom business. He wants us all free in every meaning of the word, especially from sin. Crying out to God for help in repenting does work. In fact, as you mature in God, he will continue to touch various areas in your life and require you to give up a certain thing. At that point in time, that certain thing suddenly becomes sinful for you. You repent from that certain thing and continue on with God. So repentance will be an ongoing project in your life.

At the beginning of your calling to enter the kingdom of heaven, you repent for all the sins you are aware of. Later, God begins to remove other sins as you receive revelations about them. An example is that many people who come to know God still swear and use curse words. But soon after their conversions, they become convicted within their spirits from the work of the Holy Spirit about the use of foul words. They stop using these words or repent from the use of these words.

I used to be addicted to watching TV. Then one day in 1988, the Holy Spirit began to convict me for watching TV. I was fifteen years old in the Holy Spirit and maturing in God. Suddenly God was telling me to repent from watching TV. For me, TV became sinful. I was personally directed by God to repent from TV. I did as commanded and have never watched it since.

Since 1988, I have continued to mature and increase with God. Because I repented from TV as directed, I've gone on to be able to spend more time in prayer and Bible study. This led to me receiving the twenty-five visions from God in *America's Resurrection-A Modern-Day Prophecy*. This book was a result of having matured in God and is helping countless people move on into maturity with God. It wouldn't have been possible to write this book had I not repented for watching TV. This is not to say that everyone who reads this book is to repent for watching TV. This is an example about how God will continue asking you to repent from certain things when the time arrives to do so. End of preaching.

Remember that these scriptures in Hebrew 6:1–2 were written to believers all throughout Israel and the Roman Empire. Hebrew and Greek were the spoken languages of Israel and the Roman Empire during the first church. Dead works had apparently become a problem for many of the Hebrew believers scattered throughout Rome. This was probably because many of the new converts in Christ came from Judaism. But they also came from the Gentile world, which worshiped pagan religions. They spent their entire lives practicing all the religious rites and rituals of the pagan religions or the Old Testament as well as the rules of the Sadducees and Pharisees.

Once saved through Jesus, they were suddenly plunged into God's kingdom. Like most of us who come out from religious backgrounds, we tend to take some of the rites and customs from the former religion and attempt to incorporate them in our new life in God. These are the dead works that the writer of Hebrews was talking about. We are required to repent from these dead works.

I tell you, no; but unless you repent you will all likewise perish. (Luke 13:3, NKJV)

Notice that repentance is a requirement to moving on into life with God, but repenting alone will not save you from death. To repent is the first of several steps to perform as we shall see in the following chapters.

CHAPTER 4

Faith

Faith is probably the most mentioned word of the Bible. Faith is also the most misunderstood word used throughout history, especially since Jesus first came. Even in Jesus's days on earth, most didn't have a proper definition of faith.

Surprisingly, faith is one of the most difficult words to define. To make it worse, much is lost when translating it from Greek to English. First, I'm going to provide a definition of faith, and then we will dive into the scriptures to see just exactly how it works. Most modern writers (since Martin Luther) dive into the scriptures without providing a proper definition of faith. This produces a lot of false doctrines. Why would you read anything without proper definitions of the writers' words? You end up guessing at what they are talking about and end up misinterpreting what they were writing about.

A New Outline for Faith:
What is faith?

Why is it so important?
How does it work?
When does it work?
Where do I apply it?
Who is faith for?
What other words are used in connection with faith?

> But without faith it is impossible to please Him, for
> he who comes to God must believe that He is, and
> that He is a rewarder of those who diligently seek
> Him. (Hebrews 11:6, NKJV)

> But the just shall live by his faith. (Habakkuk 2:4,
> NKJV)

This is the verse that Martin Luther used as the main point in the articles he nailed to the papal church doors that ultimately dislodged the power of the Church in Rome that went on to be called the Protestant Reformation.

Faith is a requirement from God, but so few people understand the definition of faith. In turn, they don't understand what faith is. I'll define what faith really means. You may have to re-read the definition several times till you understand the definition because the word *faith* can be involved.

The Greek verb *pistis* is translated into the English as faith. The literal definition of *pistis* is "to be persuaded to believe." (Persuasion is an action that has occurred within the mind and heart of someone.) That's it. But what does all this persuasion entail? Herein lies the difficulty of understanding faith or persuasion.

Persuasion involves two words: being swayed. To be persuaded requires a few steps of a process that has to happen. To be persuaded requires a few events to occur. Once the two words (persuasion and believing) are defined, you will learn the true meaning of faith.

Persuasion is being swayed from one idea to another idea, from one thought to a different thought, or confirming an idea as true. A repeated experience of the same testimony makes your persuasion all the more solid. This involves the use of the mind. Persuasion occurs within the mind. Persuasion is a decision made within the mind.

How we become persuaded in our thinking or change of thinking can come from many different sources. We may see something happen that we only thought about, but now we have become actual witnesses of the event. We become persuaded instead of just guessing or wondering. That witness of the event persuades our mind that something has happened. Persuasion involves all five senses. We have to experience an event or occurrence to have a persuasion. To not have an experience is to only make a theory and attempt to believe the theory. Persuasion must involve a fact. Faith involves being persuaded by the testimony of another person. Persuasion also involves ultimately believing what someone has told you, not by you personally witnessing such an event. You change your thinking based upon the testimony of another person. This form of persuasion in conjunction with faith involves trust in another person's testimony as being true.

The difficulty with the definition of faith is with the word *believe*. The word *persuasion* must be used in conjunction with another word, *believe*, which has several definitions in English but just one in Greek: "to place one's trust in another" (*Holman Treasury of Key Bible Words*). In Greek, to believe is based on an experience and facts of persuasion from another. It's not guessing, hoping, or trying to picture something. It is accepting facts as told by another person.

Most English-speaking people use the word *believe* differently from the way the Greeks used it. The English word *believe* means "to accept as true or real" (*The American Heritage Dictionary*). For example, people who want to believe there is extraterrestrial life say they believe in life on other planets. No one really knows if there is extraterrestrial life, and to believe there is creates a belief based on conjecture. In Greek, someone would have to say, "I *think* there is life on other planets."

The difference from Greek and English is in the word *accept* in the English form. In English, you choose to accept something to be true or real regardless of having any facts to prove its existence. The Greeks would hear someone's experience and then place their trust in those spoken words.

In ancient Greek days, when you saw or experienced an event, you witnessed it. When you told someone about the experience you saw, heard, tasted, smelled, or felt, you were telling about your experience. The person who has had the experience has a fact and thus is persuaded. If another person accepts what you say about your experience they become persuaded and they are a believer of your words or a believer of what you said occurred. If he or she trusts your testimony, that becomes persuasion and belief which is Greek faith.

In Greek faith, belief always involves hearing another's testimony. In English, belief doesn't just place trust in another's testimony; instead, it accepts whatever they want to be factual regardless of whether there are any facts to support the belief. *The American Heritage Dictionary* defines English faith as "confident belief." This definition of faith has nothing to do with persuasion from someone's testimony. Thus, the English form of faith is to believe whatever you choose to accept as true or real, with or without facts. In English, there is no persuasion involved to believe in something as told from another.

In Greek, *belief* is hearing another's testimony and acknowledging those words to be true, factual, of an event or a thing, and being persuaded that the experience occurred; you believe the testimony of the experience. When you accept their experience and believe it, you are trusting in their testimony even though you do not have any facts or proof.

Greek faith is having been persuaded to believe. If you continue to believe, you continue to have faith. If you stop believing in that person's testimony, you no longer have faith in it. In Greek faith, it's impossible to not choose to believe or disbelieve in a testimony; ultimately, you can only believe or not believe. Any uncertainty about a testimony is disbelieving.

You must be careful to not use the English definition of *believe*. We all either place Greek faith in people's testimony every day or we don't. The Greeks were trying to explain the mechanics of believing, the steps that occur in an individual that make that person become persuaded.

Plain Greek faith is having been persuaded to believe due to someone's experience (usually to change from one belief or idea to another). Try to remember that the word *believe* I will be using is the Greek version, not the modern English definition.

All of us live using Greek faith daily. Humans experience others' testimonies and believe or doubt their experiences. People tell us things, and we either believe or reject what is said. This is what the Greeks considered daily occurrences in their lives.

The process of persuasion is to make an observation through being a witness of an event. That event is registered within our mind's memory. Next, we conclude the witness or experience of the event to be factual—it indeed occurred. The final process is that we choose to believe in that observation. If we accept the fact and believe it, we are thus persuaded. If we choose not to believe what we observed, then we are not persuaded by the event or experience; thus, we are not persuaded. Observation plus fact plus belief equals persuasion. In Greek, it is hearing testimony plus persuasion plus believing equals faith. This is the process of Greek faith.

Many of us grow up experiencing a multitude of facts. We are persuaded in all that we have experienced. But there also are a lot of things we never experience and only have what others have made theories about or told us about. We have yet to be truly persuaded regarding these theories or sayings. Sometimes we experience different facts that cause us to change our thinking or ideas, and our persuasion is changed. For example, there is a common belief today that there is life on other planets. This is only a theory that is not backed by any facts. Many people choose to believe in this theory even though they have never witnessed or experienced any extraterrestrial life. But we are not truly persuaded by this theory because there are no facts to support the belief.

Men and women today are still actively involved in searching the cosmos for signs of other life. The fact is that there are no facts of life on other planets to date. I'm persuaded by the facts that no life exists in the cosmos. We are alone. So this is my current belief. My belief is based upon the facts that have thus formed my persuasion. My persuasion will be changed if an observation is made of finding life on another planet. Presently I have faith that mankind and planet earth are the only life in all the cosmos. To believe that life is on another planet is to believe in a theory of empty facts. It is impossible to have faith that there is life on another planet without some facts.

Another example is witnessing an event on TV. In an advertisement for pizzas, we watch people enjoying the pizza they are eating. We see the food as being something wonderful to eat. We conclude that what we are seeing and being told is factual. We believe that this must be a great meal to partake of. We are thus persuaded that the pizza is not a theory.

Then we go to that pizza restaurant and order the pizza we saw and witnessed on TV. We don't experience all the cheer and joy that the actors portrayed in the TV ad. Then we take our first bite of the food and discover that it's not to our liking. In fact, it's nothing what we thought it might taste like. The bread is bland, the cheese is not mozzarella, the sauce has no spices, and the meat toppings are of a different base of spices that we are not accustomed too. In our experience, the pizza is totally not to our liking. We thus conclude that we are persuaded that the pizza we experienced is awful. Our persuasion has now changed. It's not what we were first persuaded of when we viewed it on TV. Our idea of persuasion has been changed based upon experience and facts. We leave the pizza restaurant with gloom and sadness—not with cheer and joy. We thus no longer have faith in that pizza TV advertisement.

I hope this will give a good working definition of Greek faith. Remember that this is strictly a definition of the word *faith*. Next I'll show you how faith is used in the Bible. This is where faith becomes more difficult to understand. I'll call the faith used in the Bible—Bible Faith. From this point on when I use the word *faith,* I'm referring to the Greek definition.

Bible Faith

God requires all people to exercise faith in him. Without faith in God, nothing will ever happen to you from God. All God can do is try to get you to have faith in him. You may have experienced a few actions that came from God, but that does not make you alive in God. All this means is that you conclude that there is a God. You have faith that God exists, but it doesn't mean you have faith in God. Without faith in God, it is impossible to please him.

So what does having faith in God entail? I'll add this question to our outline.

This is why most people never come to a full understanding of faith in God. Faith in God is having experienced God personally. What does personally really mean here? You have to have God communicate to you directly. God has to speak to you. This is not witnessing outward signs such as miracles. Faith is literally having God speak to you. This is a personal experience of God. Another personal experience would be God suddenly appearing to you and you get to see him. God has only done this for one human in all history. His way with mankind is to speak to us. Seeing a miracle occur to someone else or observing a miracle is not a personal experience with God. When God speaks to you personally, you then have God's testimony.

When God speaks to you within, you know that he spoke or is speaking to you. You are hearing or experiencing his voice. You have the fact that this experience is happening or has happened. You can choose to accept this fact or reject it. Accepting the fact is being persuaded in God or having faith in God that he spoke to you. So far, this is easy to understand—even though you may never have had an experience from God. The big difficulty is that much is lost in translation from Greek to English. This is where 99 percent of the church has messed up faith and turned faith into one fat false doctrine.

In the Bible, there are many places that teach that we are to place faith in God's Word. The big error most people make is placing faith in the written Bible. But you ask, "isn't the Bible teaching us to place our faith in God's Word?" You will find many verses that say exactly just that in our English translations. Many people attempt this only to end in futility, frustration, and failure because none of it works. Here is the problem.

In the Greek New Testament, there are two different words that are translated into our one English word: *word*. In Greek, there are two separate words for our one word—*word*. In Greek, one of the words we translate into word is *logos.* The other word in Greek is *rhema,* which we translate into English as *word.* Both *logos* and *rhema* are translated into our only one word—*word.* Thus the meanings of both *logos* and *rhema* become lost in our English translations. This happens with several other words from Greek to English, such as love. In Greek, there are three words for love— *philia, eros,* and *agape.* In Greek, these describe physical love, spiritual affection of love, and the caring for the other person as love. In English, there are no separate words for love that describe these three different Greek words. The same occurs for the word *word* in English.

The Greek *logos* means "written words." It is used to usually describe the scriptures as written in the Bible. Writing letters and notes on clay tablets, parchment, or even in the dirt back then was *logos* or written words. Today, we use paper, electronic tablets, etc. to write *logos* (written words).

The Greek *rhema* means "spoken words." The Greek word is used when a conversation is occurring or has occurred. *Rhema* is a direct personal spoken word of conversation of words from one person to another or to many others, such as preaching, that are all hearing the spoken words at the same moment in time. *Rhema* is to experience personally a spoken word from someone else.

When these Greek words are translated into English, their meanings become lost in translation. To read the Bible in English, you will easily become lost in the understanding of what is truly being taught in the Bible. In fact, many of the verses will become confusing when reading them in English because it doesn't make sense with the use of the other English words in scripture. You will only be able to make conclusions about what the scriptures are seemingly teaching in English.

Unless you have the correct words of *rhema* and *logos* used in the English form, you will never gain the proper understanding of God's doctrine. When I use the following verses, I will be using two words in English to make the differential description of the two Greek words. These two words will be "written word" and "spoken word." With this corrected translation, you will clearly see what the Bible is truly teaching.

Since the Bible has been translated into English, these two lost words have caused more confusion than ever before. New false doctrines arose just because of the King James Version and all following Bible versions in that students of the Bible failed to understand faith in God. Even to this day, I'm amazed by how this error continues. In short, many people are in hell because of the confusion. Remember that false doctrines will send you to hell because the practice of them will only displease God. You will never obtain life in him through the practice of false doctrines. It becomes critically important that we get faith correct so we don't miss out on going to physical heaven. Remember that faith in God is how we please God. We are to live by faith in God.

For most of those who read this chapter, this will be the first time you will have heard a true definition of faith. This is not easy to grasp. When we go through the scriptures, it will become more obvious that *logos* and *rhema* are in use. Reread this chapter as many times as you have to. Many of you will have to cut through all the different definitions that the church has attempted to teach you regarding faith in God. There are countless attempts to define faith in

God because most of these clergymen were never taught the true definition at their Bible schools. The Bible schools don't even know the definition of faith and how it is used in the Bible. This even happened to me when I attended Bible school.

To sum up, the definition of faith is to be persuaded (observation plus the fact plus belief equals persuasion). Bible faith is having God personally speak to us (an experience). Faith used in the Bible is being persuaded by what God speaks. (Faith plus spoken word equals Bible faith). We personally experience this act, which is a fact. We choose to believe in what God has said to us. Hence, we are persuaded that God spoke words to us.

Bible faith is not reading God's written words as found in the Bible. Faith used in the following verses is only used in conjunction with the Greek word *rhema* (spoken words). Faith is never used with the Greek word *logos* (written words). I go into great detail about faith in *America's Resurrection-A Modern-Day Prophecy*. If you are still struggling with this shortened version of the definition of faith, read the chapter about faith in *America's Resurrection*.

So let's begin to go through the many verses that faith in God is used. As we examine each of the verses, the true definition of Bible faith will become very clear.

In many of these verses, we see the use of other words, such as hope. I'll touch on these other words and their definitions as we come across them. Hope is future tense. Faith is present tense. Hope is an attitude of expectancy in that it is aimed to the future. Faith is something we have within us in the now, that we possess within us in the present. Faith in God is the spoken word of God within our hearts and spirits. Hope is just in the mind. Hope knows something will occur in the future and we have yet to experience it.

I'm going to dig out all the verses that use the Greek word *rhema* so you will get a good true understanding of why you are to place your faith in such as faith in God. Then I'll go on to show the scriptures that use the word *faith*. You will better understand all these verses and clear up all the confusion for those who have already read the Bible.

The following verses are those with the use of *rhema* (spoken word). So when you see the English word *word*, use the phrase "spoken word."

> But He answered and said, "It is written, 'Man shall not live by bread alone, but by every word that proceeds from the mouth of God.'" (Matthew 4:4, NKJV)

> But if he will not hear, take with you one or two more, that "by the mouth of two or three witnesses every word may be established." (Matthew 18:16, NKJV)

> And Peter remembered the word of Jesus who had said to him, "Before the rooster crows, you will deny Me three times." So he went out and wept bitterly. (Matthew 26:75, NKJV)

> But he answered him not one word, so that the governor marveled greatly. (Matthew 27:14, NKJV)

Then Mary said, "Behold the maidservant of the Lord! Let it be to me according to your word." And the angel departed from her. (Luke 1:38, NKJV)

Lord, now You are letting Your servant depart in peace, according to Your word. (Luke 2:29, NKJV)

While Annas and Caiaphas were high priests, the word of God came to John the son of Zacharias in the wilderness. (Luke 3:2, NKJV)

But Jesus answered him, saying, "It is written, 'Man shall not live by bread alone, but by every word of God.'" (Luke 4:4, NKJV)

But Simon answered and said to Him, "Master, we have toiled all night and caught nothing; nevertheless at Your word I will let down the net." (Luke 5:5, NKJV)

For He whom God has sent speaks the words of God, for God does not give the Spirit by measure. (John 3:34, NKJV)

For if you believed Moses, you would believe Me; for he wrote about Me. But if you do not believe his writings, how will you believe My words?" (John 5:46–47, NKJV)

It is the Spirit who gives life; the flesh profits nothing. The words that I speak to you are spirit, and they are life. (John 6:63, NKJV)

He who is of God hears God's words; therefore you do not hear, because you are not of God." (John 8:47, NKJV)

And if anyone hears My words and does not believe, I do not judge him; for I did not come to judge the world but to save the world. He who rejects Me, and does not receive My words, has that which judges him—the word that I have spoken will judge him in the last day. (John 12:47–48, NKJV)

Do you not believe that I am in the Father, and the Father in Me? The words that I speak to you I do not speak on My own authority; but the Father who dwells in Me does the works. (John 14:10, NKJV)

If you abide in Me, and My words abide in you, you will ask what you desire, and it shall be done for you. (John 15:7, NKJV)

But Peter, standing up with the eleven, raised his voice and said to them, "Men of Judea and all who dwell in Jerusalem, let this be known to you, and heed my words." (Acts 2:14, NKJV)

Then Ananias, hearing these words, fell down and breathed his last. So great fear came upon all those who heard these things. (Acts 5:5, NKJV)

Go, stand in the temple and speak to the people all the words of this life. (Acts 5:20, NKJV)

Who will tell you words by which you and all your household will be saved. And as I began to speak, the Holy Spirit fell upon them, as upon us at the beginning. Then I remembered the Word of the Lord, how He said, "John indeed baptized with water, but you shall be baptized with the Holy Spirit." (Acts 11:14–16, NKJV)

So when the Jews went out of the synagogue, the Gentiles begged that these words might be preached to them the next Sabbath. (Acts 13:42, NKJV)

But he said, "I am not mad, most noble Festus, but speak the words of truth and reason." (Acts 26:25, NKJV)

But what does it say? "The word is near you, in your mouth and in your heart" (that is, the word of faith which we preach). (Romans 10:8, NKJV)

So then faith comes by hearing, and hearing by the word of God. (Romans 10:17, NKJV)

But I say, have they not heard? Yes indeed: "Their sound has gone out to all the earth, and their words to the ends of the world." (Romans 10:18, NKJV)

This will be the third time I am coming to you. "By the mouth of two or three witnesses every word shall be established." (2 Corinthians 13:1, NKJV)

For all the law is fulfilled in one word, even in this: "You shall love your neighbor as yourself." (Galatians 5:14, NKJV)

Let him who is taught the word share in all good things with him who teaches. (Galatians 6:6, NKJV)

In Him you also trusted, after you heard the word of truth, the gospel of your salvation; in whom also, having believed, you were sealed with the Holy Spirit of promise. (Ephesians 1:13, NKJV)

That He might sanctify and cleanse her with the washing of water by the word. (Ephesians 5:26, NKJV)

And take the helmet of salvation, and the sword of the Spirit, which is the word of God. (Ephesians 6:17, NKJV)

Who being the brightness of His glory and the express image of His person, and upholding all things by the word of His power, when He had by Himself purged our sins, sat down at the right hand of the Majesty on high. (Hebrews 1:3, NKJV)

And have tasted the good word of God and the powers of the age to come. (Hebrews 6:5, NKJV)

By faith we understand that the worlds were framed by the word of God, so that the things which are seen were not made of things which are visible. (Hebrews 11:3, NKJV)

But the word of the LORD endures forever. Now this is the word which by the gospel was preached to you. (1 Peter 1:25, NKJV)

But you, beloved, remember the words which were spoken before by the apostles of our Lord Jesus Christ. (Jude 1:17, NKJV)

Surprisingly, there are not very many scriptures that employ the use of *rhema* as opposed to the use of logos. Please don't get me wrong that these other verses that use *logos* are not important in your Christian walk. All scripture is important. I'm just focusing on the usage of *rhema* so that you can get a clear understanding of how we are to have faith in God.

Now I'll chose the more important verses from this listing so that we can move on to understand faith in God. I'll be expounding on each of these verses. Remember to use the translation "spoken word" for the use of the word "word."

But He answered and said, "It is written, "Man shall not live by bread alone, but by every word (spoken word) that proceeds from the mouth of God." (Matthew 4:4, NKJV)

This verse pretty much says it all. Jesus is saying that man is to not just live by food but by every spoken word that proceeds from the mouth of God. You are going to have to get God to talk to you and give you guidance for your life. This is having faith in God. God speaks to you, and you now have faith in that particular word. If God doesn't speak to you, then it is impossible to have faith in God. Notice also that we are commanded to live by God's spoken words (which we can sum up as guidance in your personal life.) Notice that it does not say "but by every word that proceeds from the Bible."

So then faith comes by hearing, and hearing by the word (spoken word) of God. (Romans 10:17, NKJV)

Again, this verse summarizes what causes us to have faith in God. You have to hear God speak. When God speaks and you are persuaded, you have faith in that spoken word of God. Notice that it does not say faith comes by reading and reading the written Word of God.

And take the helmet of salvation, and the sword of the spirit, which is the word (spoken word) of God. (Ephesians 6:17, NKJV)

This verse is using a Roman soldier's armor and weapon for an example of our spiritual armor and weaponry in Christ. Everyone I have ever met thinks that the sword of the spirit, which is the word of God, is referring to the Bible. How wrong they are. The sword of the Spirit are God's spoken words to you. It has nothing to do with the written Word of God. In other words, a Christian's only offensive weapon is having faith in God's personal spoken words. If you don't have any spoken words from God, you have no offensive weapon-you have no sword.

These three key verses are what give us insight to God's *rhema* to us. This is how we obtain faith in God.

We understand that the way we get faith in God is to have God speak to us. These spoken words from God are for us to obey and do.

Sometimes God's *rhemas* are for future reference or promises that will happen in your lifetimes. Sometimes *rhemas* are for an immediate action, usually as a warning to stay away from someone or something, to avoid injury and possible death. Sometimes *rhema* is in the form of a revelation about God.

When I was thirteen years old, God suddenly spoke to me while I was at a Baptist church service. He spoke to me and said that he wanted me to go as a missionary to other parts of the world. There was a visiting missionary at the church who did work in Africa in the jungle regions. He was telling us about his experiences and was raising money for his missionary work.

After his message, God spoke to me. I knew within my spirit that God had spoken to me. For the next several months, I struggled with that spoken word because all I understood at that time was that God wanted me to be a missionary to the jungles of Africa. I just didn't want to do that—even at the age of thirteen—but God kept nudging me to accept his call.

I finally gave in and confessed that I would go to Africa to be a missionary. Suddenly the pressure from God subsided. I was at peace again. A few years later, after I became Spirit-filled at the age of twenty, I understood that I would not be going to do missionary work in the jungles of Africa. God then added to the word and revealed that I was called to go to several other countries on his behalf.

In my thirties, I came to know all about my calling after fasting for forty days, having received more rhema words from God. That first *rhema* word is still alive within as of the writing of this book. It will always be there and will always give me hope for my calling till the day I die on earth. Since that first word, I have received many other words pertaining to this calling of which I'm able to add to. I now have many faiths that deal with this calling God has upon me.

I have had warning *rhemas* from God to suddenly stop what I'm doing and get away from that area. It turned out that some of these warnings did in fact save me from death and injuries. God is truly amazing. There have been warnings that I've ignored and had to pay a price for ignoring those words.

The number one objective of every believer is to get God to speak to them. This is also the most difficult thing to do since most of the time it requires a lot of work. It also requires time and maturity in God. For me, getting God to speak once required a forty-day fast while praying all the time during those forty days. Try that sometime. That was a lot of work, but it paid off. We believers are commanded by Jesus to live by God's words. Not too many people ever obtain such faith because of the work involved.

Once you understand how to get faith in God, we can move on to understanding the use of faith in many other scriptures. It will become very plain as I guide you through the following verses that deal with faith. Many of you who read this will finally understand just what the Bible is saying and teaching on the subject of faith. When this happens, you'll be excited to understand what the Bible is teaching.

You'll want to have God speak words (*rhema*) to you. So let's dig in and learn what faith can do.

Examples of Faith from the Bible

And a certain centurion's servant, who was dear to him, was sick and ready to die. So when he heard about Jesus, he sent elders of the Jews to him, pleading with Him to come and heal his servant. And when they came to Jesus, they begged Him earnestly, saying that the one for whom He should do this was deserving, "For he loves our nation, and has built us a synagogue." Then Jesus went with them. And when He was already not far from the house, the centurion sent friends to Him, saying to Him, "Lord, do not trouble Yourself, for I am not worthy that You should enter under my roof. Therefore, I did not even think myself worthy to come to You. But say the word, and my servant will be healed. For I also am a man placed under authority, having soldiers under me. And I say to one, "Go," and he goes; and to another, "Come," and he comes; and to my servant, "Do this," and he does it." When Jesus heard these things, He marveled at him, and turned around and said to the crowd that followed Him, "I say to you, I have not found such great faith, not even in Israel!" And those who were sent, returning to the house, found the servant well who had been sick. (Luke 7:2–10, NKJV)

Here is a perfect example in the Bible of a real true event. The centurion totally understood the definition of faith. He went to work, attempting to get God to speak to him; in this case, it was Jesus. The centurion also understood who Jesus is. When the centurion learned that Jesus was responding to his request, he sent a few friends to Jesus. In verse 7, the centurion sent another message to Jesus (*But say the word and my servant will be healed*).

In verse 9, we read an astonishing thing about Jesus. Jesus is marveling and is so excited that he says to the crowd that was following him, "I have not found such great faith not even in all Israel." The servant was at that point healed. Jesus had spoken the word, and that was all that the centurion needed. The centurion received the faith in God when he knew that Jesus was coming to heal the servant. Then understanding that Jesus didn't even need to personally come to the centurion (since he already knew that God would heal the servant), he sent a message for Jesus just to speak the word.

Here are the mechanics of what happened. The centurion knew that Jesus was the Son of God. He requested that Jesus come and heal the servant. The centurion was asking God for a request. Once the centurion learned that Jesus was coming to the servant, he knew that God had heard and answered his request. The centurion then sent out the next request, stating that all he needed was a spoken word from Jesus. Because the centurion knew that Jesus was coming, he understood that God had heard his request and was on the way to perform the healing.

This was faith in God. The servant was immediately healed. God chose to heal the servant immediately and not even give a spoken word—even though the centurion understood the mechanics of faith. The centurion understood that because God heard his request that all that needed be done was speaking the word.

Our task as believers is to ask God for our needs. Our job is to get God to hear and respond to our requests. Once God hears a request, it will either be done immediately or the process will begin and take time. We must wait for a set time in the future to see the fulfillment of the answer.

Once God acknowledges the request, we have faith in God. (We are persuaded by the spoken word of God). Some faiths are immediately answered. Some faiths require a few days or weeks till they are fulfilled. And other faiths require several years to see their fulfillment. I have a few faiths that will require another twenty to thirty years till they are fulfilled. Once God hears your request and acknowledges you, you have a spoken word from God—or you have faith in God. Whether the fulfillment happens immediately or over several years, your job is to keep the faith of that spoken word. Once that faith is fulfilled that specific faith is finished and completed.

Because of the nature of my calling as a prophet and pastor, I have many faiths that are yet to be fulfilled. My task is to keep the faith of each of those words of God. If I stop believing in the spoken words of God, then I have stopped having faith in those spoken words. I jeopardize not seeing the spoken word of God being fulfilled.

I want to add one more point before moving on to other examples. Once you receive a spoken word and it is not immediate fulfilled, you are required by God for a set date for the fulfillment of that spoken word—whether it be a day or a year. This waiting time is for several reasons. This kind of faith is thus categorized as a promise. Many times when you read through the Bible and the Bible refers to the promises of God, the scriptures are referring to the personal promises of your faith and not the written promises of God in the Bible.

> Now the next day, when they had come out from Bethany, He was hungry. And seeing from afar a fig tree having leaves, He went to see if perhaps He would find something on it. When He came to it, He found nothing but leaves, for it was not the season for figs. In response Jesus said to it, "Let no one eat fruit from you ever again." And His disciples heard it. (Mark 11:12–14, NKJV)

> Now in the morning, as they passed by, they saw the fig tree dried up from the roots. And Peter, remembering, said to Him, "Rabbi, look! The fig tree which You cursed has withered away." So Jesus answered and said to them, "Have faith in God. For assuredly, I say to you, whoever says to this mountain, 'Be removed and be cast into the sea,' and does not doubt in his heart, but believes that those things he says will be done, he will have whatever he says. Therefore, I say to you, whatever things you ask when you pray, believe that you receive them, and you will have them." (Mark 11:20–24, NKJV)

This example is really a lesson from the Father intended for the disciples to learn from. On the surface, it appears that all Jesus did was curse the fig tree of his own volition. But let's examine the mechanics of what really happened. Jesus was hungry and wanted some breakfast. So he went over to the fig tree to get some figs to eat since the tree was already leafing but it was not in season to have produced fruit. Jesus went to the tree because the Spirit was directing him to do so. It would not make sense to walk to a tree looking for fruit when it is not in season.

Jesus didn't find any figs growing. He probably intended to walk onward. But suddenly as Jesus is standing at the fig tree, the Holy Spirit tells him to say, "Let no one eat fruit from you ever again."

Jesus repeats what the Holy Spirit told him. Jesus was receiving a spoken word from the Father through the Holy Spirit and just repeated exactly what he heard. Jesus wasn't given any details about what would happen to the tree. He just knew that no one would ever eat fruit from it again. Then Jesus moves on.

The disciples saw and heard what Jesus did. The disciples probably looked at each other, knowing that this was a very strange thing to see Jesus do especially knowing that the fig tree was not in season yet with its fruit. The Father wanted to teach the disciples (and us) all about faith. God had Jesus curse the fig tree in the sight of the disciples. Nothing happened to the fig tree at that point in time.

Jesus was repeating the spoken word of God. Jesus had faith in the spoken word of God. All Jesus was doing was confessing the spoken word of the Father exactly as the Father spoke the words to Jesus. The faith was not yet fulfilled. The next morning (twenty-four hours later), Jesus and the disciples passed by the same fig tree. But then, the disciples observed that the fig tree had dried up from its roots. The entire tree had died. Peter made this observation known to Jesus. Jesus explained the mechanics of faith to them. Jesus said, "Have faith in God."

Jesus went on to explain faith in a little more detail. In verse 24, he said, "Therefore, I say to you, whatever things you ask when you pray, believe that you receive them, and you will have them." When you see the word *therefore* in scripture, this is summing up all that is being said in previous verses. First, you start asking God in prayer for God to meet your need. Then once God gives a spoken word for your need, you must believe that you will receive the answer to that need. This is the function of faith. You must believe the spoken word of God till the fulfillment of that spoken word happens. In this example, Jesus received a spoken word from the Father, spoke it openly, and continued to believe the spoken word. Part of our job is to confess the spoken words of God.

In verse 23, we read, "For assuredly, I say to you, whoever says to this mountain, 'Be removed and be cast into the sea,' and does not doubt in his heart, but believes that those things he says will be done, he will have whatever he says." Jesus is teaching the disciples that if you need to have a mountain removed, you first ask God to do this. If God says he will remove the mountain, then you have a spoken word from God. You next speak to the object the spoken word of God, in this case the mountain, and repeat exactly the spoken word from God. (In this example, *Be removed and be cast into the sea*.) From that point on, your job is to believe the spoken word of God. At some point in time, whether immediately or in the future, that mountain will be cast into the sea. All you have to do is repeat the spoken word once. Then you continue to believe that spoken word and never doubt it.

If you read these verses without having a proper definition of faith, you will have to conclude that Jesus cursed the fig tree on his own volition. The next day, the fig tree was dead. Jesus said, "Have faith in God. For assuredly, I say to you, whoever says to this mountain, 'Be removed and be cast into the sea' and does not doubt in his heart, but believes that those things he says will be done, he will have whatever he says."

Therefore, whatever you ask when you pray, believe that you receive them, and you will have them. It would appear in verse 23 that Jesus was saying that all believers had to do was see something and make some command concerning that something. If you don't doubt what you have said even to the core of your heart, and also believe what you command, then that something will happen. In verse 24, you would also conclude that all you have to do is ask God, in some prayer, for something and then go about believing that you receive that something and it will happen. We would have to conclude that "having faith in God" is something we strictly do of our own volition.

This is what churches teach today, which is all false teaching. You can read this phrase of verses, and without any teaching from the church, you will also conclude the above explanation is really what is being taught in the English translation. Millions of people have attempted this false understanding only to end up in failure because they don't have a proper definition of faith.

I would like to mention that the usual way of getting faith from God is seeking God in prayer till he gives a spoken word. As we mature in God's kingdom, there will be times that we will be doing our normal routines, and God will suddenly speak to us a spoken word. These spoken words come to us from God without us asking God for anything in prayer.

These spoken words are intended for God to perform his acts through his servants. This was the case when Jesus cursed the fig tree. He didn't pray about the fig tree before this encounter. The Father just suddenly spoke to Jesus, and Jesus did as instructed.

> While He spoke these things to them, behold, a ruler came and worshiped Him, saying, "My daughter has just died, but come and lay Your hand on her and she will live." So Jesus arose and followed him, and so did his disciples. And suddenly, a woman who had a flow of blood for twelve years came from behind and touched the hem of His garment. For she said to herself, "If only I may touch His garment, I shall be made well." But Jesus turned around, and when He saw her He said, "Be of good cheer, daughter; your faith has made you well." And the woman was made well from that hour. (Matthew 9:18–22, NKJV)

> But as He went, the multitudes thronged him. Now a woman, having a flow of blood for twelve years, who had spent all her livelihood on physicians and could not be healed by any, came from behind and touched the border of his garment. And immediately

her flow of blood stopped. And Jesus said, "Who touched Me?" When all denied it, Peter and those with him said, "Master, the multitudes throng and press You, and You say, 'Who touched Me?'" But Jesus said, "Somebody touched Me, for I perceived power going out from Me." Now when the woman saw that she was not hidden, she came trembling; and falling down before Him, she declared to Him in the presence of all the people the reason she had touched Him and how she was healed immediately. And He said to her, "Daughter, be of good cheer; your faith has made you well. Go in peace." (Luke 8:42–48, NKJV)

The woman had been praying to God to be healed of her bleeding. We are not told how long she had been praying, but it was probably for most of the twelve years. Then she heard about Jesus as everyone had at this point in time. The Father gave her a spoken word. He probably said, "Touch the hem of his garment, and you shall be made well."

There were many people all around Jesus and obviously touching him. Jesus knew that someone had received a healing because he felt power flow through him and into someone else. Jesus ended up saying to her that her faith made her well. This is also an example that some of us may find ourselves praying for a long period of time for our needs. Notice that others were touching Jesus as he was walking along, and none of them received any kind of healing (though there probably were many who needed a healing of some kind). The task of this woman was to make her way up to Jesus and just touch the hem of his garment. This she accomplished and thus was healed.

Another example of faith:

> Then Jesus went out from there and departed to the region of Tyre and Sidon. And behold, a woman of Canaan came from that region and cried out to Him, saying, "Have mercy on me, O Lord, Son of David! My daughter is severely demon-possessed." But He answered her not a word. And his disciples came and urged Him, saying, "Send her away, for she cries out after us." But He answered and said, "I was not sent except to the lost sheep of the house of Israel." Then she came and worshiped Him, saying, "Lord, help me!" But he answered and said, "It is not good to take the children's bread and throw it to the little dogs." And she said, "Yes, Lord, yet even the little dogs eat the crumbs which fall from their masters' table." Then Jesus answered and said to her, "O woman, great is your faith! Let it be to you as you desire." And her daughter was healed from that very hour. (Matthew 15:21–28, NKJV)

This woman was not an Israelite. She had heard of Jesus's ministry, how Jesus even cast out demons, and at some point, the Father gave her some spoken word instructing her to go to Jesus to have her daughter delivered from the demon. We are not given the spoken word that God gave to her. She knew this would be difficult—if not impossible— because she was a Canaanite. But she chose to believe what she had heard and went to Jesus.

She met up with Jesus and began to seek Jesus for deliverance of the demon. Jesus ignored her request as she expected. But she knew that the Father had spoken to her, and she continued to ask. Finally, Jesus responded and told her that she, being Canaanite, was not worthy of his healing. Jesus referred to her as a little dog. What a rude thing to say to this woman! She knew what Jesus was telling her, but she continued to implore the Lord.

In verse 27, she gets Jesus's attention and calls him Lord. Then in verse 28, we see that Jesus marveled at her great faith. The daughter was delivered that very hour. Also notice that once Jesus recognized that she had faith from the Father, he commended her for her faith. This is much like a wicked sinner who asks the Father for healing without believing in God. The Father grants the wicked sinner faith. That person goes to where God sends them, perhaps a faith healing ministry. They continually ask for such a healing and receive a healing because of the faith God gave them. God is not limited to just believers in him. He gives faith to anyone who asks.

The Old Testament and New Testament are full of examples of faith. In Hebrews 11, we are given a short list of Old Testament believers who had faith in God to do what they needed. The New Testament gospels and the book of Acts have many examples of faith from God. The key is to get God to give you a spoken word so that you can perform that function of faith. Sometimes it takes time just to get a spoken word from God, and other times, it happens almost as soon as you ask.

Present Faith

> Now faith is the substance of things hoped for, the evidence of things not seen. (Hebrews 11:1, NKJV)

This is a definition of faith in the New Testament. The word *now* can also be translated as *present*. The word *now* is referring to us who have already received a spoken word from God but have yet to see it fulfilled. This definition of faith is how it is presently working in our hearts and spirits. Faith is a substance. *Substance* can also be translated as assurance. *Evidence* can also be translated as *conviction*. Present faith is a promise that is yet to be fulfilled. Present faith is waiting for that word to happen. I like the NASB version because it is more accurate. (Hebrews 11:1, NASB)

Now faith is the assurance of things hoped for, the conviction of things not seen. This is what happens in our spirits and hearts once we have received faith. We have an assurance of what we are hoping for that it will indeed happen. We have a conviction that God has spoken to us and one day will see that happen even though we haven't seen it happen yet. All we are doing is waiting for the fulfillment of the faith to occur. We are usually not given a date or time when this will happen. We are given a promise that it will happen as long as we keep believing in that *rhema* from God. Thus our task is to believe till the promise occurs.

> For the vision is yet for an appointed time; but at the end, it will speak, and it will not lie. Though it tarries, wait for it; because it will surely come, it will not tarry. (Habakkuk 2:3, NKJV)

For the vision is yet for the appointed time; it
hastens toward the goal and it will not fail. Though
it tarries, wait for it; for it will certainly come, it will
not delay. (Habakkuk 2:3, NASB)

Here is another verse that backs up Hebrews 11:1. The
word *vision* can be the same as faith. We do not usually
know the appointed time when the faith will be fulfilled.
Instead, our job is to wait and believe till it does happen.
Once that piece of faith occurs, we say that it is fulfilled.
All faiths in God require a period of waiting. Some are very
short, and others are very long (even years). Hebrews 11
goes on to explain how the Old Testament believers had to
obtain faith and how they had to wait for the fulfillment
of that faith.

Another interesting part of faith requires an action of
the heart. The heart and spirit of each individual are closely
tied together.

For with the heart one believes unto righteousness,
and with the mouth confession is made unto
salvation. (Romans 10:10, NKJV)

We see that the heart is also involved in believing as
well as the mind being persuaded. Once you're persuaded or
have faith, the heart becomes involved as well. In the heart is
where all motives are made. When a heart accepts what the
Holy Spirit has been speaking of, the entire being of man
comes to believe in that faith. People believe with their heart
as well as their mind.

The heart sets its love on the persuasion of the Holy
Spirit. The heart never makes a decision to love something

unless it is first decided within the mind. The mind and heart work in harmony with each other. The mind usually follows the heart's experience. Many times, the mind goes before the heart. This is discussed in more detail in *God's Advanced Doctrines*. For now, all you need to understand is that believing in faith requires the heart to love the persuasion. The mind believes, and the heart believes. This is how it works within all people.

It is not enough to believe with just the mind or to mentally accept the facts of Jesus; we must be moved by heartfelt faith with the heart.

> Most assuredly, I say to you, he who believes in Me has everlasting life. (John 6:47, NKJV)

To believe in Jesus is to have heartfelt faith. When you have faith, you can feel it within your spirit and heart. Your conviction is also within the heart and spirit. It's just not with the mind. When God speaks *rhema* to you, you have the conviction also within the heart. The mind is only acknowledging what is occurring within the heart and spirit.

The point of this verse and dealing with the heart is to show you that "he who believes in me" has obtained eternal life—not *will* obtain eternal life. Eternal life is not something we hope to have in the next world, after death. When we accept the Holy Spirit baptism we begin eternal life at that very moment. Eternal life is something we already possess, something that we already enjoy, a reality, and a substance, here and now. This is the same with faith. Faith is here and now, a substance.

Walking by Faith

Once we receive faith in God, we are considered to be walking by faith or living by faith. We no longer have to live by our five senses. We keep our eyes focused upon the spoken word of God. This becomes our vision.

For we walk by faith, not by sight. (1 Corinthians 5:7, NKJV)

We have to learn to walk in faith or live in faith. This involves maturity in that we must learn to live by faith and sometimes ignore the five senses. Living in the kingdom of God takes some work and concentration to be able to master living by faith. Hebrews 11:1 says, "The evidence or conviction of things not yet seen." If we are to live in faith, we must also believe in this faith till the fulfillment arrives. Matthew 4:4 says, "Man shall not live by bread alone, but by every word that proceeds from the mouth of God."

The work of Satan is to get you to stop believing in the faith of God. He did this first with Eve. Once you stop believing, you have lost your faith—and you will never see that *rhema* fulfilled. You must learn to keep your faith alive within you.

Many times, there comes a conflict with our five senses and the revelation of God's *rhema*. Many times, God will test our faith in him by allowing us to be tempted through our five senses. I cover this in more detail in *God's Advanced Doctrines*.

An important point in this chapter is to know that we are to never doubt the faith God has given to us. If we keep to our faith, that promise will happen at the appointed time.

Another important point is that we are to believe first and then later see the result—not see first and then believe it. Man's way is to see it first then believe in it. God's way is to first believe and then see it happen. Such is the way of Bible faith.

When we receive faith in God, we enter into defiance of the five senses. There are many false teachings in the church world that are against what the Bible is really teaching us about faith. One sure test to know if you're correct is whether signs and wonders follow those who believe.

> These signs will accompany those who have believed: in My name they will cast out demons, they will speak with new tongues; they will pick up serpents, and if they drink any deadly poison, it will not hurt them; they will lay hands on the sick, and they will recover. (Mark 16:17–18, NASB)

If you are not following properly, there is something wrong with what you believe. It all starts and ends with faith. I'm going to move on to some other scriptures that show more about faith and why faith is required by God.

> But without faith, it is impossible to please Him, for he who comes to God must believe that He is, and that He is a rewarder of those who diligently seek Him. (Hebrews 11:6, NKJV)

This verse brings out several points concerning God. God is pleased when we get faith from him and then do as he has instructed. Also, this verse is teaching us that it is not enough to just practice the commands of the Bible. We have to find the will of God for our lives. This involves faith in God. Matthew 4:4 also backs up the verse.

Also notice that it says, "He who comes to God must believe that he is." The use of the word *believe* is not just acknowledging God's existence—but having already received faith that God does indeed exist and communicate with those who seek him. Remember to use the Greek form of believe. The reason you're coming to God is to get more faith or spoken words.

The last part—*He is a rewarder of these who diligently seek him*—is a promise. Those who are seeking God's will for their lives are going to be granted this request. Those who need guidance are going to receive faith from God for their situations. There is a condition with this promise—*those who diligently seek him*. Diligently seeking God involves more than a daily routine of living. You're going to probably have to set aside a few days for praying and fasting. You're going to have to do some hard work while seeking answers from God. When God finally gives you the faith, this becomes the reward for all your work while seeking him for that faith.

Also notice that God is not pleased if we don't get faith from him. We please the Father when we seek him and get faith from him before he performs those faiths. Reading the Bible does not please God. Performing random acts of kindness and good deeds does not please God. Being religious does not please God. Only walking in faith pleases God. When God is pleased, he is excited about those who have gotten faith from him.

Ask, and it will be given to you; seek, and you will find; knock, and it will be opened to you. For everyone who asks receives, and he who seeks finds, and to him who knocks it will be opened. (Matthew 7:7–8, NKJV)

The better translation is "ask and keep on asking," "seek and keep on seeking," and "knock and keep on knocking." These two verses reveal more of the work that goes into getting faith in God. There is another promise that accompanies verse 7. The condition is that you have to do the work of seeking God.

In both the above verses (Hebrews 11:5 and Matthew 7:7–8), there is no set time for how long it will require you to do the work of getting faith from God. It may only be a few days, and it may be several weeks or several months. The result is that you will be rewarded as long as you keep seeking. Also bear in mind that God is not a liar. What he promises, he will do—as long as you are doing your part of the condition.

- Principle: All promises in the Bible are accompanied by a condition.

But the just shall live by his faith. (Habakkuk 2:4, NKJV)

Those who are in the kingdom of God are considered just or righteous. You can use either word in translating the word just for righteous or vice versa. Again, there is the teaching from the Bible that those of us who are in and of God must live by faith. Living by faith is not an option; it is a requirement. Having faith in God is a requirement for making it to physical heaven. It's not enough to accept

Christ's forgiveness of sin. Those who have accepted Christ in their hearts and have never gone on to maturity and received the Holy Spirit are still headed for hell. You must go on to receive faith in God.

- Principle: We are commanded to receive faith in God in order to do the will of God for our own personal lives. Failure to receive faith from God will send you to hell.

But he who doubts is condemned if he eats, because he does not eat from faith; for whatever is not from faith is sin. (Romans 14:23, NKJV)

This can be a difficult verse to understand because the context is dealing with Jewish laws of the Old Testament versus a believer in Christ. But there is a very sound principle used in this verse that can be applied as a universal truth. Paul is teaching that Christians are no longer under the law of the Old Testament regarding various foods that cannot be eaten. Christians can be a stumbling block to those who are not in Christ. Paul is teaching believers to simply not eat what their fellow Jewish kinsmen would find illegal, who are still under the Jewish law. What we are interested in this verse is the very last eight words: "for whatever *is* not from faith is sin."

When we become alive through the Holy Spirit, we enter into an entirely new life. We are now living in the kingdom of God. God is expecting us to find out from him all that we are to do in our personal lives. We no longer are our own. We have become his slaves. You have forsaken your right to your own life.

In return for this servant hood, God gives us the things that are good for us, and many times, he gives us our hearts' desires as long as these desires are not evil. He will also require us to cease doing certain things. As we are growing and maturing in his kingdom, he will continually reveal to us what we are no longer permitted to do.

This process doesn't happen all at once. It is a gradual process based upon our maturity. God will eventually change your entire life and style of life. What you once did that was allowed by God will no longer be permitted. For every one of us, God will have us to not partake of something where others are allowed to do so. God is moving his servants into a separated walk with him. We become more and more separated from the worldly ways and changed more into godliness. This is moving into holiness. Holiness merely means separated from wickedness. Getting faith is this process. Faith is the requirement for change. As we are changed through faith we learn that whatever is not of faith is sin.

As an example, for me it was the removal of TV from my life. For me to go back to viewing TV would be a sin. If I continue in this personal sin, God will separate himself from me, which is what spiritual death is. It's the same death that Adam and Eve experienced in the Garden.

For the wages of sin is death. (Romans 6:23, NKJV)

When I was born again of the Holy Spirit, I was involved with tae kwon do and was becoming a master at it. One day shortly after becoming born again, the Holy Spirit said to me, "No more tae kwon do!" God was giving me guidance and faith regarding this sport. A few weeks later, I quit and never went back.

I always enjoy having good physical strength and wellness as part of health. I sought God for guidance. I asked if I could still work out at a gym for weight training. He rewarded my seeking him with a yes. I have faith that it is okay for me to work out with weights. For another believer, God may not want them to work out with weight training.

It took two months from the time he said, "No more tae kwon do" till he said, "Yes to weight training." Over the years, God has continued to remove things that were once permitted. These things are no longer permitted in my life. If I go back to any of them, it becomes sin for me.

For more information on this subject, see the chapter on holiness in *God's Advanced Doctrines*. For the purpose of this book I'm only interested in teaching the six basic doctrines of the Bible.

Our outline thus far:
What is faith? **Answered**
Why is it so important? **Answered**
How does it work? **Answered**
When does it work? **Answered**
Where do I apply it? **Answered**
Who is faith for? **Answered**
What other words are used in connection with faith? **Answered**
What does having faith in God entail? **Answered**

Faith and Works

A lot of people fall into a big trap when seeking to enter into heaven or to enter into the kingdom of God. The trap is the difference between faith and works. People from Israel in the Old Testament to the present day have made this blunder. Millions of churchgoing people today are still making the same mistake.

I want to focus here on the difference between faith and works since it is so easy to fall into this trap. I want you to be aware of getting caught up in works, which is so easy since most people fall into this blunder. Remember that your goal is to be blessed and to make it to physical heaven. What am I referring to when I refer to *dead works*?

In the chapter of repentance from dead works, I touched on this subject. The New Testament mentions this several times. All the prophets of the Old Testament dealt with the issue of dead works. This is a common mistake that a majority of believers fall into. The difference between faith and works is not a subject to be taken lightly. Derek Prince said, "Faith is not based on works, but works are the outcome of faith." Any attempt from people to earn salvation or any kind of blessing from God by doing good deeds is fleshly works.

Now to him who works, the wages are not counted as grace but as debt. But to him who does not work but believes on Him who justifies the ungodly, his faith is accounted for righteousness. (Romans 4:4–5, NKJV)

Remember the number line? When we are all in the negative, no matter what we do, including good works, we are still dead to God. Even for those who are at zero, all your good works are still performed in a state of death in God. No good work can possibly put you in the positive.

Once you're in the positive and you try to earn blessings from God by doing any kind of good work, you're doing this work of your own volition in an attempt to please God. God views this as sin. Verse 5 says, "His faith is accounted for righteousness."

A definition of righteousness is *that of being in a right state with God*. It is each believer's job to maintain his or her own state of being in a righteous position in the kingdom of God. When we remain in this correct state, God regards us as being righteous. This is done by doing what God reveals us to do as we ask him for guidance in our lives. Faith is hearing from God and then doing what he instructs. These faith works are works of righteousness.

It is our faith that is accounted for righteousness because we are pleasing God. (Hebrews 11:6, NKJV)

But without faith, it is impossible to please him; he who comes to God must believe that he is a rewarder of those who diligently seek him. We get God to speak to us, and then we have faith. This faith places us in a state of righteousness before God. We begin to do as God has instructed, and he is pleased with us. We are not doing what we think we should do; instead, we are doing what he is instructing us to do.

God places us in a right state with him and in his kingdom. If we do the work of getting faith, we are maintaining our right state with God. It is the job of every believer to remain in a right state with God. You must obey his personal guidance. You must get faith in God.

> But he answered and said, "It is written, 'Man shall not live by bread alone, but by every word that proceeds from the mouth of God.'" (Matthew 4:4, NKJV)

If you're in the positive on the number line and you stop getting faith in God, then you will begin to backslide and eventually end up back in death from God. A common thing that people do after moving to the positive is to get lazy and not be as aggressive as they first were with God in obtaining faith in God. We must continually get faith from God throughout our entire lives on earth. As long as we are partaking of the grace that God is providing us in this dispensation of grace, we are living God's way. If we don't do things God's way, we are doing things our way.

The Law of Moses was given to the new nation of Israel as a code of conduct for all the Israelites to abide by. Up until that point, there were no rules. Each person did as he or she pleased. But if the Israelites were going to name God as their God and not worship any other worldly god or idols, then they would have to abide under a code of conduct.

The benefits of abiding to the code or Law of Moses include several promises from God. It would go well with each person and the entire nation. You would live in peace and prosperity. God would keep you free of diseases and plagues that the rest of the world would have to suffer. God would never allow another warring people to conquer Israel. Everyone would enjoy all the benefits of new technologies as they came along. But if Israel were to cease practicing—or transgressed—these laws, then the people would fall under the curse of God and backslide into the difficult ways of the world. There would no longer be any protection from God.

If the Israelites rebelled against the Law they would be subject to whatever happened or would be subject to whatever way the cookie crumbled. This was one of the purposes of the Law of Moses to the nation of Israel, but most of the leaders and keepers of the spiritual part of Israel began to use the code of conduct as a means of being righteous before God. "See? We have obeyed the law, and we are in right standing with our fellow neighbors. Are we not also in right standing with God? Is not God pleased with our ability to obey the written code? Does this obeying the code or law not make us a better person before God?"

No! God was satisfied with them in that they had obeyed his written law, and he did all that he promised. They have done well to obey the law, and everything went well with them as promised. Besides the law, God requires us to have faith in him—and this is pleasing to him—but to think that obeying the code of conduct is going to put you in a state of rightness with God is asinine. You must get out of your state of death and become alive in God.

Here is an example using our present-day lives. In America—and most other countries—laws govern the people. America has lots of laws, and new laws are continually being added to the existing laws. Most laws are for our own protection and the protection of others if we all abide by them. By doing this, we partake of the benefits of the law.

There really are no rewards for obeying the laws in America. I've never seen anyone be exonerated in America for just obeying the laws of America. Instead, we all live in a harmonious way and enjoy much freedom. Americans are allowed to do many things with our freedom that many other countries are not allowed to do. Those of us who abide by all the laws are good law-abiding citizens. We enjoy the fruit of obedience to the laws. We are in right standing with our neighbors and the rest of the country. Some people obey the laws exactly and perfectly. For instance, there are those who are perfect at obeying all the rules and laws in traffic. They never speed or run stop signs or red lights. Any law-abiding citizen who obeys the law and decides that obedience to the laws of America will also put the person in right standing with God is in for a big mistake. Trusting in obeying the laws of America to make you right before God is total stupidity and foolishness. In fact, it is impossible that obeying the laws of America will make you right in the eyes of God. This false doctrine becomes your own self-made righteousness.

You're doing things or works your way. You are making your works righteous by obeying the laws of America. Your own righteousness is commendable, but your own works of righteousness are not the requirement for obtaining a relationship with God or a means to make it into heaven. God has set forth how we are to be righteous with him, which is totally separate from obeying the laws of America or any other country. He has a separate set of laws that pertain to righteousness in him.

> But the just shall live by his faith. (Habakkuk 2:4, NKJV)

> But the righteous will live by his faith. (Habakkuk 2:4, NASB)

> But without faith it is impossible to please Him, for he who comes to God must believe that He is, and that He is a rewarder of those who diligently seek Him. (Hebrews 11:6, NKJV)

This is what Israel did with the Law of Moses and continues to do to this very day. Obeying the Law of Moses, or America, or any other country cannot make you righteous before God.

> And if by grace, then it is no longer of works; otherwise grace is no longer grace. But if it is of works, it is no longer grace; otherwise work is no longer work. (Romans 11:6, NKJV)

God's grace is now given to us through Jesus. Through him, we can obtain life in the Holy Spirit and go on to get faith in God and begin to please him. We thus begin to live in the positive end of the number line.

> What shall we say then? That Gentiles, who did not pursue righteousness, have attained to righteousness, even the righteousness of faith; but Israel, pursuing

the law of righteousness, has not attained to the law of righteousness. Why? Because they did not seek it by faith, but as it were, by the works of the law (of Moses). For they stumbled at that stumbling stone. (Romans 9:30–32, NKJV)

A Law of Righteousness

God's righteousness and how he attributes righteousness is many times referred to as a law of righteousness. This use of the word law is to set forth that God has laws in his kingdom, which govern his kingdom. Thus there are several laws that God has enacted in his kingdom. One such law is the law of righteousness. In Romans 9:30, the Gentiles were not part of Israel. They were ignorant of all that God was doing, but Israel had all kinds of knowledge and experiences from God. In this age of grace, God is offering salvation to everyone, which includes us non-Israelite people called Gentiles. Gentiles who did not pursue righteousness are now offered righteousness. But the nation of Israel kept pursuing God's law of righteousness through the works of the law that God gave through Moses. Obeying the Law of Moses is not getting faith from God. For more in-depth information about the Law of Moses, see *God's Advanced Doctrines*.

Israel failed in all its attempts to obtain a righteous position with God. All attempts to obtain righteous positions with God will fail. Only getting faith and performing the acts that God is guiding us to do, from faith, will place us in a righteous position with him. When we perform acts of faith, we are regarded as being righteous in God. This is also referred to as the righteousness of God.

> Brethren, my heart's desire and prayer to God for Israel is that they may be saved. For I bear them witness that they have a zeal for God, but not according to knowledge (the truth about God and faith). For they being ignorant of God's righteousness, and seeking to establish their own righteousness, have not submitted to the righteousness of God. (Romans 10:1–3, NKJV)

Now having understood all I wrote above, explaining the difference between works of the law or code of conduct versus the requirements of God, I'm going to show you the error of most churchgoing or religious people today.

Millions of well-meaning, sincere people who attend church or other religious functions are making the same mistake that Israel made. This includes monks, priest, and clergy in all the other religions in existence. All church going people who are zeroed out on the number line are included. Even those who are Spirit Filled or Born Again not walking in faith are numbered with these millions. They are all doing works of their own rightness to please God, hoping to attain a place in heaven. They devote themselves to prayers of all kinds, penance, fasting, charity, self-denial, and the observance of church ordinances, but it is all in vain. They are hoping that their works of doing right will get them to heaven. Your own religious works cannot save you from sin. Your own works cannot get salvation of any kind. Your own religious works cannot get you anything. These people are just like Israel; they seek salvation not by faith, but by their own works.

> For by grace you have been saved through faith, and that not of yourselves; it is the gift of God, not of works, lest anyone should boast. (Ephesians 2:8–9, NKJV)

Paul is talking to Christians who have already received faith in God. He is not talking to those who have yet to obtain faith in God. Paul is explaining that no man can save himself.

> Where is boasting then? It is excluded. By what law? Of works? No, but by the law of faith. Therefore, we conclude that a man is justified by faith apart from the deeds of the law. (Romans 3:27–28, NKJV)

Paul is explaining that man must be justified by faith in God. The deeds of any law cannot justify anyone as being righteous before God. Justification must be done for us by another being. Also notice that there is the mention of the law of faith. This is another law within God's kingdom as a governing law for all servants in heaven.

> Not by works of righteousness which we have done, but according to His mercy He saved us, through the washing of regeneration and renewing of the Holy Spirit, whom He poured out on us abundantly through Jesus Christ our Savior, that having been justified by His grace we should become heirs according to the hope of eternal life.

This is a faithful saying, and these things I want you
to affirm constantly, that those who have believed
in God should be careful to maintain good works.
These things are good and profitable to men.
(Titus 3:5–8, NKJV)

Notice in verse 8 how there is an appeal for believers
to still do good works. This is obeying the laws, codes, and
extra things. But pay close attention to the last sentence
in verse 8. This verse does not say that they are good and
profitable to *God*.

Acts of Faith

When we receive faith in God, we begin to act upon
this guidance. These acts are works. The difference is that
these works are based upon faith in God. I call this "works
of faith" in order to distinguish them from "works of the
law" or our "own works of righteousness."

Once we receive many faiths from God, no matter how
many we get, we must do the work of these faiths. By doing
works of faith, we are regarded as being righteous before
God. We are pleasing God. When we practice faith in God
he reckons us as rightness before him. God even counts this
rightness as being in right standing in his kingdom. He calls
us, who do works of faith, "the righteousness of God."

Men and women who perform their own works of
righteousness make themselves righteous in their own eyes,
which is a good thing. God also has his own righteousness
unto himself. So when we do the works of faith, he regards us
as partakers of his own righteousness. We are considered and

called the righteousness of God. Wow! That is really great that God would go so far as to call us his own righteousness, especially when none of us deserve any of it.

Next is an example of the difference between "works of good acts" versus "works of faith." In the following scripture of James, I included parentheses to help you understand exactly what he is writing about.

> What does it profit, my brethren, if someone says he has faith but does not have works (of faith)? Can (just) faith (without the works of faith) save him? If a brother or sister is naked and destitute of daily food, and one of you says to them, "Depart in peace, be warmed and filled," but you do not give them the things which are needed for the body, what does it profit? Thus also faith by itself, if it does not have works (of faith), is dead (worthless). But someone will say, "You have faith, and I have works (of faith)." Show me your faith without your works, and I will show you my faith by my works. You believe that there is one God. You do well. Even the demons believe—and tremble! But do you want to know, O foolish man, that faith without works (of faith) is dead? Was not Abraham our father justified by works (of faith) when he offered Isaac his son on the altar? Do you see that faith was working together with his works, and by works (of faith) faith was made perfect (or fulfilled)? And the scripture was fulfilled which says, "Abraham believed God, and it was accounted to him for righteousness." And he was called the friend of God. You see then that

a man is justified by works (of faith), and not by faith only. Likewise, was not Rahab the harlot also justified by works when she received the messengers and sent them out another way? For as the body without the spirit is dead, so faith without works (of faith) is dead also. (James 2:14–26, NKJV)

In the above verses, James is teaching us that once we receive faith from God, we must act upon that faith. You can't just receive faith and do nothing, thinking that God's words are going to bring you into heaven. The problem with some of the believers James was writing to is that they were thinking that all they needed was faith from God—and they didn't have to do anything more.

James is attempting to teach these believers or any of us today that we must do the works of faith to gain merit with God. People would say, "Oh, I have heard the voice of God."

What good is hearing God's voice if you don't obey what he says? When God speaks, it is usually in the form of a command. Sometimes it is just a revelation of fact about his kingdom, but that faith is for you to change your belief because your belief is false. In this case, it becomes your work to change your belief to what God wants you to believe (regarding facts of truths). Sometimes a work of faith is waiting for the fulfillment of that faith. (Hebrews 11:1) You can't perform any other method but have to wait for God's planned method. Waiting is regarded as a work of faith. When you receive faith and act upon it, you believe in God and the faith he gave. Verse 23 explains how our works of faith are accounted to us for righteousness when we believe God's spoken words.

I would like to address a difficulty in other passages of the New Testament that that may bring confusion if not properly defined. You will come across the phrase *the righteousness of the law.*

> There is therefore now no condemnation to those who are in Christ Jesus, who do not walk according to the flesh, but according to the Spirit. For the law of the Spirit of life in Christ Jesus has made me free from the law of sin and death. For what the law could not do in that it was weak through the flesh, God did by sending His own Son in the likeness of sinful flesh, on account of sin: He condemned sin in the flesh, that the righteous requirement of the law might be fulfilled in us who do not walk according to the flesh but according to the Spirit. (Romans 8:1–4, NKJV)

In verse 2, we find *the law of the Spirit of life in Christ.* This is like the law of physics that governs the physical world in which we presently live. Just as there are laws of physics, there are laws in the Spirit life that govern the kingdom of God. There are laws that God established in the kingdom of God that all beings abide by. The laws of the Spirit life pertain to the nature of the Spirit life through the Holy Spirit. The laws of physics pertain to the natural world we live in.

Our fleshly nature also has laws that govern our fleshly ways. For example, we get sleepy and require a period of time to sleep. That is a law unto our flesh. Our bodies require food to continue living. That is a law unto our flesh. If I drop a solid object, it will fall down because of gravity.

This is a law of physics. If I apply a high enough heat to water, that water will turn into a gas substance. This is a law of physics. If the Holy Spirit directs me to pray for a dead person for that person to rise from the dead and this happens, this is a law of the Holy Spirit. If the Holy Spirit comes within me and abides with me, I will become born of the Holy Spirit. This is a law of the Holy Spirit.

What is the righteousness of the law? Any law has within itself a law. The law that verse 3 is referring to is the Law of Moses. Sin has laws that govern sin. Death has laws that govern death. The purpose of the Law of Moses was to make people in right standing with God and other people. If you do something that is opposed the Law of Moses, you are guilty of wrongdoing. This puts you under the law of sin and death. You are no longer in right standing with God and people. God and other people frown upon you under the law of sin and death. You broke the law! You must have the guilt removed in order to be placed back in good standing with God and other people.

Along with the Law of Moses, laws were instituted about how a man could go about regaining a position of having the guilt removed in order to retain a right state with God and other people. This is what the Law of Moses can do for anyone. It is limited. If we are in a right standing with God and other people, all will go well with us—and we can obtain some of God's blessings that are promises of the law. This is what the righteousness of the law is. Another translation is *the righteous requirement of the law*. The righteousness of the law is having done all the law requires.

According to Verse 4, "The righteous requirement of the law might be fulfilled in us who do not walk according to the flesh but according to the spirit." Notice the phrase *might be fulfilled in us who.* God has not done away with the Law of Moses—even to this very day. A lot of Christians think that because we are in the New Testament, the Law of Moses no longer governs us. This is a false thinking. We are still under the Law of Moses. In fact, we are under even more laws that are added in the New Testament.

Part of walking in God's kingdom is being in a right standing with God and other people. God requires us to maintain the requirements of the Law of Moses and Jesus. In other words, because we have the Spirit does not mean we can kill, worship other gods, commit adultery, etc. Maintaining the Law of Moses is meeting the righteous requirement of the law. It has nothing to do with having faith in God. In fact, keeping the righteousness of the law does nothing for you in obtaining salvation from sin and life in God. All the law can do is warn you about sin.

Now, in the age of grace, we are able to fulfill the laws work very easily. It is all done through the work of Jesus. When we receive the Holy Spirit, we obtain the Holy Spirit's nature. We now have two natures within us. We have the flesh nature and the Holy Spirit's nature. God wants us to follow the Holy Spirit's nature and not the nature of the flesh. The sum total of the Law of Moses is in the Holy Spirit's nature. This is all so cool.

When we receive the Holy Spirit, we also receive the Law of Moses and Jesus's rules and laws of the New Testament. These laws are now within us because of the nature of the Holy Spirit. If we are in the Holy Spirit and violate one of the laws, we have instant notification that we are wrong. A buzzer goes off within us. The Holy Spirit is that buzzer. We have sinned against God's law. Due to the work of Christ, we can repent from that sin and receive forgiveness. The buzzer stops, and we are no longer guilty. We don't have to go make an animal sacrifice on behalf of our transgression or violation. Jesus is the animal sacrifice required by the Law of Moses. All this comes to us in the age of grace. The righteous requirement of the law is fulfilled within us. And the righteousness of the law is fulfilled within us.

Why is obeying the law still important for us if the law can't bring us any salvation unto heaven? What is the purpose of the law? The purpose of the law is to point out any sin we may be doing. Sin brings death or separation from God. If we continue to sin and make no effort to stop sinning, God will reject us and separate him from us. We enter back into death. The law acts as a warning system within our hearts and minds.

The Holy Spirit will point out any transgression of the law. It is God's way of helping us not enter back into sin. If we go through all the work to be saved, why would we want to go back into death? If you really want to end up in heaven, you'll want all the available help you can get. God provides as much help to us as he can.

Faith and the Law

The purpose of the law or the entire reason the law was given is so that all people can enjoy a relationship with God.

> But when the Pharisees heard that he had silenced
> the Sadducees, they gathered together. Then one
> of them, a lawyer, asked Him a question, testing

him, and saying, "Teacher, which is the great commandment in the law?" Jesus said to him, "You shall love the Lord your God with all your heart, with all your soul, and with all your mind." This is the first and great commandment. And the second is like it: "You shall love your neighbor as yourself." On these two commandments hang all the law and the Prophets." (Matthew 22:34–40, NKJV)

Verse 40 shows that this is the entire purpose of the law, including the Prophets, which I haven't even touched on. If you have love for God and all people, you will automatically do what the law is asking and intended to do. You will want to do as God commands and to help other people. If you truly have love for God and other people, you will always want to do good to both to the best of your ability. You will never do anything bad to either; this is true love. This is what is called the righteousness of the law. If you ever find or see someone who loves God and other people, you will find that person automatically practicing Jesus's laws and the Law of Moses. You will also discover that the promises that accompany the laws are with that person.

I have a great love for God, especially since I have come to experience his goodness and promises. I also care about my fellow man and want to help everyone who wants to climb out of his or her sinful condition to experience all the wonders of God as I have come to do. I have a love for all people. I want to help everyone I meet come to a good understanding of who God is and how he or she can get out of a fallen state. This is one of the reasons I wrote this book. It is one of the reasons why I travel around and speak to those who want to learn. If I didn't care about others, I wouldn't have sacrificed my personal life from my own enjoyment. Instead, I sacrificed of my own self enjoyments so I can help others who want a relationship with God. One such sacrifice is that I travel to them so they don't have to travel to me. No other religion makes this kind of sacrifice. They require you to travel to them. What's really bad is that they don't even teach the truth; instead they teach false doctrines.

> Owe no one anything except to love one another, for he who loves another has fulfilled the law. For the commandments, "You shall not commit adultery," "You shall not murder," "You shall not steal," "You shall not bear false witness," "You shall not covet," and if there is any other commandment, are all summed up in this saying, namely, "You shall love your neighbor as yourself." Love does no harm to a neighbor; therefore love is the fulfillment of the law. (Romans 13:8–10, NKJV)

> If you really fulfill the royal law according to the Scripture, "You shall love your neighbor as yourself," you do well. (James 2:8, NKJV)

Notice the last three words; doing well is all you can do with the totality of the law. This has nothing to do with getting faith from God. When you do well, all will go well with you. You will be in good standing with God and other people. This has nothing to do with salvation. If you want to be blessed by God, you have to follow the law. To do even better, you have to enter into the kingdom of heaven and the kingdom of God.

I'll give you an insight that even most believers and servants don't know about. Those who have the love of God in their hearts will be given more freedoms than anyone else. Those who allow themselves to be under total control of the Holy Spirit will have more freedom to do whatever they desire. They will have matured in God and will always remain in harmony with God. In return, God pours out great amounts of freedom to do what your heart desires. You can ask for the desires of your heart, and he will grant them. That's because God has tested and proven you to be loyal and faithful to him therefore he can put his trust in you.

I will share a secret here. It is a great desire for God to be able to come to a place of trusting each person who loves him. This isn't some theory I have concocted. Below are a few verses that reveal this.

- Principle: The person whose heart is filled with the love of God and controlled by the Holy Spirit is free to do whatsoever his or her heart desires so long as these desires are in line with God's will.

But he who looks into the perfect law of liberty and continues in it, and is not a forgetful hearer but a doer of the work, this one will be blessed in what he does. (James 1:25, NKJV)

But whoever keeps His word, truly the love of God is perfected in him. By this we know that we are in Him. (1 John 2:5, NKJV)

Once again, I want to help you through the more difficult verses. I call to your attention to the difference between the Law of Moses and faith in God. The law is a tool to help you identify what sin is. The age of grace enables you to come into the new life of the Holy Spirit. Once you are in the positive end of the number line, you must continue to receive faiths from God.

The righteousness of the law cannot do anything except show you when you transgress a law and enter into sin. In the age of grace with the indwelling of the Holy Spirit, the law becomes written in our hearts. When we commit sin, we can receive forgiveness from Jesus. When we sin, repent, and receive forgiveness, we perform the righteousness of the law. The law is fulfilled in that it did what it was supposed to do.

When we receive faith from God and do the work of each faith, we receive the righteousness of God. We then go on to full maturity in God, and we go on to more freedoms and liberties. We also go on to inherit God's kingdom in its entirety. Those who have never moved on into full maturity will never know of what I'm speaking because they will never experience these things of God.

CHAPTER 5

Baptisms

Our outline concerning baptisms:
What are all the different baptisms?
What is baptism?
Who is baptism for?
When do we get baptized?
Why should we get baptized?
Is baptism a necessity in our life?
How do we get baptized?
Who baptizes us?

> Therefore, leaving the discussion of the elementary principles of Christ, let us go on to perfection, not laying again the foundation of repentance from dead works and of faith toward God, of the doctrine of baptisms, of laying on of hands, of resurrection of the dead, and of eternal judgment. (Hebrews 6:1–2, NKJV)

I'm using these two verses as our base to learn about the six basic doctrines in the Bible. Notice how verse 2 mentions *the doctrine of baptisms*. Also notice that the word *baptisms* is plural, which reveals that there is more than one baptism.

Let's first get a definition of the word baptism so that we are all on the same page. If we all have the same definition, there will be no confusion in this chapter. In English, there is no word to translate from the Greek word *baptizo*. English used the Greek word *baptizo* and changed the last letter from *o* to *e* from grammar's sake. *Baptize* was first introduced to the English language in the seventh century. In fact, to this day, *baptize* is an alien word to most other languages. The correct translation in the English form is *to baptize*.

The Greek word *baptizo* is a verb (action). In Greek, there are root words and compound words. The compound words make use of the root word, but they change the meaning into a broader use of the word. Compound words can give the root word a particular meaning. The root word for baptize is *bapto*. The compound word is adding *iz* making it *baptizo*. This change by the use of *iz* makes it into a causative meaning. The causative meaning gives the word a sense of causing something to be or to happen. The exact cause of something to be or to happen is determined by the root word.

In any Greek verb, you can change the root word into a causative meaning just by adding iz. So far, we know that *baptizo* is causing something to happen or something to be. What is that something? The root word will reveal this mystery. *Bapto* occurs only three times in the New Testament, and it means "to dip." How profound! Don't start jumping up and down yet in excitement. Here are the three scriptures with the word *bapto*:

> Then he cried and said, "Father Abraham, have mercy on me, and send Lazarus that he may dip the tip of his finger in water and cool my tongue; for I am tormented in this flame." (Luke 16:24, NKJV)

> Jesus answered, "It is he to whom I shall give a piece of bread when I have dipped it." And having dipped the bread, He gave it to Judas Iscariot, the son of Simon. (John 13:26, NKJV)

> He was clothed with a robe dipped in blood, and His name is called the Word of God. (Revelation 19:13, NKJV)

Notice anything about the use of the word dip? Notice that in each use of *dip* is to place something into a liquid and to take it back out. (In John 13:26, it was a custom when dining with others to dip a small portion of bread into a sauce, which was an extreme delicacy, and then give it to another person to eat.)

We can thus determine that *bapto* is used to dip something into a fluid. This comes from the use of the word in connection to how it is being used. It is never used with any other action in the Bible. The causative would be to cause something to be dipped into a fluid and taken back out. The literal translation of bapto is *to cause something to be dipped*. In every use of the word *bapto* or *baptize,* we find whatever is being dipped is being dipped into some kind of fluid, whether it be water, blood, food, etc. You can't dip something into a solid substance.

With this definition, we move on to the word *baptism,* which is used in several places in the New Testament. Everywhere it is used brings out three distinct features. It is an experience. It involved the whole of a person, including character and personality. It is transforming—it marks a transition of someone passing out of a stage or realm of experience into a new stage or realm of experience that was never previously entered into. An example would be someone who gets dipped totally into a large container of plaster of paris and is then pulled back out. Then they must wait till the plaster is dried. Now you have to walk and move around with the hardened plaster. This would be a new experience till all the plaster breaks and falls off your body. It's like the first time you jumped into a swimming pool. You went through the shock of the cool water. Once you came back out, you were cold for a few minutes. The act of baptism in the Bible is going from one experience to a new experience.

Hebrews 6:2 includes the plural use of baptisms. There is more than one baptism. The following verses show the different kinds of baptisms used and described in the New Testament.

John came baptizing in the wilderness and preaching a baptism of repentance for the remission of sins. Then all the land of Judea, and those from Jerusalem, went out to him and were all baptized by him in the Jordan River, confessing their sins. Now John was clothed with camel's hair and with a leather belt around his waist, and he ate locusts and wild honey. And he preached, saying, "There comes One after me who is mightier than I, whose sandal strap I am not worthy to stoop down and loose. I indeed baptized you with water, but He will baptize you with the Holy Spirit." (Mark 1:4–8, NKJV)

John baptizes with water for the forgiveness of sins. But also remember that Jesus baptized with the Holy Spirit. John wasn't baptizing people because they had come to hear what he was preaching. The purpose of John's baptism was for people to repent for their sins. These people wanted to receive forgiveness for their sins. I'll get into that later in this chapter.

But I have a baptism to be baptized with, and how distressed I am till it is accomplished! (Luke 12:50, NKJV)

They said to Him, "Grant us that we may sit, one on Your right hand and the other on Your left, in your glory." But Jesus said to them, "You do not know what you ask. Are you able to drink the cup that I drink, and be baptized with the baptism that I am baptized with?" (Mark 10:37–38, NKJV)

These passages refer to the suffering that Jesus had to undertake a suffering unto death by the hand of man. Today, Bible students call this a baptism of suffering.

And Jesus came and spoke to them, saying, "All authority has been given to Me in heaven and on earth. Go therefore and make disciples of all the nations, baptizing them in the name of the Father and of the Son and of the Holy Spirit. (Matthew 28:18–19, NKJV)

This baptism was just like John's—except it was not just for the remission of sins. Instead, it incorporated the name and authority of the Father, Son, and Holy Spirit. (It is a symbol of the death and resurrection of Jesus—we die to the old life and are born of the new life. We are buried in water and rise out of the water—just as Jesus was buried in the tomb and rose out of the tomb. Water is likened to the tomb.)

For John truly baptized with water, but you shall be baptized with the Holy Spirit not many days from now. (Acts 1:5, NKJV)

A more correct translation is baptized *in* the Holy Spirit, not *with* the Holy Spirit. We discover that the New Testament mentioned four baptisms:

- John's baptism in water for the remission of sins
- A baptism of suffering
- Christian baptism in water resembling the death and resurrection of Jesus
- The baptism in the Holy Spirit

The baptism of suffering is more for the advanced or more mature Christian and doesn't pertain to what I'm teaching in this book. But note that the two sons of Zebedee were two of Jesus's disciples who later suffered painful deaths and were numbered among the first martyrs of Jesus. Be cautious about this baptism; if you ask God for this kind of baptism, you might get what you ask for. I'm interested in focusing upon the other three baptisms because they pertain to the six basic doctrines.

I'll look at each of these baptisms in the order of the New Testament.

John's Baptism

> And it happened, while Apollos was at Corinth, that Paul, having passed through the upper regions, came to Ephesus. And finding some disciples, he said to them, "Did you receive the Holy Spirit when you believed?" So they said to him, "We have not so much as heard whether there is a Holy Spirit." And he said to them, "Into what then were you baptized?" So they said, "Into John's baptism." Then Paul said, "John indeed baptized with a baptism of repentance, saying to the people that they should believe on Him who would come after him, that is, on Christ Jesus." When they heard this, they were baptized in the name of the Lord Jesus. (Acts 19:1–5, NKJV)

Paul makes his way to Ephesus, which was a major city in the Roman province. Paul found twelve believers but soon learned that they only knew about John's baptism. Paul taught them about Jesus and all that happened after John. The believers accepted Jesus into their hearts and were again baptized into Christ's water baptism.

This passage clearly reveals that John and Christ's baptisms are two distinct and separate baptisms. Once John's ministry ended, the dispensation of grace began with the resurrection of Jesus. John's baptism is no longer likened unto the Christian baptism. In fact, anyone who had received John's baptism was required to undergo the Christian baptism. John's ministry was to usher in the dispensation of grace. His baptism was that of repentance, which is what Jesus's first command entails.

John was to usher in the Messiah. His ministry reflected much of what the Messiah was going to require of people—repentance by publicly confessing any sins. As an outward sign of this repentance, John used a water baptism as part of the public confession of sins since the water baptism was also done in public.

It's interesting to note that all the regions had heard about John and his preaching of remission of sins with baptism. Everyone had at least heard about John's ministry to baptism. This was no small event at that point in time. John was a herald to the coming Messiah and was preaching much of what Jesus was going to provide whether the people understood all that he was preaching or not. Even many of the Pharisees and Sadducees came to be baptized.

> Then Jerusalem, all Judea, and all the region around the Jordan went out to him and were baptized by him in the Jordan, confessing their sins. But when he saw many of the Pharisees and Sadducees coming to his baptism, he said to them, "Brood of vipers! Who warned you to flee from the wrath to come? Therefore, bear fruits worthy of repentance. (Matthew 3:5–8, NKJV)

John did not baptize these religious leaders because they did not repent from their sins or even confess their sins. Because of this great event of John's ministry, everyone was aware that John was a prophet and a great prophet at that. Even the Romans and kings of Israel knew about John in no small way.

People may not have understood much of what John was doing or what was happening, but John did. John had total understanding that he was a herald to the coming of the Messiah; he preached it to all the people who came to hear him. There was a special anointing upon John during his ministry and his ministry was a very powerful ministry. When people confessed their sins publicly, truly repented of their sins, and were baptized by John, they experienced a change of heart. Their hearts were changed. This prepared those hearts to be able to better receive the work of Jesus once the age of grace began on Jesus's resurrection day. One day, Jesus comes to John as everyone else did. John immediately knew who Jesus was. He said, "Behold the Lamb of God who takes away the sins of the world."

> Then Jesus came from Galilee to John at the Jordan to be baptized by him. And John tried to prevent Him, saying, "I need to be baptized by You, and are You coming to me?" But Jesus answered and said to him, "Permit it to be so now, for thus it is fitting for us to fulfill all righteousness." Then he allowed Him. When He had been baptized, Jesus came up immediately from the water; and behold, the heavens were opened to Him, and He saw the Spirit of God descending like a dove and alighting

upon Him. And suddenly a voice came from heaven, saying, "This is My beloved Son, in whom I am well pleased." (Matthew 3:13–17, NKJV)

Jesus talked to John in verse 15 and said, "It is right for us to fulfill all righteousness."

What did Jesus mean by this statement? Jesus didn't need John's baptism because there was no sin in Jesus. Jesus was instituting an example or pattern that all believers in the Messiah were to follow. Jesus was showing everyone that he would die and be resurrected. He was sinless and would take on everyone's sin to die in his or her place, which was the requirement of the law when the priest had to offer a spotless and unblemished animal for a sin offering.

Jesus told John that it is right for us to fulfill all righteousness. Jesus was referring to the law and John understood this. I have always wondered if this was the last time that John ever baptized anyone. Was this the ending of John's ministry?

Verse 16 says, "Jesus came up immediately from the water." This phrase reveals to us that Jesus had a full immersion in the water. His entire body was covered in water because he came up from the water. When we are baptized into Christ's baptism, we are fully immersed in water and then pulled back out of the water. The entire body is put underwater and then pulled back out of the water. It has nothing to do with sprinkling of water as many denominations and other religions perform. Sprinkling is just that; baptism involves dipping.

Caleb MacDonald

Water Baptism

Another interesting fact in the New Testament is that wherever you find the gospel being preached, you find baptism being taught to an individual or a group of people. Water baptism is resembling the death and resurrection of Jesus.

> Go therefore and make disciples of all the nations, baptizing them in the name of the Father and of the Son and of the Holy Spirit, teaching them to observe all things that I have commanded you. (Matthew 28:19–20, NKJV)

> Now when they heard this, they were cut to the heart, and said to Peter and the rest of the apostles, "Men and brethren, what shall we do?" Then Peter said to them, "Repent, and let every one of you be baptized in the name of Jesus Christ for the remission of sins; and you shall receive the gift of the Holy Spirit. (Acts 2:37, NKJV)

Notice that you repent before you are baptized. Once this happens, you are eligible for the next baptism of the Holy Spirit.

> And He said to them, "Go into all the world and preach the gospel to every creature. He who believes and is baptized will be saved; but he who does not believe will be condemned." (Mark 16:15–16, NKJV)

308

The command is to believe before getting baptized. This is the beginning of entering into the kingdom of heaven.

> Now an angel of the Lord spoke to Philip, saying, "Arise and go toward the south along the road which goes down from Jerusalem to Gaza." This is desert. So he arose and went. And behold, a man of Ethiopia, a eunuch of great authority under Candace the queen of the Ethiopians, who had charge of all her treasury, and had come to Jerusalem to worship, was returning. And sitting in his chariot, he was reading Isaiah the prophet. Then the Spirit said to Philip, "Go near and overtake this chariot." So Philip ran to him, and heard him reading the prophet Isaiah, and said, "Do you understand what you are reading?" And he said, "How can I, unless someone guides me?" And he asked Philip to come up and sit with him. The place in the Scripture which he read was this: "He was led as a sheep to the slaughter; and as a lamb before its shearer is silent, so He opened not His mouth. In His humiliation His justice was taken away, and who will declare His generation? For His life is taken from the earth." So the eunuch answered Philip and said, "I ask you, of whom does the prophet say this, of himself or of some other man?" Then Philip opened his mouth, and beginning at this Scripture, preached Jesus to him. Now as they went down the road, they came to some water. And the eunuch said, "See, here is water. What hinders me from being baptized?" Then Philip said, "If you believe with all your heart, you may." And he answered and said, "I believe that

Jesus Christ is the Son of God." So he commanded the chariot to stand still. And both Philip and the eunuch went down into the water, and he baptized him. (Acts 8:26–38, NKJV)

This eunuch from Ethiopia was no ordinary man; he was a man of great authority. He was a very wise man. After he accepted Jesus into his heart, he was very much aware of the next step to be baptized. And having come along the Jordan, he was baptized. He accepted Jesus into his heart and then was baptized.

Notice the three main conditions in the New Testament for Christ's baptism:

- A person must have been taught enough of the message of Jesus to understand the need for baptism.
- A person must have repented from his or her sins.
- A person must believe from the heart that Jesus is the Son of God.

The following passages of scriptures all have these three main conditions in common:

There was a certain man in Caesarea called Cornelius, a centurion of what was called the Italian Regiment, a devout man and one who feared God with all his household, who gave alms generously to the people, and prayed to God always. (Acts 10:1–2, NKJV)

So I sent to you immediately, and you have done well to come. Now therefore, we are all present before God, to hear all the things commanded you by God. (Acts 10:33, NKJV)

While Peter was still speaking these words, the Holy Spirit fell upon all those who heard the word. And those of the circumcision who believed were astonished, as many as came with Peter, because the gift of the Holy Spirit had been poured out on the Gentiles also. For they heard them speak with tongues and magnify God. Then Peter answered, "Can anyone forbid water, that these should not be baptized who have received the Holy Spirit just as we have?" And he commanded them to be baptized in the name of the Lord. Then they asked him to stay a few days. (Acts 10:44–48, NKJV)

Then he called for a light, ran in, and fell down trembling before Paul and Silas. And he brought them out and said, "Sirs, what must I do to be saved?" So they said, "Believe on the Lord Jesus Christ, and you will be saved, you and your household." Then they spoke the word of the Lord to him and to all who were in his house. And he took them the same hour of the night and washed their stripes. And immediately he and all his family were baptized. Now when he had brought them into his house, he set food before them; and he rejoiced, having believed in God with all his household. (Acts 16:29–34, NKJV)

"Therefore, let all the house of Israel know assuredly that God has made this Jesus, whom you crucified, both Lord and Christ." Now when they heard this, they were cut to the heart, and said to Peter and the rest of the apostles, "Men and brethren, what shall we do?" Then Peter said to them, "Repent, and let every one of you be baptized in the name of Jesus Christ for the remission of sins; and you shall receive the gift of the Holy Spirit. For the promise is to you and to your children, and to all who are afar off, as many as the Lord our God will call." And with many other words he testified and exhorted them, saying, "Be saved from this perverse generation." Then those who gladly received his word were baptized; and that day about three thousand souls were added to them. (Acts 2:36–41, NKJV)

But there was a certain man called Simon, who previously practiced sorcery in the city and astonished the people of Samaria, claiming that he was someone great, to whom they all gave heed, from the least to the greatest, saying, "This man is the great power of God." And they heeded him because he had astonished them with his sorceries for a long time. But when they believed Philip as he preached the things concerning the kingdom of God and the name of Jesus Christ, both men and women were baptized. Then Simon himself also believed; and when he was baptized he continued with Philip, and was amazed, seeing the miracles and signs which were done. (Acts 8:9–13, NKJV)

Then a certain Ananias, a devout man according to the law, having a good testimony with all the Jews who dwelt there, came to me; and he stood and said to me, "Brother Saul, receive your sight." And at that same hour I looked up at him. Then he said, "The God of our fathers has chosen you that you should know His will, and see the Just One, and hear the voice of His mouth. For you will be His witness to all men of what you have seen and heard. And now why are you waiting? Arise and be baptized, and wash away your sins, calling on the name of the Lord." (Acts 22:12–16, NKJV)

Now a certain woman named Lydia heard us. She was a seller of purple from the city of Thyatira, who worshiped God. The Lord opened her heart to heed the things spoken by Paul. And when she and her household were baptized, she begged us, saying, "If you have judged me to be faithful to the Lord, come to my house and stay." So she persuaded us. (Acts 16:14–15, NKJV)

Notice that baptism follows immediately within a day or a few days. There was no waiting for several weeks or months. After the baptism, there was more teaching. I'm going to give some teaching about Jesus baptism and why it is an important rite.

What shall we say then? Shall we continue in sin that grace may abound? Certainly not! How shall we who died to sin live any longer in it? Or do you not know that as many of us as were baptized into Christ Jesus were baptized into His death? Therefore, we were buried with Him through baptism into death, that just as Christ was raised from the dead by the glory of the Father, even so we also should walk in newness of life. For if we have been united together in the likeness of His death, certainly we also shall be in the likeness of His resurrection, knowing this, that our old man was crucified with Him, that the body of sin might be done away with, that we should no longer be slaves of sin. For he who has died has been freed from sin. Now if we died with Christ, we believe that we shall also live with him, knowing that Christ, having been raised from the dead, dies no more. Death no longer has dominion over him. (Romans 6:1–9, NKJV)

Paul is teaching us how we pass from the death (that we inherit from Adam's fall) into life in God. The death we inherit is a result of sin. Christ came to die for our sins and did so, taking upon himself everyone's sins. Through Christ we can appropriate the forgiveness of God.

Three days after Christ died, he rose from the dead with newness of life. When he rose, the sins he took to death were gone. He rose in newness of life. Jesus's baptism is a reflection or symbol of what Jesus did. When we are baptized as commanded, we are undergoing a death of sin and rising in newness of life. The water is likened unto a tomb; we die and are buried or placed underwater. But when we are forgiven for our sins, we rise to a newness of life or are forgiven for our sins having been cleansed. Our rising up out of the water is a representation of the resurrection from the dead only now with a clean life.

Coming back out of the water is symbolic of being raised from the dead. Our sins are gone. We are new again. On the number line, when we ask Christ for forgiveness, he takes away all our sins. We are new again or at zero on the number line. When we are buried just as Christ was, we were in the negative, but when we arise, we are at zero.

When we undergo baptism, we are doing the same thing that Jesus did on the cross. We are dying for our sins and being raised to a newness of life. The only difference is that we are not physically dying and then having to be physically raised from a grave. In Jesus's baptism, we are doing the same thing that Jesus did on the cross. Just as Jesus died, was buried, and was raised to life, so we die, are buried, and are raised to a clean pure life.

When this happens, we can conquer the results of sin that we inherited. We can now go on to receive the life of the Holy Spirit. Jesus conquers this death, and all we do is partake with Jesus this death. Death from sin is finally conquered when you receive the baptism of the Holy Spirit. You never have to go back to into death—as long as you maintain this life of the Holy Spirit. Through Christ, we gain the forgiveness of sin, and we can go on to receive life. When you receive forgiveness of your sins you become dead to those sins. They can never again be slaves to you. When you're dead to those sins, you are freed from those sins.

> For the death that He died, He died to sin once for all, but the life that He lives, He lives to God. Likewise you also, reckon yourselves to be dead

indeed to sin, but alive to God in Christ Jesus our Lord. Therefore, do not let sin reign in your mortal body, that you should obey it in its lusts. And do not present your members as instruments of unrighteousness to sin, but present yourselves to God as being alive from the dead, and your members as instruments of righteousness to God. For sin shall not have dominion over you, for you are not under law but under grace. (Romans 6:10–14, NKJV)

When we are forgiven of our sins we have died together with Christ. The next step is we must be made alive.

A common mistake that most new converts make is assuming that they have also obtained the new life. Remember that these scriptures were written to those who went on to receive the new life from the Holy Spirit. Romans 6:4 says, "Even so we also should walk in newness of life."

Notice the words *we also should walk*. This suggests that there is another experience that we must obtain.

In verse 6, Paul uses the phrase "old man." He refers to our life before we came to know God to be the "old man." Our old man is living according to the flesh. Now we are to go on and get a "new man," which can be done through the Holy Spirit. This new man is what is referred to as being born again. The new man is obtaining the nature of the Holy Spirit. Jesus used this phrase in John 3:3. Jesus answered and said to him, "Most assuredly, I say to you, unless one is born again, he cannot see the kingdom of God."

So then, those who are in the flesh cannot please God. But you are not in the flesh but in the Spirit, if indeed the Spirit of God dwells in you. Now if anyone does not have the Spirit of Christ, he is not His. And if Christ is in you, the body is dead because of sin, but the Spirit is life because of righteousness. But if the Spirit of Him who raised Jesus from the dead dwells in you, He who raised Christ from the dead will also give life to your mortal bodies through his Spirit who dwells in you. (Romans 8:8–11, NKJV)

Verse 9 says, "if indeed the Spirit of God dwells in you," and verse 11 says, "But if the Spirit of him who raised Jesus from the dead dwells in you." The use of the word *if* suggests that there is a separate experience after being forgiven for sins.

Baptism of the Holy Spirit

The baptism of the Holy Spirit is mentioned in a few verses of the Bible:

I indeed baptize you with water unto repentance, but He who is coming after me is mightier than I, whose sandals I am not worthy to carry. He will baptize you with the Holy Spirit and fire. (Matthew 3:11, NKJV)

I indeed baptized you with water, but He will baptize you with the Holy Spirit. (Mark 1:8, NKJV)

John answered, saying to all, "I indeed baptize you with water; but One mightier than I is coming, whose sandal strap I am not worthy to loose. He will baptize you with the Holy Spirit and fire. (Luke 3:16, NKJV)

I did not know Him, but He who sent me to baptize with water said to me, "Upon whom you see the Spirit descending, and remaining on Him, this is He who baptizes with the Holy Spirit." (John 1:33, NKJV)

And being assembled together with them, He commanded them not to depart from Jerusalem, but to wait for the Promise of the Father, "which," He said, "you have heard from Me; for John truly baptized with water, but you shall be baptized with the Holy Spirit not many days from now." (Acts 1:4–5, NKJV)

And as I began to speak, the Holy Spirit fell upon them, as upon us at the beginning. (Acts 11:15, NKJV)

For by one Spirit we were all baptized into one body—whether Jews or Greeks, whether slaves or free—and have all been made to drink into one Spirit. (1 Corinthians 12:13, NKJV)

Notice that in all seven passages, you find the words *with the Holy Spirit,* and in the last passage the words *by one*

Spirit. The correct translation should be *in*, which uses the correct preposition.

Why is the use of *in* so important? Some false doctrines have arisen that teach that the baptism of the Holy Spirit is a special experience that is different from what is being taught in the gospels and Acts. The claim is that the Holy Spirit is doing the baptizing—and not Jesus. This false teaching teaches that the Holy Spirit baptizes whomever he chooses at his own discretion. Another false teaching is that the baptism in the Holy Spirit was only for those of the first church era. This teaching is also suggesting that God changes. Nowhere in the Bible is it recorded that God changes. There are lots of passages that say that God doesn't change.

What do we learn from the seven passages that we read about the baptism of the Holy Spirit? Notice that six of the passages mention is compared to water baptism since the word baptism is being used. Therefore the baptism of the Holy Spirit is thus a total-immersion experience. Also, notice that in two of the passages, fire accompanies the Holy Spirit's baptism. In the last passage, notice how we "have all been made to drink into one Spirit." (This refers to partaking of what is being offered.) Also notice the use of the phrase *have all*, which proves that it is for everyone. These verses describe a total separate experience from accepting Jesus into your life. It is God's intent that we all receive the baptism of the Holy Spirit.

- False Doctrine: The Holy Spirit baptizes whomever he chooses at his own discretion.
- False Doctrine: The Holy Spirit baptism was only for the first generation believers.

On the last day, that great day of the feast, Jesus stood and cried out, saying, "If anyone thirsts, let Him come to Me and drink. He who believes in Me, as the Scripture has said, out of his heart will flow rivers of living water." But this He spoke concerning the Spirit, whom those believing in Him would receive; for the Holy Spirit was not yet given, because Jesus was not yet glorified. Therefore, many from the crowd, when they heard this saying, said, "Truly this is the Prophet." (John 7:37–40, NKJV)

Again Jesus is referring to an experience in which the believer is to receive.

Jesus answered and said to him, "Most assuredly, I say to you, unless one is born again, he cannot see the kingdom of God." Nicodemus said to Him, "How can a man be born when he is old? Can he enter a second time into his mother's womb and be born?" Jesus answered, "Most assuredly, I say to you, unless one is born of water and the Spirit, he cannot enter the kingdom of God. That which is born of the flesh is flesh, and that which is born of the Spirit is spirit. Do not marvel that I said to you, "You must be born again." The wind blows where it wishes, and you hear the sound of it, but cannot tell where it comes from and where it goes. So is everyone who is born of the Spirit." (John 3:3–8, NKJV)

Holy Spirit Baptism Is Being Born Again

In the passage above, Jesus mentions that you must be born again or born of the Spirit in order to enter into the kingdom of God. This is in harmony with receiving the baptism of the Holy Spirit.

There is no other mention of the correlation between born again and the baptism of the Holy Spirit mentioned in the entire Bible. In this verse, we learn that when we receive the baptism of the Holy Spirit, the Holy Spirit comes and dwells next to the spirit of each of us within our body. This is the beginning of spiritual life in God.

On the number line, you pass from being "zeroed out" to becoming alive in your spirit when you receive the baptism of the Holy Spirit. You enter into the positive on the number line. God refers to this new beginning as being born again. What God has wanted to do with man since the fall of Adam and Eve is now possible. The Holy Spirit can dwell within each of us. Our spirit is made alive with the Holy Spirit's baptism. Our spirit must literally grow up in maturity as from a baby to an adult. The more you mature in the Holy Spirit, the more obvious this new birth will become. I can tell you from my own personal life that this truly is an exciting event. It is wonderful to slowly feel your spirit growing and maturing in the life of God.

We see the word *baptized* in all these scriptures. Baptized means to dip. How does this relate to the Holy Spirit? This use of the word *baptize* suggests that we are dipped or immersed in the Holy Spirit. How can this happen since all we understand that baptism is physical dipping, such as a water baptism? What does it mean to be baptized by the

Holy Spirit? Is the entire body or another part of us being baptized?

Let's look at what scripture reveals, and then we may be able to draw some accurate conclusions for the above questions.

> When the Day of Pentecost had fully come, they were all with one accord in one place. And suddenly there came a sound from heaven, as of a rushing mighty wind, and it filled the whole house where they were sitting. Then there appeared to them divided tongues, as of fire, and one sat upon each of them. And they were all filled with the Holy Spirit and began to speak with other tongues, as the Spirit gave them utterance. (Acts 2:1–4, NKJV)

> Now when the apostles who were at Jerusalem heard that Samaria had received the word of God, they sent Peter and John to them, who, when they had come down, prayed for them that they might receive the Holy Spirit. For as yet, He had fallen upon none of them. They had only been baptized in the name of the Lord Jesus. Then they laid hands on them, and they received the Holy Spirit. (Acts 8:14–17, NKJV)

> While Peter was still speaking these words, the Holy Spirit fell upon all those who heard the word. And those of the circumcision who believed were astonished, as many as came with Peter, because the gift of the Holy Spirit had been poured out on the Gentiles also. (Acts 10:44–45, NKJV)

And it happened, while Apollos was at Corinth, that Paul, having passed through the upper regions, came to Ephesus. And finding some disciples, he said to them, "Did you receive the Holy Spirit when you believed?" So they said to him, "We have not so much as heard whether there is a Holy Spirit." And he said to them, "Into what then were you baptized?" So they said, "Into John's baptism." Then Paul said, "John indeed baptized with a baptism of repentance, saying to the people that they should believe on Him who would come after him, that is, on Christ Jesus." When they heard this, they were baptized in the name of the Lord Jesus. And when Paul had laid hands on them, the Holy Spirit came upon them, and they spoke with tongues and prophesied. (Acts 19:1–6, NKJV)

We notice two experiences that happened. The Holy Spirit externally fell on the believers and engulfed them. The Holy Spirit came from above and completely surrounded and immersed the believers. At the same time—on the inside of the believers—the Holy Spirit gushed into their spirits with his presence and power. These two experiences happened together.

From my own experience, there are no words that can accurately describe what happens on the inside of the believer. The only description that comes close is that you're suddenly bursting with power, joy, and excitement all at once. It's impossible to describe the power of the Holy Spirit. If you have never received the Holy Spirit's baptism, it's like nothing you have ever experienced. This baptism is an entirely new experience because it entails the new birth.

I can tell you that the power of the Holy Spirit is all over you—inside and out. As I've prayed in the Holy Spirit for the past forty years, I continually feel different levels of his power. Sometimes, it's very weak; other times, it's incredibly strong. A lot of times, it is much like a flood within you; other times, it's like a trickle. This falling of the Holy Spirit upon a believer is a literal baptism of the Holy Spirit. He comes upon the believer externally and internally at the same time. Your entire being is soaked in the Holy Spirit. There are no other words that describes it any better that the word *baptized*. If you ever have this experience, you will conclude—just as I do and others do—that this is the best word to describe the Holy Spirits work.

Remember that there are always going to be people who will not believe or accept that this is a separate experience in God's kingdom. This is why I have shown you what is recorded in the New Testament. You can believe what the Bible says or what others say in disagreement. It's your life; it's your choice. Most believers in the New Testament had received the Holy Spirit's baptism. Jesus purpose for coming and leaving was for this reason of receiving the Holy Spirits baptism.

Outward Manifestations of the Holy Spirit

Along with this baptism are outward manifestations of the Holy Spirit's baptism. By manifestations, I mean that there is evidence of what is happening or has just happened.

Let's look at an example that Jesus gave about the Holy Spirit's manifestation.

> Jesus answered, "Most assuredly, I say to you, unless one is born of water and the Spirit, he cannot enter the kingdom of God. That which is born of the flesh is flesh, and that which is born of the Spirit is spirit. Do not marvel that I said to you, "You must be born again." The wind blows where it wishes, and you hear the sound of it, but cannot tell where it comes from and where it goes. So is everyone who is born of the Spirit." (John 3:5–8, NKJV)

Verse 8 is an example of such a manifestation that is compared to wind. You can hear and feel the wind. The wind stirs up dust, the trees bend, leaves rustle, and even waves are created. You can feel the wind against your body, but you can't see the wind because it is invisible. It's the same with the Holy Spirit. He is invisible, but you can feel him and see outward and inward manifestations just as the wind produces manifestations.

> Therefore, being exalted to the right hand of God, and having received from the Father the promise of the Holy Spirit, He poured out this which you now see and hear. (Acts 2:33, NKJV)

Once you receive the baptism of the Holy Spirit, you can see and hear these manifestations just as you can with the wind. One who has the Holy Spirit can sense that manifestation of the Holy Spirit with the five senses.

And my speech and my preaching were not with persuasive words of human wisdom, but in demonstration of the Spirit and of power. (1 Corinthians 2:4, NKJV)

But the manifestation of the Spirit is given to each one for the profit of all. (1 Corinthians 12:7, NKJV)

Notice in the above two scriptures that there is: *but in demonstration of the Spirit and of power* and there is: *the manifestation of the Spirit.* These two verses show us that the Holy Spirit can produce effects that can be felt by the five physical senses.

Now we can look at these experiences in the New Testament.

When the Day of Pentecost had fully come, they were all with one accord in one place. And suddenly there came a sound from heaven, as of a rushing mighty wind, and it filled the whole house where they were sitting. Then there appeared to them divided tongues, as of fire, and one sat upon each of them. And they were all filled with the Holy Spirit and began to speak with other tongues, as the Spirit gave them utterance. (Acts 2:1–4, NKJV)

While Peter was still speaking these words, the Holy Spirit fell upon all those who heard the word. And those of the circumcision who believed were astonished, as many as came with Peter, because the gift of the Holy Spirit had been poured out on the Gentiles also. For they heard them speak with tongues and magnify God. Then Peter answered. (Acts 10:44–46, NKJV)

And when Paul had laid hands on them, the Holy Spirit came upon them, and they spoke with tongues and prophesied. (Acts 19:6, NKJV)

In all three of the above passages, we find the same reoccurring manifestation: that those who received the Holy Spirit spoke in other tongues or other languages. There are other manifestations mentioned that are important and can happen even today, but we are interested in the manifestation that is the same in all three passages. Notice in the second passage that the Holy Spirit is also given to the Gentiles and is not restricted to just Jews. This truly means that the Holy Spirit and salvation is for anyone—regardless of race or national citizenship.

There is much controversy today regarding the baptism of the Holy Spirit, especially regarding the manifestation of speaking in tongues. A lot of people don't like the fact that you have to speak in tongues to have the baptism of the Holy Spirit. There are other controversies that are prevalent today that I regard as false doctrines.

Remember one important fact before I attack these false teachings. It is Satan's goal to keep you from ever getting saved, especially from receiving the Holy Spirit. The most powerful people who can do much damage to him are those who have the baptism of the Holy Spirit. Satan is going to focus on keeping anyone from ever gaining the Holy Spirit baptism. To counter the truth, he has spent the last two thousand years subtly introducing false doctrines into the church to keep people ignorant of the truth—and he has been very successful.

Satan is the major influence behind all the false doctrines. You have to see the false doctrines, look at what the Bible is teaching, and embrace what the Bible is truly teaching if you want to go on with God. No matter how many strange things may be in the Bible, there are reasons why God chooses to do them. If God required these strange things, then so be it. Once you practice these strange things, you will come to understand why God chose or required things like speaking in tongues.

- False Doctrine: When people receive Jesus into their lives, they automatically receive the Holy Spirit along with Jesus.

This false teaching gives the belief that you do not need any additional experiences or evidence of manifestations with the Holy Spirit. But herein lays the basis of this false teaching-"you do not need." Let's look at some scriptures that deal with the "need of the Holy Spirit." Let's see what the Bible teaches.

Then, the same day at evening, being the first day of the week, when the doors were shut where the disciples were assembled, for fear of the Jews, Jesus came and stood in the midst, and said to them, "Peace be with you." When He had said this, He showed them His hands and His side. Then the disciples were glad when they saw the Lord. So Jesus said to them again, "Peace to you! As the Father has sent Me, I also send you." And when He had said this, he breathed on them, and said to them, "Receive the Holy Spirit. If you forgive the sins of any, they are forgiven them; if you retain the sins of any, they are retained." (John 20:19–23, NKJV)

In verse 22, Jesus breathes on them and says, "Receive the Holy Spirit." This is not receiving the *baptism of the Holy Spirit* because Jesus commands them to return to Jerusalem to wait for the Holy Spirit's baptism. This is revealed in the following passages.

> Then He said to them, "Thus it is written, and thus it was necessary for the Christ to suffer and to rise from the dead the third day, and that repentance and remission of sins should be preached in His name to all nations, beginning at Jerusalem. And you are witnesses of these things. Behold, I send the Promise of My Father upon you; but tarry in the city of Jerusalem until you are endued with power from on high." (Luke 24:46–49, NKJV)

> And being assembled together with them, He commanded them not to depart from Jerusalem, but to wait for the Promise of the Father, "which," He said, "You have heard from Me; for John truly baptized with water, but you shall be baptized with the Holy Spirit not many days from now." (Acts 1:4–5, NKJV)

> But you shall receive power when the Holy Spirit has come upon you; and you shall be witnesses to Me in Jerusalem, and in all Judea and Samaria, and to the end of the earth. (Acts 1:8, NKJV)

If those disciples received the baptism of the Spirit before going to Jerusalem, why would Jesus command them to go to Jerusalem to wait for the baptism of the Holy Spirit? At that point, the believers gathered together in some place outside of Jerusalem and received a part of the Holy Spirit. The Holy Spirit was now with them—but not inside them.

Was there any experience that accompanied this? Jesus breathes on them and says, "Receive the Holy Spirit." There is no mention of any kind of experience that occurred when Jesus breathed on them, but when they received the baptism of the Holy Spirit in Jerusalem, they received an experience.

When they received the baptism of the Holy Spirit, they also received a promise of the Father and a portion of power of God. Accompanying the baptism of the Holy Spirit each person is endowed with the power of the Holy Spirit.

All believers are going to need the power of the Holy Spirit. You will need the power to overcome your flesh nature (the old man) and to defeat Satan and the demons because they all have a portion of power. This is discussed in length in *God's Advanced Doctrines*.

Notice also the mention of the *Promise of the Father* in verses Luke 24:49 and Acts 1:4. Luke 24:49 notes that you will have *power from on high*, and Acts 1:8 says that *you shall receive power*.

- Bible principle: When each person receives the Baptism of the Holy Spirit they also receive the power of the Holy Spirit.

This promise was prophesied in the Old Testament:

> And it shall come to pass afterward that I will
> pour out My Spirit on all flesh; your sons and
> your daughters shall prophesy, your old men
> shall dream dreams, your young men shall see
> visions. And also on My menservants and on My
> maidservants I will pour out My Spirit in those
> days. (Joel 2:28–29, NKJV)

The Holy Spirit and the work of redemption through
Jesus are the two main goals of the age of grace. John the
Baptist also preaches this in the passage found in Mark: "I
indeed baptized you with water, but He will baptize you
with the Holy Spirit." (Mark 1:8, NKJV)

> Then Peter said to them, "Repent, and let every one
> of you be baptized in the name of Jesus Christ for
> the remission of sins; and you shall receive the gift
> of the Holy Spirit. For the promise is to you and to
> your children, and to all who are afar off, as many as
> the Lord our God will call." (Acts 2:38–39, NKJV)

These above passages clearly reveal that the baptism
of the Holy Spirit is a separate experience than that of
receiving Jesus into the repenting heart. Two examples in
the New Testament clearly show that you can receive the
work of Jesus's redemption and not have the Holy Spirit.
In fact, every passage in the New Testament that deals
with believing in Jesus and then receiving the Holy Spirit
describes two completely separate experiences. It is never

mentioned anywhere that you receive the Holy Spirit when you accept Jesus into your heart.

- Bible Truth: You do not receive the Holy Spirit baptism when you when you accept Jesus into your heart.
- Bible Truth: Receiving Jesus's work of cleansing your spirit of sin is a separate work of receiving the baptism of the Holy Spirit.
- Bible Truth: The Holy Spirit can visit you outwardly without you receiving the baptism of the Holy Spirit but He cannot dwell inside you till you receive His baptism.
- Bible Truth: You can only receive the baptism of the Holy Spirit until after you have repented of your sins and received Jesus into your life.
- Bible Truth: When you receive the baptism of the Holy Spirit is when you pass from death into life with God.

And it happened, while Apollos was at Corinth, that Paul, having passed through the upper regions, came to Ephesus. And finding some disciples, he said to them, "Did you receive the Holy Spirit when you believed?" So they said to him, "We have not so much as heard whether there is a Holy Spirit." And he said to them, "Into what then were you baptized?" So they said, "Into John's baptism." Then Paul said, "John indeed baptized with a baptism of repentance, saying to the people that they should believe on Him who would come after him, that is, on Christ Jesus." When they heard this, they were baptized in the name of the Lord Jesus. And when Paul had laid hands on them, the Holy Spirit came upon them, and they spoke with tongues and prophesied. (Acts 19:1–6, NKJV)

Paul goes to Ephesus and finds twelve believers who only knew about John's baptism. Paul tells them about Jesus and all that Jesus did. They receive the work of Jesus and get water baptized. Following this, Paul lays hands on them, and they receive the baptism of the Holy Spirit. These clearly are two separate experiences.

- False Doctrine: We receive the baptism of the Holy Spirit when we receive Jesus into our hearts. There is no record in the New Testament that supports this false doctrine.

But there was a certain man called Simon, who previously practiced sorcery in the city and astonished the people of Samaria, claiming that he was someone great, to whom they all gave heed, from the least to the greatest, saying, "This man is the great power of God." And they heeded him because he had astonished them with his sorceries for a long time. But when they believed Philip as he preached the things concerning the kingdom of God and the name of Jesus Christ, both men and women were baptized. Then Simon himself also believed; and when he was baptized he continued with Philip, and was amazed, seeing the miracles and signs which were done. Now when the apostles who were at Jerusalem heard that Samaria had received the word of God, they sent Peter and John to them, who, when they had come down, prayed for them that they might receive the Holy Spirit. For as yet He had fallen upon none of them. They had only been baptized in the name of the Lord Jesus. Then they laid hands on them, and they received the Holy Spirit. (Acts 8:9–17, NKJV)

There was a certain man in Caesarea called Cornelius, a centurion of what was called the Italian Regiment, a devout man and one who feared God with all his household, who gave alms generously to the people, and prayed to God always. About the ninth hour of the day he saw clearly in a vision an angel of God coming in and saying to him, "Cornelius!" And when he observed him, he was afraid, and said, "What is it, Lord?" So he said to him, "Your prayers and your alms have come up for a memorial before God. Now send men to Joppa, and send for Simon whose surname is Peter. He is lodging with Simon, a tanner, whose house is by the sea. He will tell you what you must do." And when the angel who spoke to him had departed, Cornelius called two of his household servants and a devout soldier from among those who waited on him continually. So when he had explained all these things to them, he sent them to Joppa. The next day, as they went on their journey and drew near the city, Peter went up on the housetop to pray, about the sixth hour. Then he became very hungry and wanted to eat; but while they made ready, he fell into a trance and saw heaven opened and an object like a great sheet bound at the four corners, descending to him and let down to the earth. In it were all kinds of four-footed animals of the earth, wild beasts, creeping things, and birds of the air. And a voice came to him, "Rise, Peter; kill and eat." But Peter said, "Not so, Lord! For I have never eaten anything common or unclean." And a voice spoke to him again the second time, "What God has cleansed you must not call common." This was done three times. And the object was taken up into heaven again. Now while Peter wondered within himself what this vision which he had seen meant, behold, the men who had been sent from Cornelius had made inquiry for Simon's house, and stood before the gate. And they called and asked whether Simon, whose surname was Peter, was lodging there. While Peter thought about the vision, the Spirit said to him, "Behold, three men are seeking you. Arise therefore, go down and go with them, doubting nothing; for I have sent them." Then Peter went down to the men who had been sent to him from Cornelius, and said, "Yes, I am he whom you seek. For what reason have you come?" And they said, "Cornelius the centurion, a just man, one who fears God and has a good reputation among all the nation of the Jews, was divinely instructed by a holy angel to summon you to his house, and to hear words from you." Then he invited them in and lodged them. On the next day Peter went away with them, and some brethren from Joppa accompanied him. And the following day they entered Caesarea. Now Cornelius was waiting for them, and had called together his relatives and close friends. As Peter was coming in, Cornelius met him and fell down at his feet and worshiped him. But Peter lifted him up, saying, "Stand up; I myself am also a man." And as he talked with him, he went in and found many who had come together. Then he said to them, "You know how unlawful it is for a Jewish man to keep company with or go to one of another nation. But God has shown me that I should not call any man common or unclean. Therefore, I came without objection as soon as I was sent for. I ask, then, for what reason have you sent for me?" So Cornelius said, "Four days ago I was fasting until this hour; and at the ninth hour I prayed in my house, and behold, a man stood before me in bright clothing, and said, "Cornelius, your prayer has been heard, and your alms are remembered in the sight of God. Send therefore to Joppa and call Simon here, whose surname is Peter. He is lodging in the house of Simon, a tanner, by the sea. When he comes, he will speak to you." So I sent to you immediately, and you have done well to come. Now therefore, we are all present before God, to hear all the things commanded you by God." Then Peter opened his mouth and said, "In truth I perceive that God shows no partiality. But in every nation whoever fears Him and works righteousness is accepted by Him. The word which

God sent to the children of Israel, preaching peace through Jesus Christ—He is Lord of all—that word you know, which was proclaimed throughout all Judea, and began from Galilee after the baptism which John preached: how God anointed Jesus of Nazareth with the Holy Spirit and with power, who went about doing good and healing all who were oppressed by the devil, for God was with Him. And we are witnesses of all things which He did both in the land of the Jews and in Jerusalem, whom they killed by hanging on a tree. Him God raised up on the third day, and showed Him openly, not to all the people, but to witnesses chosen before by God, even to us who ate and drank with Him after He arose from the dead. And He commanded us to preach to the people, and to testify that it is He who was ordained by God to be Judge of the living and the dead. To Him all the prophets witness that, through His name, whoever believes in Him will receive remission of sins." While Peter was still speaking these words, the Holy Spirit fell upon all those who heard the word. And those of the circumcision who believed were astonished, as many as came with Peter, because the gift of the Holy Spirit had been poured out on the Gentiles also. For they heard them speak with tongues and magnify God. Then Peter answered, "Can anyone forbid water, that these should not be baptized who have received the Holy Spirit just as we have?" And he commanded them to be baptized in the name of the Lord. Then they asked him to stay a few days. (Acts 10:1–48, NKJV)

Notice that Cornelius already knew about the message of Jesus. He had already believed in Jesus and received forgiveness for sins along with the entire household because of the statement "that word you know." Cornelius is seeking God for something more as is stated in verse 4: "your prayers have been heard."

In verse 6, the angel instructs, "Now send men to Joppa, and send for Simon whose surname is Peter. He is lodging with Simon, a tanner, whose house is by the sea. He will tell you what you must do." The fact that *he will tell you what you must do* suggests that Cornelius is asking God for something.

After hearing what Peter is preaching, we find the Holy Spirit falling upon Cornelius and all those present just as on the day of Pentecost. The only difference is that these are Gentiles and not Jews. Here we find two separate experiences. Also notice that God has to communicate to Cornelius via an angel of God.

From the study of all these verses above, we draw four conclusions:

- It is normal for a believer to receive the baptism of the Holy Spirit as a separate experience following conversion of repentance and belief in Jesus.
- It is possible to receive the baptism of the Holy Spirit immediately following conversion of repentance and belief in Jesus.

- When a believer receives the baptism of the Holy Spirit, the manifestation and evidence of receiving the Spirit is speaking in tongues.
- The fact that a person has a genuine conversion to Christ does not mean that that person has also received the baptism of the Holy Spirit.

These four conclusions are based upon the book of Acts. These conclusions are in full harmony with the teaching of Jesus in the four Gospel books. There are supporting scriptures that deals with the baptism of the Holy Spirit in other parts of the New Testament:

If you then, being evil, know how to give good gifts to your children, how much more will *your* heavenly Father give the Holy Spirit to those who ask Him! (Luke 11:13, NKJV)

Receiving the Baptism of the Holy Spirit

Notice that sometimes you must ask for the baptism of the Holy Spirit. If you have repented and received forgiveness of your sins, you are eligible to receive the Holy Spirit baptism. In fact, it is a believer's right to obtain the Holy Spirit. If you want to continue on with God you must receive the baptism of the Holy Spirit. Because everyone must ask for the baptism of the Holy Spirit it is clear to conclude that it is not scriptural to assume that a believer automatically receives the baptism of the Holy Spirit along with repentance and forgiveness.

On the last day, that great day of the feast, Jesus stood and cried out, saying, "If anyone thirsts, let him come to Me and drink. He who believes in Me, as the Scripture has said, out of his heart will flow rivers of living water." But this He spoke concerning the Spirit, whom those believing in Him would receive; for the Holy Spirit was not yet given, because Jesus was not yet glorified. (John 7:37–39, NKJV)

It is clear that you must first be a believer in Jesus. Verse 38 mentions "he who believes in me," and verse 39 refers to "whom those believing in him would receive." (*Would receive* is better translated *about to receive* or *later receive* or *were to receive*. *Would receive* is a bad English translation.

It is clear that Jesus is speaking about two separate experiences. Reading these two passages from a summarized point of view would lead a new convert to think that they also receive the Holy Spirit. You have to remember to read the entire context of scripture to see that there are two separate experiences. John 7:38 is a conclusion of a believer doing everything God is providing.

If you love Me, keep My commandments. And I will pray the Father, and He will give you another Helper, that He may abide with you forever—the Spirit of truth, whom the world cannot receive, because it neither sees Him nor knows Him; but you know Him, for He dwells with you and will be in you. (John 14:15–17, NKJV)

Notice that Jesus is telling the disciples that the Holy Spirit is presently dwelling with you and will be in you. This clearly shows that Jesus is speaking about two separate times. Also notice that *dwelling with you* is not that same as *being inside you*. Up until now, the Holy Spirit is a companion, but he is not dwelling within each of their bodies. Notice also that it is the desire of the Father to have the Holy Spirit dwell within every man.

If you choose to believe that the infilling of the Holy Spirit is not a separate experience, then you are going against scripture. You will not experience the power of the Holy Spirit. None of the signs and wonders will ever follow you. You will not have power against the attacks of Satan. You will never grow or mature in the Holy Spirit or in God's kingdom. You will not be born again. You may upon occasion have God speak to you. You will never have the fruit of the Holy Spirit within you, instead you will have to make mental attempts to mimic what is written in the New Testament about the fruit of the Holy Spirit.

Another false doctrine comes from a passage in Galatians.

> I say then: Walk in the Spirit, and you shall not fulfill the lust of the flesh. For the flesh lusts against the Spirit, and the Spirit against the flesh; and these are contrary to one another, so that you do not do the things that you wish. But if you are led by the Spirit, you are not under the law. Now the works of the flesh are evident, which are: adultery, fornication, uncleanness, lewdness, idolatry, sorcery, hatred, contentions, jealousies, outbursts of wrath, selfish

ambitions, dissensions, heresies, envy, murders, drunkenness, revelries, and the like; of which I tell you beforehand, just as I also told you in time past, that those who practice such things will not inherit the kingdom of God. But the fruit of the Spirit is love, joy, peace, longsuffering, kindness, goodness, faithfulness, gentleness, self-control. Against such there is no law. And those who are Christ's have crucified the flesh with its passions and desires. If we live in the Spirit, let us also walk in the Spirit. Let us not become conceited, provoking one another, envying one another. (Galatians 5:16–26, NKJV)

• False doctrine: If you believe in Jesus, you will have the fruit of the Holy Spirit.

Verses 22–23 say, "But the fruit of the Spirit is love, joy, peace, longsuffering, kindness, goodness, faithfulness, gentleness, self-control." To believe that all believers have the fruit of the Holy Spirit without the baptism of the Holy Spirit, you have to take this verse out of the context of the entire passage.

In verse 16, Paul teaches us to walk in the Holy Spirit. This is to follow what the Holy Spirit will direct you to do. We are to war against the flesh nature of man. The Holy Spirit provides us with the power of God to do just this and to triumph over the flesh nature.

In verse 18, we are to be led by the Holy Spirit. How do we know we are following the Holy Spirit? The fruit or works of the flesh are listed in verses 19–21. If you don't have the Holy Spirit then you have no choice but to still live by the strength of the flesh. You may be able to suppress the flesh but this will be of your own strength. But if you have the Holy Spirit then you also have his power to control the strength of the flesh and this becomes very easy to do. In other words if the Spirit is not within you then you are subject to the flesh and any type of sin as a result of the flesh. Verse 25 shows clearly that "If we live in the Spirit, let us also walk in the Spirit." We all need to understand what walking in the Holy Spirit entails. For now, I want to show here that when a believer receives the baptism of the Holy Spirit there is fruit that comes as a result of having the Holy Spirit. Also fruit is a slow gradual process that requires time to be developed. The gift of the baptism of the Holy Spirit is a onetime event or single experience. But to believe that we all have the fruit of the Spirit—just from believing in Jesus—is completely taken out of context and used as a false doctrine.

- False doctrine: Speaking in tongues is not necessarily the evidence of having received the baptism of the Holy Spirit.

If this false doctrine is true, you must provide another form of evidence of receiving the Holy Spirit. What is the test or evidence provided in the Bible? The only evidence provided in the Bible is that of speaking with other tongues or in other languages. None of the apostles write about or speak about any other outward evidence of the baptism of the Holy Spirit. The evidence is that all the believers spoke in tongues. To say that there are other outward evidences is false because there are none listed in the Bible. Over time, as you mature in the Holy Spirit, the fruit of the Spirit becomes more and more apparent, which is considered evidence of the Holy Spirit. The fruit of the Spirit is an inward evidence of having received the baptism of the Holy Spirit. Another inward evidence of having received the baptism of the Holy Spirit is seeing the signs and wonders that follow the believer.

A common scripture that is used in this false doctrine is found in Acts.

> Now when the apostles who were at Jerusalem heard that Samaria had received the word of God, they sent Peter and John to them, who, when they had come down, prayed for them that they might receive the Holy Spirit. For as yet He had fallen upon none of them. They had only been baptized in the name of the Lord Jesus. Then they laid hands on them, and they received the Holy Spirit. (Acts 8:14–17, NKJV)

It is taught that there is no mention of the believers speaking in tongues when they received the Holy Spirit. Also notice that these Samaritans had already had accepted Jesus, but they had not received the Holy Spirit. This refers to two separate experiences. Again, there is direct mention of people speaking in tongues and having the power of the Spirit accompany the receiving of the Holy Spirit.

> And when Simon saw that through the laying on of the apostles' hands the Holy Spirit was given, he offered them money, saying, "Give me this power also, that anyone on whom I lay hands may receive the Holy Spirit." (Acts 8:18–19, NKJV)

These two verses make it clear that Simon saw that the Holy Spirit was given through the laying on of the apostles' hands. He wanted to have the same ability to lay his hands on people to receive the Holy Spirit.

Simon had to have witnessed an outward manifestation of the Holy Spirit. If the people of Samaria did not speak with tongues, there is no way to know what other evidence they may have experienced. But Simon did witness outward evidence because it said, "And when Simon saw."

In verse 19, Simon wants to do the same as the apostles for which he is rebuked because his motive was of the flesh. Because the only evidence of tongues is in other passages, we must conclude that the Samaritans did speak with tongues. What else could Simon have witnessed? To suggest that there is other outward evidence without describing it is total foolishness because it would be out of harmony with the rest of the New Testament. What Simon saw was right then and there.

Another part of scripture that is used to back this false doctrine is found in the book of Acts.

> And Ananias went his way and entered the house; and laying his hands on him he said, "Brother Saul, the Lord Jesus, who appeared to you on the road as you came, has sent me that you may receive your sight and be filled with the Holy Spirit." Immediately there fell from his eyes something like scales, and he received his sight at once; and he arose and was baptized. (Acts 9:17–18, NKJV)

False teachers use this verse in an attempt to explain that Paul never spoke in tongues. It is not recorded that Paul never spoke in tongues when he received the Holy Spirit. It is recorded that he did receive the Holy Spirit. But in other passages of the New Testament, we find that Paul confessed in personal testimony that he spoke in other tongues.

> I thank my God I speak with tongues more than you all. (1 Corinthians 14:18, NKJV)

> And when Paul had laid hands on them, the Holy Spirit came upon them, and they spoke with tongues and prophesied. (Acts 19:6, NKJV)

In this verse Paul lays his hands upon other believers to receive the baptism of the Holy Spirit which they do and is evidenced by them speaking in tongues. It would be foolish to think that Paul is able to provide an experience that he never had. Just because it is not recorded that Paul never spoke in tongues when he first received the Holy Spirit baptism, does not mean that Paul didn't speak in tongues at the very moment that Ananias laid hands on him. Paul later confesses that he speaks in tongues. When did Paul start speaking in tongues? Just as all the other passages of evidence of receiving tongues, Paul started speaking in tongues when Ananias laid hands on him. What was the reason that Ananias came to Paul? That Paul might receive sight only? No—so that Paul might receive the baptism of the Holy Spirit and his sight.

- False doctrine: Receiving the baptism of the Holy Spirit is evidenced by a strong, intense emotional experience.

The teaching of an intense joy or emotion is an evidence of the baptism of the Holy Spirit is not in harmony with the New Testament. There is no other record of outward evidence except that of speaking in tongues. There is not any mention anywhere of a strong emotional display or any kind of emotional display when receiving the baptism of the Spirit. There are passages where believers were rejoicing and continuing to rejoice for days after the baptism in the Holy Spirit.

> Therefore, those who were scattered went everywhere preaching the word. Then Philip went down to the city of Samaria and preached Christ to them. And the multitudes with one accord heeded the things spoken by Philip, hearing and seeing the miracles which he did. For unclean spirits, crying with a loud voice, came out of many who were possessed; and many who were paralyzed and lame were healed. And there was great joy in that city. (Acts 8:4–8, NKJV)

Notice that signs and wonders followed Philip who had previously received the Holy Spirit baptism in Jerusalem. Shortly following Philip's work, Peter and John traveled to Samaria and continued the work of teaching about the baptism of the Holy Spirit (Acts 8:14–17).

Before moving on to the next chapter, I would like to touch on one subject that few ever really ask. Why does God choose to use the tongue of man when receiving the baptism of the Holy Spirit? Why not some other part of the body? Why must we speak in other languages?

I'll list a few principles of the Bible that deal with man's tongue that may provide some insights as to why God chooses to use other tongues in the Holy Spirit's baptism.

> Brood of vipers! How can you, being evil, speak good things? For out of the abundance of the heart the mouth speaks. (Matthew 12:34, NKJV)

> But no man can tame the tongue. It is an unruly evil, full of deadly poison. With it we bless our God and Father, and with it we curse men, who have been made in the similitude of God. Out of the same mouth proceed blessing and cursing. My brethren, these things ought not to be so. Does a spring send forth fresh water and bitter from the same opening? Can a fig tree, my brethren, bear olives, or a grapevine bear figs? Thus no spring yields both salt water and fresh. (James 3:8–12, NKJV)

> And do not present your members as instruments of unrighteousness to sin, but present yourselves to God as being alive from the dead, and your members as instruments of righteousness to God. (Romans 6:13, NKJV)

Notice in Matthew that what is in the heart comes out of the mouth of man. Also notice in James that the tongue is untamable by any man. And in Romans, we are to present our members (different parts of our bodies) as instruments of righteousness to God. All these verses deal with man's tongue.

If the Holy Spirit chooses to use the tongue of man to speak in other tongues, then you can say that the Holy Spirit is taming the tongue of man. If you have really received the baptism of the Holy Spirit, then God's first job is to tame that wicked tongue of man. If you've received the Holy Spirit baptism, then the Holy Spirit has begun to dwell within your body. So out of your heart, you are able to speak the things of God and his kingdom. And when you speak of your experiences of God, you are going to be talking all about God's righteousness. When you speak about God, you are going to have to use your tongue. The more mature you are in God and the more revelations you receive through the Holy Spirit, the more you will proclaim all that is happening through the member called the tongue.

The Purpose of the Baptism of the Holy Spirit

Thus far, in this chapter, we have looked into baptisms. We have seen the three different baptisms. We have learned that the Bible only mentions one piece of immediate evidence of the baptism of the Holy Spirit. I revealed some of the false teachings that are taught today, and I used scripture to disprove them. But what I haven't taught is the entire purpose of the baptism of the Holy Spirit. I'm going to deal with that now. I'm going to be writing as though you—a believer in Jesus—have gone on to receive the baptism of the Holy Spirit.

Again I will be addressing false doctrines that are being taught in various church groups today. I'm going to begin by attacking false doctrines in order to clear up some misunderstandings that I hear often from other Spirit-filled believers.

- False doctrine: The Holy Spirit plays the role of an ogre or a dictator in anyone.

Some groups are teaching that the Holy Spirit is now in charge of everything you do. You have no say in what you're led to do. You either do or die. You have no freedom of any kind. The Holy Spirit must be in charge of every aspect of your life and being.

None of this is ever mentioned in the Bible. The Holy Spirit is a guide, teacher, and helper in your life. The Holy Spirit will never force you to do anything.

However, when He, the Spirit of truth, has come, He will guide you into all truth; for He will not speak on his own authority, but whatever He hears He will speak; and He will tell you things to come. He will glorify Me, for He will take of what is Mine and declare it to you. (John 16:13–14, NKJV)

But the Helper, the Holy Spirit, whom the Father will send in My name, He will teach you all things, and bring to your remembrance all things that I said to you. (John 14:26, NKJV)

If you love Me, keep My commandments. And I will pray the Father, and He will give you another Helper, that He may abide with you forever—the Spirit of truth, whom the world cannot receive, because it neither sees Him nor knows Him; but

you know Him, for He dwells with you and will be
in you. (John 14:15–17, NKJV)

It is the job of the Holy Spirit to guide us into all the
truth. The Holy Spirit can be our helper. The Holy Spirit
is a teacher unto each one of us. The Holy Spirit provides
us with power and liberty. Does this sound like an ogre or
dictator? The Holy Spirit will never force us to do something
against our own will. He is gentle and peaceful and always
guides those who are willing to be guided.

You can easily ignore or refuse to follow the advice of
the Holy Spirit. All these things I will touch on later. For
now, I want to show the believer that the Holy Spirit desires
to be Lord of your life—but not through forcing his will
upon each believer.

Now the Lord is the Spirit; and where the Spirit of
the Lord is, there is liberty. (2, NKJV)

For now understand that there are three separate Beings
that we call god. They are the Father, the Son, and the Holy
Spirit. All three comprise of the same nature, making them
deities to us. See *God's Advanced Doctrines* for more about
this subject. For now, I want to show you how "the Lord is
the spirit" refers to the Holy Spirit being the Lord of your
life. If you allow the Holy Spirit to become the Lord of your
life, he becomes your Lord, just as Jesus is also referred to as
the Lord of your life.

Wherever the Spirit of the Lord of your life is, there
is liberty. This verse is saying that there is always liberty if
you make the Holy Spirit Lord of your life and follow him.
In order to make the Spirit the Lord a true reality in your

daily life, you must continually yield your life to the Holy Spirit's guidance and help. Just receiving the infilling of the Holy Spirit at the beginning is just the beginning, and not the end.

- False doctrine: Once we receive the Holy Spirit, there is nothing more we need to do.
- False doctrine: God will only do for us certain things that we need.

We will see how wrong these false doctrines truly are. This is where most Pentecostal and Spirit Filled Churches get messed up. I will show you where in the Bible God makes full provisions for every one of our needs in every area and aspect of life. God has no limitations; in fact, he goes beyond the natural limits of physics that we call miracles.

And God is able to make all grace abound toward you, that you, always having all sufficiency in all things, may have an abundance for every good work. (2 Corinthians 9:8, NKJV)

Wow! What a fact. Either this is true—or it is a lie. Either God can provide all sufficiency in all things—or he can't. Notice how it does not say *in some things*. It says *in all things. May have an abundance* is teaching us that God will supply our needs and supply an abundance for these needs. The context is for believers who are giving a portion of their possessions or income. For the believer who does this, God responds that he will provide sufficiency in all things. The principle is that you give to God, and God will give back in your time of need (in abundance).

As His divine power has given to us all things that
pertain to life and godliness, through the knowledge
of Him who called us by glory and virtue. (2 Peter
1:3, NKJV)

This verse reveals that there is nothing that God can't
provide to us through his divine power. As long as we are
doing what God is asking, he will be providing for us.
There is nothing that he can't provide as long as these needs
pertain to righteousness and godliness. I call this teaching
the total provision of God.

It becomes a false doctrine when believers think that
one part of God's provision becomes a substitute for another
part of provision. You can't apply part of a provision in place
of another provision. If you do, it will not work. Millions
of Christians are trying to make this happen in their lives.
The following verses are examples of God's provision to
believers and demonstrate how many born again Christians
apply part of the provision as a substitute for another part
of the provision.

Finally, my brethren, be strong in the Lord and in
the power of His might. Put on the whole armor of
God, that you may be able to stand against the wiles
of the devil. For we do not wrestle against flesh and
blood, but against principalities, against powers,
against the rulers of the darkness of this age, against
spiritual hosts of wickedness in the heavenly places.
Therefore, take up the whole armor of God that you
may be able to withstand in the evil day, and having
done all, to stand. (Ephesians 6:10–13, NKJV)

Notice that we are exhorted to be strong in the Lord and the power of his might. Most Christians pass over this verse and ignore it. It is your job to be strong in the power of God. Most Spirit-filled Christians don't even know how to do this.

Next, we see that we are to put on all our armor—not just some of it. Most Spirit-filled Christians only use part of their armor. Would you ever go into combat with only a part of your armor? It is our job to stand against the devil. It is not God's job to stand against the devil for us.

In verse 12, we see that there are four different categories of wickedness that we must wrestle against. I'm amazed by how most Christians shrink or back away from doing this work when they learn what they must do in this part of their lives. They think that Christianity is a flowery world. The fact is that Satan is going to try to destroy you because you are now with God, and he knows that if you ever learn of your power and how to use it and your armor, you can do some very serious damage to him. Just by you doing your job, God can do some major damage to Satan. If you don't utilize all the provisions of God in just this one area of your life, you are doomed to be defeated in your walk with God. This is one reason so many millions of people fail in their lives with God.

Understand that this passage is only providing you protection in your Christian life. It has nothing to do with being on the offensive against Satan. If a believer omits just one of these six parts of armor mentioned in verses 14–16, then his protection is not complete. Satan isn't stupid. He will quickly discover your omission and concentrate his attacks to that missing part of armor. He will defeat you.

You cannot omit a part of the armor and think that having the rest will provide full protection.

The armor was a metaphor that Paul used after observing all the armor that Roman soldiers put on before entering into battle. Roman armor made the Roman soldiers dangerous on the battlefield. New developments and new technologies for battle made it difficult for enemies to cut through all this armor. This made the Roman soldiers extremely dangerous and effective in battle. Rome was able to win many battles due to this armor.

> Epaphras, who is one of you, a bondservant of Christ, greets you, always laboring fervently for you in prayers, that you may stand perfect and complete in all the will of God. (Colossians 4:12, NKJV)

You cannot omit any of the provisions of God and expect to stand perfect and complete in all the will of God.

Receiving the Spirit does not mean that we can omit Bible studying or praying. To be effective in your life with God, you must do all the provisions that he provides. What are the provisions that God provides to every believer? These are all the commands and ordinances that are written throughout the Bible. We have to be careful not to get caught up in just the works of these provisions, which is easy to do. You can't repent from all your sins except one. You must repent from *all* your sins to receive the forgiveness of God, and then you are able to be eligible to receive the baptism of the Holy Spirit. The provision is to repent for all your sins. You do all of your part, and God will do all of his part. I see many Christians asking for the baptism of the Holy Spirit and can't receive it. This is because most of these Christians still hang onto a few sins.

> And God is able to make all grace abound toward you, that you, always having all sufficiency in all things, may have an abundance for every good work. (2 Corinthians 9:8, NKJV)

You must do all that God is asking. There are several purposes that are provided for the believer through the baptism in the Holy Spirit. The Holy Spirit is only going to be good for the benefits and blessings that God intends when the Holy Spirit is utilized with all the other provisions that God is supplying for each believer. The Holy Spirit is part of the total provision God has given to people in order to obtain all the blessings of God. To separate the Holy Spirit from the rest of God's provisions will cause the Christian to fail to achieve success in God's kingdom.

The promises of God are based upon his provisions. All promises are conditional in that they require us to do our part in order that God will do his part. There are several thousand promises throughout the Bible. None of them are lies. They are all true and will work—provided you do all the provisions that pertain to those promises.

I'm not going to list and explain all the promises of God because that would take an entire book, but you can do this by reading through the Bible and taking notes. Write the reference of the promise as well as the promise—and then study to see what the provisions are to meet the requirements of that promise. You'll be amazed by what you will learn.

I can't live your life for you, but I can tell you how to do many things. It's your life, and you can live in liberty and abundance—or you can live as a slave and in poverty. I see the second choice daily. I'm amazed by the amount of Christians who choose to live defeated, as slaves, and in poverty. The main reason is that these people are lazy and refuse to do the work of the provisions.

Remember that there are doers of the Word—and there are hearers of the Word. Which are you? Let's go one step farther. Of all the Christians in your acquaintance, how many are doers of the Word? You'd be amazed to learn how few Christian actually are doers of the Word. You will also notice that the doers of the Word are the ones who are greatly blessed of God. The doers of the Word will discover that they have access to the provision of the power of the Holy Spirit.

To Receive the Power of the Holy Spirit

The first person to receive the Holy Spirit was Jesus.

> Then Jesus, being filled with the Holy Spirit, returned from the Jordan and was led by the Spirit into the wilderness, being tempted for forty days by the devil. And in those days He ate nothing, and afterward, when they had ended, He was hungry. And the devil said to Him, "If you are the Son of God, command this stone to become bread." But Jesus answered him, saying, "It is written, 'Man shall not live by bread alone, but by every word of God.' Then the devil, taking Him up on a high

mountain, showed Him all the kingdoms of the world in a moment of time. And the devil said to Him, "All this authority I will give You, and their glory; for this has been delivered to me, and I give it to whomever I wish. Therefore, if You will worship before me, all will be Yours." And Jesus answered and said to him, "Get behind me, Satan! For it is written, 'You shall worship the LORD your God, and Him only you shall serve. Then he brought Him to Jerusalem, set Him on the pinnacle of the temple, and said to Him, "If you are the Son of God, throw Yourself down from here. For it is written: 'He shall give his angels charge over you, to keep you' and 'In their hands they shall bear you up, lest you dash your foot against a stone.'" And Jesus answered and said to him, "It has been said, 'You shall not tempt the LORD your God.' Now when the devil had ended every temptation, he departed from Him until an opportune time. Then Jesus returned in the power of the Spirit to Galilee, and news of Him went out through all the surrounding region. (Luke 4:1–14, NKJV)

Notice that the very first thing that happens is that Jesus is filled with the Holy Spirit. Next the Holy Spirit leads Jesus into the wilderness. The devil spends forty days constantly tempting Jesus. Jesus was undergoing a battle against Satan.

After the forty days, Jesus's body was at a point of complete starvation. Satan attacked Jesus with three of his most powerful attacks since Jesus was at his greatest point of physical weakness. Jesus responded with the use of the written Word. This is like the armor we discussed earlier. Jesus is now using the shield of faith and the sword of the Spirit, which is the spoken word of God. (Ephesians 6:17, NKJV) Notice that the sword is a weapon of the Holy Spirit. It works when Satan attacks. The Holy Spirit tells you how to respond by speaking to Satan. The Holy Spirit usually gives you words to repeat to Satan. Jesus is merely repeating what the Spirit is personally speaking to Jesus within his spirit. Jesus speaks the words of the Holy Spirit. The difference is that when Jesus speaks these words of the Holy Spirit, an anointing of power accompanies these words.

Satan is blasted with the written Word of God and with the power of God through the Holy Spirit. If Jesus spoke words of his own volition, there would be no anointing of power to accompany his words. Jesus said later to the disciples, "The words I speak to you are spirit and life."

Satan tries three different times, but he is defeated each time because of the power of the Holy Spirit. The power of the Holy Spirit is far greater than anything Satan has. Satan has to back away from Jesus. Even Jesus himself has to rely upon the power of the Holy Spirit.

After all this spiritual battling, Jesus returns in the power of the Spirit in verse 14. Jesus enters the wilderness just full of the Spirit, but he returns in the power of the Spirit. Jesus had entered into a higher level of spiritual authority. He had the power of the Spirit at his disposal as another weapon to be used in his ministry.

The warfare that Jesus underwent is an example for us who are following the Holy Spirit. The lesson to learn here is that we are going to do battle with spiritual enemies because of receiving the baptism of the Holy Spirit. We must learn how to successfully battle Satan and his kingdom through the use of the Holy Spirit. Through each battle we encounter, we mature and learn how to be effective, successful warriors in God's kingdom—as long as we learn how to use the Holy Spirit. It's too bad that Adam and Eve didn't know how to do this in the Garden of Eden. So, one of the purposes of the Holy Spirit is to learn how to defeat Satan and his horde of demons. Satan and all his demons are alive on the earth. So we must learn how to successfully battle and defeat them. Just as Jesus relied upon the power of the Holy Spirit so too we must rely upon the power of the Spirit. This also applies to all the other wickedness within the earth.

> For we do not wrestle against flesh and blood, but against principalities, against powers, against the rulers of the darkness of this age, against spiritual hosts of wickedness in the heavenly places. (Ephesians 6:12, NKJV)

The other wicked people and demons within the earth are going to have to be dwelt with. They are in control of the earth and the lives of others. As you mature in God and become successful in warfare through use of the Holy Spirit, God will begin to use you to tear down all these wicked people and powers. If you don't allow God to do this, they will eventually rise up to destroy the righteous on the earth. I go more into this subject in *God's Advanced Doctrines*. This becomes part of the Christian life.

We who accept Jesus are plunged into warfare against Satan. Throughout the remainder of Jesus's life, you will read how he always had to deal with wicked people, Satan's demons, and Satan. Along with all these events, Jesus had the power of the Holy Spirit. He was not on his own; the Spirit was with him.

Flowing in Power

Behold, I send the Promise of My Father upon you; but tarry in the city of Jerusalem until you are endued with power from on high. (Luke 24:49, NKJV)

But you shall receive power when the Holy Spirit has come upon you; and you shall be witnesses to Me in Jerusalem, and in all Judea and Samaria, and to the end of the earth." (Acts 1:8, NKJV)

The second purpose of the baptism in the Holy Spirit is to provide power to the disciples at that point in time in order to perform their ministries. Their ministries were to preach repentance and remission of sins in Christ to all the nations beginning in Jerusalem. "And that repentance and remission of sins should be preached in his name to all nations, beginning at Jerusalem." (Luke 24:47, NKJV)

This was the calling of the eleven disciples. They were performing all that God called them to do and to have the power of the Holy Spirit just as in Jesus's ministry because that power was going to be needed. It's interesting that today we don't find men or women going into the ministry with an anointing of power from the Holy Spirit. Why? Because they are ignorant of the power of God—or they really are not called. You would be amazed by how many people are in the ministry because they want to be there and are not called of God. These people never get to experience the glorious victories of battling the evil forces. They almost always end up with a dead church. These people have never learned much about the Holy Spirit.

The task of the eleven disciples was to evangelize the entire world. This was their calling and ministry. It is important to understand that this was to be accomplished through the power of the Holy Spirit. The principle being taught is that everyone with a calling from God to perform a task or ministry must be empowered by the Holy Spirit if they are to succeed.

- Principle: To perform a calling or task from God, you must be empowered by the Holy Spirit to successfully accomplish this work.

One of the purposes of the baptism in the Holy Spirit is to be empowered when God calls you to perform a task for him. Let's look at more Bible passages that reveal this purpose.

Now Peter and John went up together to the temple at the hour of prayer, the ninth hour. And a certain man lame from his mother's womb was carried, whom they laid daily at the gate of the temple which is called Beautiful, to ask alms from those who entered the temple; who, seeing Peter and John about to go into the temple, asked for alms. And fixing his eyes on him, with John, Peter said, "Look at us." So he gave them his attention, expecting to receive something from them. Then Peter said, "Silver and gold I do not have, but what I do have I give you: In the name of Jesus Christ of Nazareth, rise up and walk." And he took him by the right hand and lifted him up, and immediately his feet and anklebones received strength. So he, leaping up, stood and walked and entered the temple with them—walking, leaping, and praising God. And all the people saw him walking and praising God. Then they knew that it was he who sat begging alms at the Beautiful Gate of the temple; and they were filled with wonder and amazement at what had happened to him. Now as the lame man who was healed held on to Peter and John, all the people ran together to them in the porch which is called Solomon's, greatly amazed. (Acts 3:1–11, NKJV)

Peter went on to preach a sermon that pretty much reviewed all that had occurred since the death and resurrection of Jesus. The wicked rulers had the disciples held in detention for an evening to be questioned the next day by all the rulers of Jerusalem. In the meantime, as a result of the lame man's healing and the preaching of Peter, some five thousand people became believers.

However, many of those who heard the word believed; and the number of the men came to be about five thousand. (Acts 4:4, NKJV)

After the questioning and threats, the disciples were released. They returned to all the new converts and began to give further instructions. They were praying together during the first few days. They asked God to perform more miracles as Jesus had done. At this request, God shook the entire building, which was no small building. Below verse

33 says, "With great power the apostles gave witness to the resurrection of the Lord Jesus."

> Now, Lord, look on their threats, and grant to Your servants that with all boldness they may speak Your word, by stretching out Your hand to heal, and that signs and wonders may be done through the name of Your holy Servant Jesus." And when they had prayed, the place where they were assembled together was shaken; and they were all filled with the Holy Spirit, and they spoke the word of God with boldness. Now the multitude of those who believed were of one heart and one soul; neither did anyone say that any of the things he possessed was his own, but they had all things in common. And with great power the apostles gave witness to the resurrection of the Lord Jesus. And great grace was upon them all. (Acts 4:29–33, NKJV)

In this passage, the disciples prayed for a lame man who was healed. Everyone saw this, came running, and gathered together to see the miracle that had occurred. Peter preached the gospel of Jesus, and suddenly there were five thousand new converts in Jerusalem. This angered the wicked synagogue leaders (Sadducees and Pharisees who controlled the church back then) because God was performing miracles through other people rather that the synagogue leaders.

The synagogue rulers tried to suppress this great event by ordering the disciples to not speak anymore. This was a great embarrassment to the religious rulers because they believed that God was supposed to work through them, but they had been doing things their way and not God's way. The disciples all got together afterward and prayed. As they were praying, the power of God shook the place that they were meeting at. The power of God was at play. All this happened because the disciples were operating in the power of the Holy Spirit. They were doing what they were called to do.

Let's look at how the power of the Holy Spirit actually worked to bring about this amazing work.

> Now Peter and John went up together to the temple at the hour of prayer, the ninth hour. And a certain man lame from his mother's womb was carried, whom they laid daily at the gate of the temple which is called Beautiful, to ask alms from those who entered the temple; who, seeing Peter and John about to go into the temple, asked for alms. And fixing his eyes on him, with John, Peter said, "Look at us." So he gave them his attention, expecting to receive something from them. Then Peter said, "Silver and gold I do not have, but what I do have I give you: In the name of Jesus Christ of Nazareth, rise up and walk." And he took him by the right hand and lifted him up, and immediately his feet and anklebones received strength. So he, leaping up, stood and walked and entered the temple with them—walking, leaping, and praising God. And all the people saw him walking and praising God. (Acts 3:1–9, NKJV)

Peter and John were going to the temple to meet with the three thousand new believers to pray and minister to those who had become converts a few days earlier. A lame man from birth was always taken to the gate of the temple to beg for money. The lame man had probably been doing this for years. It is obvious that most people walked past him and noticed him in his daily routine.

It appears that most people in Jerusalem knew this man by sight. In verse 10, we read, "Then they knew that it was he who sat begging alms at the Beautiful Gate of the temple; and they were filled with wonder and amazement at what had happened to him."

Even Peter and John had walked past him several times but paid no attention to him. Jesus probably passed by this same man. But on this particular day, Peter walked by the lame man. Suddenly the Holy Spirit spoke to Peter, commanding him to heal the lame man.

Peter was hearing from the Holy Spirit. He stopped and fixed his eyes on the lame man. This action clearly shows that something was suddenly happening inside Peter. The Holy Spirit was speaking to Peter to tell this lame man to "rise up and walk."

The Spirit instructed Peter to take hold of the man's right hand and lift him up. As Peter did this action, the man's feet and anklebones were healed. The lame man began walking, leaping, and praising God as he walked with Peter and John into the temple courtyard. Would you start doing this if this happened to you? For the first time in this man's life, he could walk. The power of God healed the lame man. This caused such a stir in the temple that the news of this miracle spread thought all Jerusalem quickly within minutes, and many thousands of people came running to see what had happened.

I know this is how the Spirit worked within Peter because of the scriptures and my own experiences. There are many examples of Jesus healing people in the four gospels. Every time Jesus did this, it was Jesus doing as he was directed by the Holy Spirit. Jesus never did anything of his own accord except for one time (turning water into wine). *"The things I do, it is because I was directed to do them."*

Every time I see the power of God working through me, it is because the Holy Spirit is directing me to do those exact things. When I was young in the Lord, I tried to do things of my accord and saw nothing happen. As I matured, I learned that when the Spirit tells you to do something, obey the spirit. That's when I witness the power of God flowing through me.

This is also in line with how faith operates in a believer's life as was discussed earlier in this book. When the Holy Spirit speaks to you, this is faith in present action. This entire event was orchestrated by the Father, and as a result of the obedience of Peter to the Holy Spirit, five thousand new converts entered into God's kingdom.

Therefore, those who were scattered went everywhere preaching the word. Then Philip went down to the city of Samaria and preached Christ to them. And the multitudes with one accord heeded the things spoken by Philip, hearing and seeing the miracles which he did. For unclean spirits, crying with a loud voice, came out of many who were possessed; and many who were paralyzed and lame were healed. And there was great joy in that city. (Acts 8:4–8, NKJV)

Notice how the power of God was flowing through Philip. Philip had learned how to hear the voice of the Holy Spirit and obeyed the spirit. As a result, he saw the power of God manifested in those who the Spirit would point out.

> Now it happened, as we went to prayer, that a certain slave girl possessed with a spirit of divination met us, who brought her masters much profit by fortunetelling. This girl followed Paul and us, and cried out, saying, "These men are the servants of the Most High God, who proclaim to us the way of salvation." And this she did for many days. But Paul, greatly annoyed, turned and said to the spirit, "I command you in the name of Jesus Christ to come out of her." And he came out that very hour. (Acts 16:16–18, NKJV)

After many days of tolerating this demon-possessed woman, Paul turned and commanded the demon to leave her—and the demon left the slave girl. Again the Holy Spirit was speaking to Paul to cast out the demon just by speaking to it.

When Paul does this, the power of God flows through Paul, and the demon was now in confrontation with the power of the Holy Spirit. This powerful demon was no match for the power of God, and he left the slave girl. This one act of power from God ended up creating a mighty stir in the entire city.

Later, God sent an earthquake to shake the town. Again, the power of God is demonstrated through Paul. Many people heard the message of God, but there is no record about how many people converted to Christianity. Again, this was the Holy Spirit working within Paul. The Spirit spoke to Paul, and Paul had faith in God. Paul was able to cast out the demon from the girl.

> And my speech and my preaching were not with persuasive words of human wisdom, but in demonstration of the Spirit and of power, that your faith should not be in the wisdom of men but in the power of God. (Acts 16:16–18, NKJV)

These are a few examples of one of the purposes of the baptism in the Holy Spirit, which is to see the power of God displayed to people. I would also like to point out that when God demonstrates his power through a person in the presence of other non-believers, it becomes a very effective method of catching their attention. This also occurs among believers. Those people are obviously doing something right and know what they are doing.

The Exaltation of Jesus

When Jesus is exalted, God can begin to draw people to himself. When a believer receives the baptism in the Holy Spirit, he or she has a continual assurance and personal evidence that Jesus is with the Father.

> Therefore, being exalted to the right hand of God, and having received from the Father the promise of the Holy Spirit, He poured out this which you now see and hear. (Acts 2:33, NKJV)

And what is the exceeding greatness of His power toward us who believe, according to the working of His mighty power which He worked in Christ when He raised Him from the dead and seated Him at His right hand in the heavenly places, far above all principality and power and might and dominion, and every name that is named, not only in this age but also in that which is to come. And He put all things under His feet, and gave Him to be head over all things to the church, which is His body, the fullness of Him who fills all in all. (Ephesians 1:19–23, NKJV)

And being found in appearance as a man, He humbled himself and became obedient to the point of death, even the death of the cross. Therefore, God also has highly exalted Him and given Him the name which is above every name, that at the name of Jesus every knee should bow, of those in heaven, and of those on earth, and of those under the earth, and that every tongue should confess that Jesus Christ is Lord, to the glory of God the Father. Therefore, my beloved, as you have always obeyed, not as in my presence only, but now much more in my absence, work out your own salvation with fear and trembling; for it is God who works in you both to will and to do for His good pleasure. (Philippians 2:8–13, NKJV)

Nevertheless I tell you the truth. It is to your advantage that I go away; for if I do not go away, the Helper will not come to you; but if I depart, I will send Him to you. And when He has come, He will convict the world of sin, and of righteousness, and of judgment: of sin, because they do not believe in Me; of righteousness, because I go to My Father and you see Me no more; of judgment, because the ruler of this world is judged. I still have many things to say to you, but you cannot bear them now. However, when He, the Spirit of truth, has come, He will guide you into all truth; for He will not speak on His own authority, but whatever He hears He will speak; and He will tell you things to come. He will glorify Me, for he will take of what is Mine and declare it to you. All things that the Father has are Mine. Therefore, I said that He will take of mine and declare it to you. (John 16:7–15, NKJV)

Why is the exaltation of Jesus so important as a reason for the purpose of the Holy Spirit? There is the constant knowing of the Father, the Son, and the Holy Spirit once baptized in the Holy Spirit. This is a great help to us as we go about our daily lives, working or doing God's work. Satan's goal is to get us to turn away from God. We are going to encounter many of his attacks, and most of these attacks will come in the form of doubt. Satan will attempt to get you to doubt that God has done any of these things. He will attempt to get you to deny God.

There will come times when you don't feel the presence of the spirit. I call these desert experiences. These spiritual deserts are designed to test your faith. For more information on the testing of your faith, see *God's Advanced Doctrines*.

During these spiritual deserts, you don't sense the presence of the Spirit or the Father. This is also when the devils can attack you.

During these spiritual deserts, your walk with God becomes difficult because you seem dead to him. Once you have completed a spiritual desert, you are plunged back into the sensing the spirit. This is all part of maturing in God. This is how God chooses to mature us.

During the spiritual desert, we all long for the constant sensing of being with God or the continual knowing that we are in the Holy Spirit. This is the life of God in us. If you're no longer experiencing this continual feeling, something is definitely wrong. You're no longer walking in the spirit. Along with this feeling, there is the continual knowing that Jesus has been exalted. Jesus is the King of kings. Jesus is the Lord of lords.

A Foretaste of Things to Come

> For it is impossible for those who were once enlightened, and have tasted the heavenly gift, and have become partakers of the Holy Spirit, and have tasted the good word of God and the powers of the age to come, if they fall away, to renew them again to repentance, since they crucify again for themselves the Son of God, and put Him to an open shame. (Hebrews 6:4–6, NKJV)

> In Him you also trusted, after you heard the word of truth, the gospel of your salvation; in whom also, having believed, you were sealed with the

Holy Spirit of promise, who is the guarantee of our inheritance until the redemption of the purchased possession, to the praise of His glory. (Ephesians 1:13–14, NKJV)

We gain an inheritance from God. We will one day be living in physical heaven. I previously discussed how we end up getting to heaven. Having the baptism in the Holy Spirit provides us with a foretaste of things to come. We have a continual knowing of our inheritance. As long as we are maturing and walking in the spirit, there is always a sense that we are on our way to the next age—and then on to physical heaven.

We know that we are already in the kingdom of God and have a continual awareness through the Holy Spirit that we are royal subjects of God. Only the Holy Spirit does this for each one who is baptized. Having this continual knowing keeps the believer excited and full of joy. This joy is a strength to us who are baptized. Sensing this joy and knowing our destiny acts as a seal. We obtain heaven within us once we are baptized in the Holy Spirit.

Effective Praying in the Holy Spirit

Likewise, the Spirit also helps in our weaknesses.

For we do not know what we should pray for as we ought, but the Spirit Himself makes intercession for us with groanings which cannot be uttered. Now He who searches the hearts knows what the mind of the Spirit is, because He makes intercession for the saints according to the will of God. (Romans 8:26–27, NKJV)

What kind of praying is this? This is what I call "praying in the spirit." I get this phrase from the Book of Jude.

But you, beloved, building yourselves up on your most holy faith, praying in the Holy Spirit. (Jude 1:20, NKJV)

Praying always with all prayer and supplication in the Spirit, being watchful to this end with all perseverance and supplication for all the saints. (Ephesians 6:18, NKJV)

Speaking in tongues is a prayer language of the Holy Spirit. Very few scriptures explain our prayer language in the New Testament, so I'm going to provide my testimony of what I have learned about praying in the spirit. This will help you understand what praying in the Holy Spirit is all about—and how effective and powerful it is.

When I was first baptized in the Holy Spirit, I spoke in tongues for several days. It was glorious. As the days passed, I noticed that there was something about always speaking in tongues, though I didn't understand what it was. I asked my fellow believers, but they didn't know much about speaking in tongues. My church didn't know much about it either.

Two years later, I attended a Bible school that was comprised of Spirit-filled believers. After the first week, the school had an all-day prayer meeting. Since I had never heard of this, I went. About thirty believers were there, and all they did was speak in tongues while praying all day long.

I joined with them and quickly learned that they were actually praying to God in their tongues. After about a half hour, the power of God fell on all of us. I had never had that happen before. When the Spirit would lift, we were all full of joy. This would happen several times during the day. It was the best prayer meeting I had ever gone to. All kinds of things happened that day. The school would do this once a month, and it was powerful.

I learned that speaking in tongues is a prayer language. When the school had to make serious decisions, they would call for a day of fasting and prayer in order to get guidance from God. We would gather together to fast and pray in the Spirit. A few days later, the school would receive the guidance from God, and it was always right on track with God. This went on for the two years that I attended that school.

Before I left Bible school, I spent a few days fasting and praying because I had received my calling when I was thirteen years old. Was it time for me to enter into the ministry? I didn't even know what I was called to do except to go to other parts of the earth. To make things more difficult, I was presented with three requests from other churches to enter the ministry as an associate pastor.

I needed guidance and spent time praying in the spirit. I received guidance after a few days of praying and fasting. The Holy Spirit instructed me to go home and not enter into the ministry at that point in my life. That was not an expected answer since I assumed that God was going to show me which of the three churches I was to go to. Nonetheless, I had heard from God and told everyone that it was not time for me to go into the ministry. I was to return home. Everyone was shocked and thought that I hadn't heard from God correctly. I did as instructed—despite what my fellow students and instructors thought.

Later, I discovered that I was to be working at the Post Office. One evening, I was reading the Bible and came across a scripture in Ephesians:

> Praying always with all prayer and supplication in the spirit, being watchful to this end with all perseverance and supplication for all the saints. (Ephesians 6:18, NKJV)

I knew that God wants us to always be praying in the Holy Spirit. I knew what praying in the Holy Spirit was, but how could I always be praying in the Holy Spirit? I began to pray in the Holy Spirit as much as possible. I would quietly pray in my tongue throughout each day as the years passed working at the Post Office.

In a few months after applying this, God began to speak to me more than I had ever thought was possible. This was great. Bible school had never taught me that kind of praying. I began to live just to hear his voice. An opportunity came along for me to spend forty days fasting and praying. As a result of those forty days, I learned all about what God has called me to do. It wasn't anything like I had expected. I continued to pray.

As the months turned into years. I was learning all kinds of things about God. He would reveal the past, much of the present, and the future to me. I discovered that the more you pray, the more you will know, the less you pray, the less you know, and if you don't pray at all, you know nothing.

As I began this continual praying, I experienced the power of Satan's kingdom like never before. I had all kinds of encounters with his horde of demons. I learned a lot about Satan and the demons. I also become powerful against Satan and was constantly defeating his every attempt against me. Even to this day, I am always going through some kind of battle against Satan and his horde of demons.

After a few years of practicing this kind of praying, in 1994, I received the twenty-five visions that are written in *America's Resurrection-A Modern Day Prophecy*. I have continued to mature in wisdom and knowledge. God has gone on to show me more of what he would have me do. As I continue to pray in the Holy Spirit, he continues to reveal things to me. There are so many things that have happened that it would take an entire book to write them all down. I have seen countless miracles. I have gained a wealth of knowledge.

One amazing thing that will happen to anyone who prays in the Spirit is that they will understand many of the seemingly difficult parts of the Bible. As you read through the Bible, many seemingly mysterious verses become clear to you. God opens your understanding of his written Word. It's truly wonderful.

All that I have learned about effective prayer in my personal life was a result of praying in the Spirit. The more I pray the more I know and understand. One of the reasons you will want the baptism in the Holy Spirit is to become effective and successful in prayer. What I find even more amazing is how few of even the Spirit-filled believers understand what I have discovered about praying in tongues.

To Receive Teaching

> But the Helper, the Holy Spirit, whom the Father will send in My name, He will teach you all things, and bring to your remembrance all things that I said to you. (John 14:26, NKJV)

> However, when he, the Spirit of truth, has come, He will guide you into all truth; for He will not speak on his own authority, but whatever He hears he will speak; and He will tell you things to come. (John 16:13, NKJV)

One of the purposes of the Holy Spirit is to guide us into the truth about ourselves. He will teach us what we need to learn. He will bring what Jesus spoke about to our remembrance. He will even bring to our remembrance what we read in the Bible. One of the tasks of the Holy Spirit is to mature us and cause us to grow in wisdom and knowledge. To accomplish this, we have to be changed from a lot of our ideas thoughts, and beliefs. This doesn't happen all at once. God does this one idea at a time. It may happen in a few weeks or a year. The more you pray in the Spirit the sooner it will happen.

Before any of us accept Jesus into our lives, we take on quite a lot of false beliefs. Once saved and born again, we begin to grow in the Holy Spirit. It is during this growing that God deals with all the false beliefs we collected before we met Jesus. The Holy Spirit will point out a belief you have and then begin to show you the truth. These false beliefs bind up our thoughts and cause confusion and bondage. Once we get free of one of them, we experience much liberty.

God is a god of freedom, and he doesn't want to see us living in bondage. The more God is able to free us from these false beliefs, the more we can enjoy freedom—and then we can go on to learn the true knowledge of God. It truly is wonderful to have been set free from the ideas that entangle our minds. Without freedom from these beliefs, we cannot continue to mature in the Spirit. The Spirit will do this for us, but we must work with the Spirit.

Study the life of Paul to see how he had to undergo this process. It took a good twenty-five years for the Spirit to accomplish this in Paul's life before God could use Paul. Paul was around fifty-five years old when he entered into the ministry, and he was used to evangelize the Roman Empire.

Also notice the phrase at the end of (John 3:16) *and He will tell you things to come.* This becomes a very nice advantage since you can also learn of future events.

It's the Holy Spirit's task to be our teacher of the kingdom of God. He becomes our teacher and will never stop teaching us.

Guidance

For as many as are led by the Spirit of God, these are sons of God. (Romans 8:14, NKJV)

But He answered and said, "It is written, 'Man shall not live by bread alone, but by every word that proceeds from the mouth of God.'" (Matthew 4:4, NKJV)

Another advantage of the Holy Spirit's role is to give us guidance. Earlier in this chapter, I wrote about how God revealed to me that I had to go back home after Bible school. I sought the Lord's guidance and learned that I was to return home and not go into the ministry at that point in time. Had I disobeyed, I probably would never have come to learn what I have learned. While I was working at the Post Office, the Spirit led me into what I understand today about praying in the Spirit; even Bible school didn't know this.

Guidance is our number one goal in God's kingdom. Guidance is also one of the most difficult areas to master in life. You must learn the voice of the Holy Spirit, and that takes a long time. Much of this learning is through trial and error. Then there is the work of praying and fasting just to get God to speak something to you. In addition, many times you need an answer—and you don't have much time to pray properly to make the important decision. Guidance is a difficult subject to master.

The church today teaches us to do the opposite. They teach that we make a plan for our lives, and then we pray a superficial prayer asking God to bless our efforts and activities to fulfill our plans. I call this humanistic reasoning.

> For we are His workmanship, created in Christ Jesus for good works, which God prepared beforehand that we should walk in them. (Ephesians 2:10, NKJV)

What do you think this verse is speaking about? Our good works are not just doing good things; they involve doing the works that God has planned for your life that "we should walk in them." We are to find out from God what he would have us do in our lifetimes. It was the will of God for Jesus to first be a carpenter for the first thirty years of his life on earth. It was the will of God for Paul to cease being a Pharisee and become a tentmaker before being used in the ministry. You will read in the Bible that every person used by God first had a daily job before being called to enter into the assigned ministry. Noah was a farmer and a preacher before he was called to build the Ark.

Many of us come to be born again at middle age and God helps us change careers. This happened to Moses and Paul. Some of us are fortunate enough to become baptized in the Spirit at an early age and find out what we are supposed to do. This happened to me.

Thousands of born again believers become baptized in the Holy Spirit at an early age, but they don't understand that this is one of their tasks. They do as most others do and plan out their lives. There is no seeking God to get an answer. Since the church does not know to do this, they don't teach it. How many Christians have ruined their lives because of the failure to do this task?

All this guidance pays off later in life, which I'll show you in the next scriptures.

Now when they had gone through Phrygia and the region of Galatia, they were forbidden by the Holy Spirit to preach the word in Asia. After they had come to Mysia, they tried to go into Bithynia, but the Spirit did not permit them. So passing by Mysia, they came down to Troas. And a vision appeared to Paul in the night. A man of Macedonia stood and pleaded with him, saying, "Come over to Macedonia and help us." Now after he had seen the vision, immediately we sought to go to Macedonia, concluding that the Lord had called us to preach the gospel to them. (Acts 16:6–10, NKJV)

God's plan for each of us involves a much larger plan that he has regarding the earth for many decades to come. It is important to be exactly where God wants you to be and do what God wants you to do.

In the above passage, we see that Paul was not permitted to go into Asia. Later, God taught through Paul in Ephesus to some believers for two years, and these believers took the gospel to Asia.

(Paul) departed from them and withdrew the disciples, reasoning daily in the school of Tyrannus. And this continued for two years, so that all who dwelt in Asia heard the word of the Lord Jesus, both Jews and Greeks. (Acts 19:9–10, NKJV)

If you study the missionary trips of Paul with an atlas of the Roman times of Paul, you can see that Paul was confined to the Roman Empire. This was God's will for Paul. Look it up in the book of maps in your Bible.

Derek Prince said, "It is not enough to merely do the right thing, or to have the right purpose. In order to enjoy success and the blessing of God, we must do the right thing at the right time; we must carry out the right purpose at the right season." It is the responsibility of each believer to get guidance from God regarding his or her life. God has a timing and plan for everything on earth. What would our generation be like if the church had been doing this for the past two thousand years since Christ returned to the right hand of the Father?

To Walk in Divine Health and Divine Healing

> But if the Spirit of Him who raised Jesus from the dead dwells in you, He who raised Christ from the dead will also give life to your mortal bodies through His Spirit who dwells in you. (Romans 8:11, NKJV)

A big argument that continues in the church: is it the will of God to heal our bodies from sickness and disease. Is it the will of God that we live in divine health? Jesus and the disciples went about healing people from diseases, sickness, and infirmities. Jesus said that we are to do as he did.

Jesus said, "These signs and wonders will follow them that believe... they will lay their hand upon people, and they will be healed."

Do you think that this is still the will of God today? The church tries to teach us that healing died out after the apostles. Healings and other miracles did not die out after the apostles.

If Jesus and the apostles did all these works of healing—and the command is for us to also do these signs and wonders—where is the problem? It's not with God. It's with mankind. Do I need to say anything more? If you want to live in divine health and divine healing, then fast and pray in your prayer language until you get your healing. This is your task to perform. You do your job, and God will do his job. If you don't want to live in divine health and divine healing, simply do nothing—and it will not happen for you.

To Walk in God's Love

God wants all his believers to deal with each other as God deals with each believer. The Holy Spirit gives us this role and is always needling us to be loving toward all people.

Now hope does not disappoint, because the love of God has been poured out in our hearts by the Holy Spirit who was given to us. (Romans 5:5, NKJV)

In the Greek language, there are three separate words for love. In English, we have just one word for love. In Greek, *eros, philia,* and *agape* all mean love. Eros is physical love from sexual desires. *Philia* is the affections of love within the heart. *Agape* is the caring and concern for others. *Agape* is the kind of love that Romans 5:5 is talking about.

Beloved, let us love one another, for love is of God; and everyone who loves is born of God and knows God. He who does not love does not know God, for God is love. (1 John 4:7–8, NKJV)

When a believer receives the baptism in the Holy Spirit, he or she will immediately sense the caring and gentle love of God. It's much like *agape*, but God's love has a power to it. God's love is something we can't mimic because we don't have the power to manufacture it. The love of God becomes our motive to do anything that God would command. If you don't care about someone, you're not going to do anything for that person.

> Though I speak with the tongues of men and of angels, but have not love, I have become sounding brass or a clanging cymbal. And though I have the gift of prophecy, and understand all mysteries and all knowledge, and though I have all faith, so that I could remove mountains, but have not love, I am nothing. And though I bestow all my goods to feed the poor, and though I give my body to be burned, but have not love, it profits me nothing. Love suffers long and is kind; love does not envy; love does not parade itself, is not puffed up; does not behave rudely, does not seek its own, is not provoked, thinks no evil; does not rejoice in iniquity, but rejoices in the truth; bears all things, believes all things, hopes all things, endures all things. Love never fails. (1 Corinthians 13:1–8, NKJV)

The love of God in us, through the Holy Spirit's baptism, fulfills the entire law of the Old Testament and all the commands in the New Testament. The Holy Spirit gives us the power of God's love. We are never without it unless we are not walking in the Spirit.

In the above verses, we see the fruit of love in a believer. Because we begin to live by the Spirit, we begin to take on the fruit of this love, and it changes our hearts. The love of God is powerful. This love is meant to change our hearts. The more we flow in God's love, the more meaning we have in our lives. I have told many people who have asked for the meaning of life that the love of God is the meaning of life. When you see a mature person walking in the Holy Spirit, you will find a very loving person. This is one way to know that they are truly walking in the Spirit. An anointing also comes with this love of God.

If you do all the things of the Holy Spirit without the love of God, you begin to enter into just works. But if you're filled with the love of God, there is great satisfaction for every work you perform. You become fulfilled with your tasks being completed. This becomes a great and precious reward in your life.

There is no greater joy in all existence than to be full of the love of God through the Holy Spirit. We all enjoy being cared for, and the world offers barely any care. In the Spirit, we always have an ever-present awareness that God is watching over us and caring for us. This being cared for and being loved by God brings great satisfaction and meaning into our hearts and minds through the Holy Spirit.

> And we have known and believed the love that God has for us. God is love, and he who abides in love abides in God, and God in him. Love has been perfected among us in this: that we may have boldness in the day of judgment; because as He is, so are we in this world. There is no fear in love; but perfect love casts out fear, because fear involves torment. But he who fears has not been made perfect in love. We love Him because He first loved us. (1 John 4:16–19, NKJV)

This love of God supersedes all other things. The first, most important activity for God is to love. God likes being loved. He loves us and receives great satisfaction when love is returned to him. What good are we if we lose our love for God? God no longer can rejoice because of us. When we stop loving, our hearts turn to stone. Ever tried to love a stone? You get nothing in return. If we stop loving there is no more fulfillment or satisfaction for God. He helps us love him by providing a portion of this same power of love to us through the Holy Spirit.

When we love the brethren, we receive back of that love in return. We all become very blessed and full of joy. You will never know what this is like until you are baptized in the Holy Spirit and fellowship with others who are Spirit-filled and keep their love of God alive and strong. It's truly an incredible state to be in.

There are times that I pray in the Spirit just to be filled with the love of God. The more you mature in the Spirit, the better it gets—and the more powerful God's love becomes. It's like he has a volume control to turn up the power of his love.

To Be Changed and Bear Fruit of the Spirit

I was never taught that God is very interested in changing you as a person. I discovered this only after years of walking in the Holy Spirit. The Holy Spirit taught me later that God is very interested in changing you to be more like him.

You don't lose your personality, instead you are molded and shaped to become godly. God removes all the wicked ways from your life and creates a new person. Being changed into this new person eventually loses even the smallest ways of wickedness. You will discover that becoming godly is a very exciting characteristic to obtain.

The more you mature and develop, the more you are changed. See more details in *God's Advanced Doctrines*. The more like God you become, the more he begins to show you of his kingdom. God is full of goodness. He loves to share all that he has and the plans he has for those who become more like him. God is incredibly pure, and when you begin to experience bits of this purity, you will be amazed by how good and wonderful it truly is. The Holy Spirit's baptism will begin to change you. This becomes the working of the fruit of the Spirit.

> For the fruit of the Spirit is in all goodness, righteousness, and truth. (Ephesians 5:9, NKJV)

> But the fruit of the Spirit is love, joy, peace, longsuffering, kindness, goodness, faithfulness, gentleness, self-control. Against such there is no law. (Galatians 5:22–23, NKJV)

All these words describe just one fruit of the Spirit. Many people think that these are different fruits of the Spirit. Notice in verse 22 that the word *fruit* is singular. When you are undergoing change, the Holy Spirit produces these characteristics within you. You don't have to mimic them. They happen *for* you. This happens over a long period of time.

In Ephesians 5:9, we see other characteristics of the Holy Spirit's fruit. We become good by always doing good. We become more righteous in our right doing. And we walk more and more in the truth as the Spirit guides us into all the truth.

> I am the true vine, and My Father is the vinedresser. Every branch in Me that does not bear fruit He takes away; and every branch that bears fruit He prunes, that it may bear more fruit. You are already clean because of the word which I have spoken to you. Abide in Me, and I in you. As the branch cannot bear fruit of itself, unless it abides in the vine, neither can you, unless you abide in Me. I am the vine, you are the branches. He who abides in Me, and I in him, bears much fruit; for without Me you can do nothing. If anyone does not abide in Me, he is cast out as a branch and is withered; and they gather them and throw them into the fire, and they are burned. If you abide in Me, and My words abide in you, you will ask what you desire, and it shall be done for you. By this My Father is glorified, that you bear much fruit; so you will be My disciples. (John 15:1–8, NKJV)

One of our goals in life with God is to bear much fruit. This is pleasing to the Father. In verse 8, we learn that God is so pleased with our lives bearing fruit that he is glorified. Wow! How can God be glorified by us bearing fruit? It's simple. God gets very excited, and it is very satisfying to him to see each one of his believers go on to produce much fruit. This is God's work within each of us through the Holy Spirit.

When God sees the change happen, he is greatly pleased because we allowed the Spirit to do this in our lives. I want you to notice what happens to those who do not produce fruit. In verse 2, we find that God removes that person and takes him or her away. He casts that branch into the fire. You can enter into the kingdom of heaven and then enter into the kingdom of God, and if you stop advancing in God, he will discard you and toss you out of his kingdom. In other words, you can lose your salvation. See *God's Advanced Doctrines* for more information about losing your salvation.

We do not produce fruit by our own works. All we do is walk in the Holy Spirit, and God—through the Spirit—causes the fruit to develop. He even goes as far as pruning us in order for us to produce much fruit. This is a pleasing thing for God to do in our lives. Do not take this purpose of the Spirit lightly. This is a very serious work that God is most interested in performing within each believer.

The Gifts of the Holy Spirit

> For the gifts and the calling of God are irrevocable. (Romans 11:29, NKJV)

> But the manifestation of the Spirit is given to each one for the profit of all: for to one is given the word of wisdom through the Spirit, to another the word of knowledge through the same Spirit, to another faith by the same Spirit, to another gifts of healings by the same Spirit, to another the working of miracles, to another prophecy, to another discerning of spirits, to another different kinds of tongues, to another the interpretation of tongues. But one and the same Spirit works all these things, distributing

to each one individually as he wills. (1 Corinthians 12:7–11, NKJV)

As each one has received a gift, minister it to one another, as good stewards of the manifold grace of God. (1 Peter 4:10, NKJV)

The purpose of gifts is to build up the body of Christ. Notice that the entire body or church needs to have gifts performed in the midst of the believers. These gifts are provided for the profit of all (as mentioned in verse 7).

Why is this an important purpose of the spirit? In a body of believers, you have some who are more mature than others. The younger believers need to be encouraged and inspired by those who are more mature. When the gifts are manifested in a church body, everyone benefits. Everyone becomes encouraged and excited at the moving of the Spirit of God in outward signs and wonders. Seeing these manifestations is always inspiring and encouraging. They work to encourage the younger believers to continue on in growth. They also encourage those who may be lethargic or complacent. The gifts always offer encouragement.

Some of the gifts are messages for the entire body; these are edifying and uplifting. The body of believers becomes one unit and needs to be treated as such. We are all part of one body. We all need to be ministered too as one body as well as separate individuals.

Some of the gifts are for individuals. When all the gifts are in full function, everyone benefits. All are encouraged, inspired, and built up. When the gifts are in operation within a body of believers, it is safe to say that this particular body is right on course with God's will.

When the gifts are not present, something is very wrong with that body of believers. Every dead church I have ever seen has not had any of the gifts being manifested. I've seen churches where everyone is trying to "pump up" the manifestation of the Spirit, but this doesn't happen because the gifts and the power of the Holy Spirit are not present.

I have been in churches that are right on with God, and the gifts are in full play. Those churches are experiencing the glory of God in visitations of power. I personally usually flow in words of wisdom, but this mostly happens in churches that flow in the Spirit. Some churches allow me to flow in my gift, but this is difficult because most of them don't believe in this. When I minister to others through my gift - words of wisdom, people are greatly encouraged and amazed by God's power. Sometimes I flow in other gifts as well, but I usually am used in the Spirit with the gift of wisdom. God has thus given me the gift of wisdom from the Holy Spirit.

I'm not going to go into each gift and explain exactly what each is. Most are self-explanatory. I'm merely pointing out the purpose of the gifts of the Spirit. Many people who read this have never ever heard of such a thing.

I have covered eleven purposes of the baptism of the Holy Spirit. As you can see, we covered a lot of what the Holy Spirit can do for each believer. The Holy Spirit doesn't just do one thing; instead, he does multiple things. Talk about multitasking!

The Holy Spirit's baptism covers many areas for a believer in Christ. Without the baptism in the Holy Spirit, you will never make it in God's kingdom. The baptism of the Holy Spirit is a requirement for ending up in physical heaven. He is the one who moves the believer onto the positive side of the number line. He is the total fullness of the life of God that comes as a result of Jesus's work and redemption. Failure to receive the Holy Spirit's baptism will cost you eternity in hell.

Many people have seen a congregation speak in tongues. Whether that body was right on course with God or way off course can be tested by the signs and wonders of God. But to those who only see others speaking in tongues, this is a strange and weird observation for the first time. And if the manifestation of God was not present in some way (as discussed in this chapter), it is even stranger for a new visitor.

If all I've written about the baptism of the Holy Spirit is new to you, remember that this is God's way as is spelled out in the New Testament. This is not something that I manufactured. All I've done is point out what is written in the New Testament. Go back and read this chapter as many times as needed till you see that this is truly God's way spelled out in the New Testament.

Satan doesn't want you to know about any of the workings of the Holy Spirit. Satan has gone to great lengths to try to stop me from getting this book printed just to keep you, the reader, from learning what I'm revealing. If your church doesn't teach or practice any of what I've shown you in the New Testament, then that church is in total error. If you've concluded that what I've revealed here in the New Testament is true and want more of God, you need to pray that God will lead you to a group of believers that is flowing in the power of the Holy Spirit and practices the totality of the New Testament. You can also contact my ministry, and we can help provide you with more information to get you in touch with other Spirit-filled believers.

CHAPTER 6

The Laying on of Hands

What is laying on of hands in the Bible? What is the purpose of laying on of hands? Laying on of hands is the act of a person or persons placing their hands on another person while praying or prophesying for that person. In the Bible, there are three main reasons why someone lays his or her hands upon another person:

- It is for the transmission of a spiritual blessing or authority from the giving person to the receiving person.
- The person or persons doing the laying on of hands is publicly acknowledging a spiritual blessing or authority being given by God by the one laying on their hands.
- For publicly committing to God for some special task or ministry the one whom hands are laid upon. There are times when all these reasons are done at once.

And Joseph took them both, Ephraim with his right hand toward Israel's left hand, and Manasseh with his left hand toward Israel's right hand, and brought them near him. Then Israel stretched out his right hand and laid it on Ephraim's head, who was the younger, and his left hand on Manasseh's head, guiding his hands knowingly, for Manasseh was the firstborn. And he blessed Joseph, and said: "God, before whom my fathers' Abraham and Isaac walked, the God who has fed me all my life long to this day, the angel who has redeemed me from all evil, bless the lads; let my name be named upon them, and the name of my father's Abraham and Isaac; and let them grow into a multitude in the midst of the earth." Now when Joseph saw that his father laid his right hand on the head of Ephraim, it displeased him; so he took hold of his father's hand to remove it from Ephraim's head to Manasseh's head. And Joseph said to his father, "Not so, my father, for this one is the firstborn; put your right hand on his head." But his father refused and said, "I know, my son, I know. He also shall become a people, and he also shall be great; but truly his younger brother shall be greater than he, and his descendants shall become a multitude of nations." So he blessed them that day, saying, "By you Israel will bless, saying, 'May God make you as Ephraim and as Manasseh!'" And thus he set Ephraim before Manasseh. (Genesis 48:13–20, NKJV)

This is an example of passing on a blessing to the next generation. Also notice that the blessing contained a prophecy and faith from God. This is the first reason for laying on of hands, which is passing along a spiritual blessing of some authority to another person.

> Then Moses spoke to the Lord, saying: "Let the LORD, the God of the spirits of all flesh, set a man over the congregation, who may go out before them and go in before them, who may lead them out and bring them in, that the congregation of the LORD may not be like sheep which have no shepherd." And the LORD said to Moses: "Take Joshua the son of Nun with you, a man in whom is the Spirit, and lay your hand on him; set him before Eleazar the priest and before all the congregation, and inaugurate him in their sight. And you shall give some of your authority to him, that all the congregation of the children of Israel may be obedient. He shall stand before Eleazar the priest, who shall inquire before the LORD for him by the judgment of the Urim. At his word they shall go out, and at his word they shall come in, he and all the children of Israel with him—all the congregation." So Moses did as the LORD commanded him. He took Joshua and set him before Eleazar the priest and before all the congregation. And he laid his hands on him and inaugurated him, just as the LORD commanded by the hand of Moses. (Numbers 27:15–23, NKJV)

Toward the end of his life, Moses imparted some of the anointing he had from God onto Joshua. Again, this is an example of passing on a blessing to the next generation.

> So Moses the servant of the LORD died there in the land of Moab, according to the Word of the LORD. And He buried him in a valley in the land of Moab, opposite Beth Peor; but no one knows his grave to this day. Moses was one hundred and twenty years old when he died. His eyes were not dim nor his natural vigor diminished. And the children of Israel wept for Moses in the plains of Moab thirty days. So the days of weeping and mourning for Moses ended. Now Joshua the son of Nun was full of the spirit of wisdom, for Moses had laid his hands on him; so the children of Israel heeded him, and did as the LORD had commanded Moses. (Deuteronomy 34:5–9, NKJV)

Notice that the first and third reason of laying on of hands is in use in this passage.

> Elisha had become sick with the illness of which he would die. Then Joash the king of Israel came down to him, and wept over his face, and said, "O my father, my father, the chariots of Israel and their horsemen!" And Elisha said to him, "Take a bow and some arrows." So he took himself a bow and some arrows. Then he said to the king of Israel, "Put your hand on the bow." So he put his hand on it, and Elisha put his hands on the king's hands. And he said, "Open the east window"; and he opened it. Then Elisha said, "Shoot"; and he shot. And he

said, "The arrow of the LORDS'S deliverance and the arrow of deliverance from Syria; for you must strike the Syrians at Aphek till you have destroyed them." (2 Kings 13:14–17, NKJV)

Elisha placed his hands on Joash's hands and prophesied that Joash would deliver Israel from Syria (the first reason for laying on of hands).

To Bring Healing to the Sick

And these signs will follow those who believe: In My name they will cast out demons; they will speak with new tongues; they will take up serpents; and if they drink anything deadly, it will by no means hurt them; they will lay hands on the sick, and they will recover. (Mark 16:17–18, NKJV)

Verse 18 says, *"they will lay hands on the sick, and they will recover."* Jesus is giving a commission to His believers to lay hands on the sick in order that the sick may be healed.

In verse 17, the laying on of hands becomes a sign to non-believers as well as believers, which was intended for the work of evangelizing and developing maturity of the church.

And they went out and preached everywhere, the Lord working with them and confirming the Word through the accompanying signs. Amen. (Mark 16:20, NKJV)

> And my speech and my preaching were not
> with persuasive words of human wisdom, but in
> demonstration of the Spirit and of power, that your
> faith should not be in the wisdom of men but in the
> power of God. (1 Corinthians 2:4–5, NKJV)

We can conclude that the laying on of hands brings healing to the sick for the unconverted or new believers.

Healings come in all kinds of variations. Some will be instantaneous, and others require a longer length of time. Two people may suffer from the exact same illness, and both may have hands laid on them. One person may be instantly healed, and the other may recover in a week. There are reasons why God chooses to do this, but he will be glorified in both cases.

To Receive the Baptism in the Holy Spirit

Laying on of hands helps a believer in Jesus receive the Holy Spirit baptism.

> Now when the apostles who were at Jerusalem heard
> that Samaria had received the word of God, they
> sent Peter and John to them, who, when they had
> come down, prayed for them that they might receive
> the Holy Spirit. For as yet He had fallen upon none
> of them. They had only been baptized in the name
> of the Lord Jesus. Then they laid hands on them,
> and they received the Holy Spirit. (Acts 8:14–17,
> NKJV)

And Ananias went his way and entered the house; and laying his hands on him he said, "Brother Saul, the Lord Jesus, who appeared to you on the road as you came, has sent me that you may receive your sight and be filled with the Holy Spirit." (Acts 9:17, NKJV)

And it happened, while Apollos was at Corinth, that Paul, having passed through the upper regions, came to Ephesus. And finding some disciples, he said to them, "Did you receive the Holy Spirit when you believed?" So they said to him, "We have not so much as heard whether there is a Holy Spirit." And he said to them, "Into what then were you baptized?" So they said, "Into John's baptism." Then Paul said, "John indeed baptized with a baptism of repentance, saying to the people that they should believe on Him who would come after him, that is, on Christ Jesus." When they heard this, they were baptized in the name of the Lord Jesus. And when Paul had laid hands on them, the Holy Spirit came upon them, and they spoke with tongues and prophesied. (Acts 19:1–6, NKJV)

Sometimes the Holy Spirit instructs a believer to lay hands upon another person in order to receive the baptism of the Holy Spirit. At other times, there will be no laying on of hands to receive the baptism of the Holy Spirit. This usually happens when there are many people gathered to receive the baptism of the Holy Spirit together. In the New Testament, there are two other passages where the Spirit baptizes believers in the Spirit without the laying on of hands.

> When the Day of Pentecost had fully come, they were all with one accord in one place. And suddenly there came a sound from heaven, as of a rushing mighty wind, and it filled the whole house where they were sitting. Then there appeared to them divided tongues, as of fire, and one sat upon each of them. And they were all filled with the Holy Spirit and began to speak with other tongues, as the Spirit gave them utterance. (Acts 2:1–4, NKJV)

> While Peter was still speaking these words, the Holy Spirit fell upon all those who heard the Word. And those of the circumcision who believed were astonished, as many as came with Peter, because the gift of the Holy Spirit had been poured out on the Gentiles also. For they heard them speak with tongues and magnify God. Then Peter answered. (Acts 10:44–46, NKJV)

Notice in both circumstances that the Spirit is poured out on all of them from above. The first group is of Jewish descent. The second group is Gentiles. These two outpourings were directly from God. The first was obvious because no one knew about laying on of hands to receive the spirit. God had no other choice but to just do it. The second group entailed Gentiles of which the Jewish believers were very hesitant to do anything about receiving the baptism of the Holy Spirit. This is apparent in verse 45. No one knew that the baptism in the Spirit was also intended for the Gentiles. God had to just do it as he did with the first outpouring.

In all other recordings, we find the use of laying on of hands.

For the Imparting of Spiritual Gifts

> For I long to see you, that I may impart to you some spiritual gift, so that you may be established—that is, that I may be encouraged together with you by the mutual faith both of you and me. (Romans 1:11–12, NKJV)

Spiritual gifts are for comfort, strengthening, and encouragement. The operation and the effects of spiritual gifts are for everyone within a congregation or a group of believers.

In the New Testament, the Roman Christians endured a lot of struggles in this first church. There was much suffering in their daily lives. Who knew how long the suffering was to continue for the Roman believers? What was in store for them? What was happening throughout the rest of the Roman Empire as far as the spreading of the news about Jesus? All they had at that time were letters or visitations from other believers. Spiritual gifts provided relief from the daily pressures and trials of life. Those people were not in a free country like America. Harsh Roman dictators ruled them all. They never knew what was going to happen. Their lives were lived in poverty and bondage. Receiving gifts from the Holy Spirit was like a refreshing, cool river in the middle of a desert. Paul always wanted to help further establish their walk in the kingdom of God. He needed results from spiritual gifts. Gifts of prophecy, words of wisdom, and knowledge can go a long way for mature believers.

We still need gifts from the Holy Spirit for encouragement and inspiration. Satan is still working to destroy all of God's workings. There are many different types of challenges that face the modern church. The modern-day believer needs to receive encouragement directly from the Holy Spirit.

> Do not neglect the gift that is in you, which was given to you by prophecy with the laying on of the hands of the eldership. (1 Timothy 4:14, NKJV)

> Therefore, I remind you to stir up the gift of God which is in you through the laying on of my hands. (2 Timothy 1:6, NKJV)

> This charge I commit to you, son Timothy, according to the prophecies previously made concerning you, that by them you may wage the good warfare. (1 Timothy 1:18, NKJV)

In these three passages, Timothy received a spiritual gift from God through the laying on of hands. We notice that the imparting of this spiritual gift also was done with prophecy. Usually prophecies include special instructions. It is clear that God had placed a calling upon Timothy to do a work.

In the next verse, we find that Paul is referring to these prophecies. Any work or calling of God involves warfare against Satan's kingdom. This is proof that Timothy had a calling to do a work or ministry for God. The entire purpose of these three verses is to encourage Timothy to move into his calling and use the authority of the gift that God was providing. I like to refer to spiritual gifts as tools of the Holy Spirit.

God was equipping Timothy with all the tools he was going to need when his time came to minister. All this was done through the laying on of hands. Later, we learned that a great persecution against all the Christians broke out from Emperor Nero. Many Christians died as a result of this persecution. Timothy probably played a major role with this madness. Timothy had to deal a lot with fear—his own fear and the fear of the other believers. His spiritual gift was a powerful aid to the other believers in their struggles through this horrible time.

For God has not given us a spirit of fear, but of power and of love and of a sound mind. (2, NKJV)

Was Paul prophesying here to Timothy about fear? This all began with the laying on of hands.

Every generation is confronted with different challenges. Wicked forces are forever at work to steal, destroy, plunder, and enslave each believer in Christ. Paul was called to evangelize the Roman Empire, and his challenges were going up against pagan worshipers and their pagan gods, which was no easy task. The Jewish believers had to deal with the unbelief and rejection of their own countrymen, which was an extremely difficult task (and finally ended up in persecution). Timothy had to deal with an empire's persecution of the Christians.

What about today in America? What are the challenges of the church? We are dealing with a nation steeped in the worship of money, materialism, pride, and arrogance. Wickedness is the order of the day. Hatred, anger, selfishness, drug abuse, idol worship, and sexual sins are but a few of the difficulties that fill the hearts of the wicked in America. Are gifts needed for the church today? Look at the church. It is weak and powerless. Most people in the church are still involved in secret sins. Pastors have turned Jesus into a business. These pastors want grand buildings with beautiful architecture that cost millions of dollars.

Where are the mature, mighty people of God who will lay their hands on the believers so that we can be empowered, full of authority and strength? Where are they? Are there any? The gifts are needed more today in our filth-crazed nation.

Recognizing Those Called for a Work from God

> Now in the church that was at Antioch there were certain prophets and teachers: Barnabas, Simeon who was called Niger, Lucius of Cyrene, Manaen who had been brought up with Herod the tetrarch, and Saul. As they ministered to the Lord and fasted, the Holy Spirit said, "Now separate to Me Barnabas and Saul for the work to which I have called them." Then, having fasted and prayed, and laid hands on them, they sent them away. (Acts 13:1–3, NKJV)

Notice that there are five men mentioned as certain prophets and teachers at the church in Antioch. These men, along with others in the church, for some reason chose to minister to the Lord with fasting. During this time, the Holy Spirit spoke to them. God's will, at that point in time, was to use two men who had already known that they had a calling in their lives. We know this because verse 2 mentions "for the work to which I have called them." This is past tense. These two men had already been spoken to, and their time had come. The Greek word that is used for "sending out" is *apostle*. Today, the church uses the word *missionary*. Also notice in verse 3 that after more fasting and praying, the church laid hands on them.

In Acts 14, we find Paul and Barnabas being called apostles. So what does all this have to do with laying on of hands?

In verse 3, we see another period of fasting and praying. Everyone involved wants to provide a blessing before Barnabas and Paul depart. There was probably the imparting of some type of spiritual gifts of wisdom or anointing. The fact that there was more praying and fasting proves that they were seeking God for something. Why else would they be praying and fasting?

God must have spoken more to these teachers and prophets and other members of the Antioch church because they laid their hands on them. As Moses did with Joshua, there must have been some further passing along of spiritual gifts. You don't lay hands upon someone unless it has something to do with the workings of the Holy Spirit. It's not mentioned what was passed on to Barnabas and Paul, but clearly something from the Holy Spirit was passed on to them.

What is clearly established is that everyone in the church knew that Barnabas and Paul were called to do work for God. Their time to perform God's calling had come. The church was able to send them off after passing along an extra blessing of some kind from the Holy Spirit.

> From there they sailed to Antioch, where they had been commended to the grace of God for the work which they had completed. Now when they had come and gathered the church together, they reported all that God had done with them, and that He had opened the door of faith to the Gentiles. So they stayed there a long time with the disciples. (Acts 14:26–28, NKJV)

Notice that they first were commended to the grace of God for the work. When it was finished, they did what God had originally commanded of them. Therefore, they must have known when God was first calling them that they were to visit a select number of cities. God must have revealed this to them at the beginning. God opened the door of faith to the Gentiles through Barnabas and Paul. Also notice that they didn't rush out again to do another work. Instead, the two remained in Antioch for a long time. All this work employed the laying on of hands by the elders in Antioch.

> Now in those days, when the number of the disciples was multiplying, there arose a complaint against the Hebrews by the Hellenists, because their widows were neglected in the daily distribution. Then the twelve summoned the multitude of the disciples and said, "It is not desirable that we should leave the word

of God and serve tables. Therefore, brethren, seek out from among you seven men of good reputation, full of the Holy Spirit and wisdom, whom we may appoint over this business; but we will give ourselves continually to prayer and to the ministry of the word." And the saying pleased the whole multitude. And they chose Stephen, a man full of faith and the Holy Spirit, and Philip, Prochorus, Nicanor, Timon, Parmenas, and Nicolas, a proselyte from Antioch, whom they set before the apostles; and when they had prayed, they laid hands on them. Then the word of God spread, and the number of the disciples multiplied greatly in Jerusalem, and a great many of the priests were obedient to the faith. And Stephen, full of faith and power, did great wonders and signs among the people. (Acts 6:1–8, NKJV)

The number of believers had increased to the point where the twelve disciples needed helpers. Seven men who were full of the Holy Spirit and wisdom were chosen. This freed up the twelve disciples to spend more time in prayer and fasting. As a result, the church multiplied, and many of the priests became believers. The church was multiplying.

These seven men also did many miracles among the people. The believers appointed the seven men, but only the twelve disciples laid hands upon them. It was understood that the twelve disciples were in authority and were passing along the authority to other men in positions that required recognition and authority with the title of deacon.

To sum up the laying on of hands, we have seen in various passages of scripture that there are five purposes for the use of laying on of hands:

1. to minister healing to the sick
2. to help those seeking the baptism of the Holy Spirit
3. to impart spiritual gifts
4. to send out apostles
5. to ordain leaders

The laying on of hands is always done by those who are more mature or placed in a higher position of authority than those who are having hands laid upon.

CHAPTER 7

The Resurrection of the Dead

Eternity and Time

Before explaining the resurrection of the dead, I would like you to understand the difference between eternity and time. By having a working idea of time and eternity, you will better understand the resurrection of the dead and eternal judgment in chapter 8.

Eternity is difficult to explain because it involves existence in a realm that none of us has experienced. The Bible doesn't provide a definition for eternity. We only get pieces of eternity in the Bible. But on the subject of time, we get a lot examples and definitions in the Bible. I will try to provide a definition of eternity by using the Bible and logical thinking.

Time involves decay or aging. Eternity has no decay or aging. Beings in eternity do not undergo any decay or any aging. All beings in eternity always remain the same. There is no need for time. Time only marks the beginning of an event till the end of that event, and the nature of this event requires decay or aging.

There is no waiting in eternity. If we pass from time into eternity, we step out of the domain of time and into the domain of eternity. There is no past tense or future tense in eternity. The nature of time has a past, present, and future tense. The nature of eternity is always present tense. There is no beginning or ending of anything in eternity. For believers who enter into the kingdom of God, our only beginning is that of a new creation—we are born again— and we suddenly begin in eternity. There is no end for believers and those who end up in hell. All we know is present tense. Our bodies are in the realm of time, but our newborn spirits are now members of eternity. We taste and partake of eternity. Eternity is not counting time as far distant into the future. Eternity has no future because there is no time in eternity. Those who live in eternity do not decay or age.

When God created the heavens and earth, he created them in a realm involving time. This realm of time is separate from the realm of eternity. It is understood that in eternity, this creation of heavens and earth will have a start and a finish. At the end, that creation will be done away with, but for the inhabitants in the kingdom of God, there is always eternity. We cannot apply time to the domain of eternity because eternity knows no time. When God makes something with a beginning and an end, it involves the domain of time—and it will either decay or age. Beings in eternity are constantly observing the present of that creation of time. They watch it come and go. They do not age or decay. You have to remember not to compare eternity to time. There is no comparing.

A physical example is that you watch an animal being born. That animal has a beginning and an end. The animal lives a few years, and then it dies. It has an end. You, as the observer of that animal, are like living in eternity in comparison to the animal. You are always in the present, knowing there is a beginning and an end to the animal's life. Once the animal has died, you continue on in your realm of the present.

I hope this understanding of the difference between time and eternity will help you understand God's realm of eternity and what he is doing with the creation of the angels and mankind. It may help you better understand this chapter in dealing with the resurrection of the dead.

In the beginning God created the heavens and the earth. (Genesis 1:1, NKJV)

This is the creation of our universe (all the galaxies, suns, planets, meteors, comets, etc.) and the earth.

The angel whom I saw standing on the sea and on the land raised up his hand to heaven and swore by Him who lives forever and ever, who created heaven and the things that are in it, the earth and the things that are in it, and the sea and the things that are in it, that there should be delay no longer, but in the days of the sounding of the seventh angel, when he is about to sound, the mystery of God would be finished, as He declared to His servants the prophets. (Revelation 10:5–7, NKJV)

Verse 6 mentions that "there should be delay no longer," but time is a more accurate word in translation the word delay. We also see in this scripture that all things on earth will come to an end.

Remember that eternity is a difficult word for us because we have no experience with it. The time of the heavens and earth are just an event for the beings that are living in eternity. They never change, decay, or age. There is no need to count time in eternity. The beings that reside in eternity only know present tense. This isn't much for us to define eternity, but it is all we have.

The Resurrection of the Dead

So with this understanding of eternity, we may have a better understanding of other passages in the Bible that deal with resurrection of the dead.

> And as it is appointed for men to die once, but after this the judgment. (Hebrews 9:27, NKJV)

> For to this end Christ died and rose and lived again, that He might be Lord of both the dead and the living. (Romans 14:9, NKJV)

> And now, Christ hath risen out of the dead—the firstfruits of those sleeping he became, for since through man is the death, also through man is a rising again of the dead, for even as in Adam all die, so also in the Christ all shall be made alive. (1 Corinthians 15:20–22, Young's Literal Translation)

In this verse, it appears that every human will be raised back from the dead—not just the believers in Jesus.

> Behold, I tell you a mystery: We shall not all sleep, but we shall all be changed—in a moment, in the twinkling of an eye, at the last trumpet. For the trumpet will sound, and the dead will be raised incorruptible, and we shall be changed. For this corruptible must put on incorruption, and this mortal must put on immortality. (1 Corinthians 15:51–53, NKJV)

Notice that all men will die one death. Also notice that Christ is able to resurrect people from the dead. The Christians undergo a resurrection from the dead, but do those who are non-Christians undergo a resurrection from the dead? Who gets raised from the dead? To become Lord of everyone, there must be a ceremony or event that recognizes Jesus being Lord of everyone.

Only those believers who have not died when Christ returns will not undergo a resurrection from the dead. What then is the purpose of all people being resurrected?

> Truly, these times of ignorance God overlooked, but now commands all men everywhere to repent, because He has appointed a day on which He will judge the world in righteousness by the Man whom He has ordained. He has given assurance of this to all by raising Him from the dead. (Acts 17:30–31, NKJV)

All people must face a judgment, including all Christians. Even the believers in God will undergo a judgment.

> But why do you judge your brother? Or why do you show contempt for your brother? For we shall all stand before the judgment seat of Christ. For it is written: "As I live," says the LORD, "every knee shall bow to Me, and every tongue shall confess to God." So then each of us shall give account of himself to God. (Romans 14:10–12, NKJV)

> For we must all appear before the judgment seat of Christ, that each one may receive the things done in the body, according to what he has done, whether good or bad. (2 Corinthians 5:10, NKJV)

Again we read that all people are to appear before Christ in a time of judgment. When does this event of judgment occur? We also know that when the body dies, it decomposes and returns back to the earth into the original elements of the earth. We also know that the invisible, immaterial soul or spirit is released from the body. Where does this living part go?

In every place the Bible mentions the resurrection of the dead, there immediately follows the judgment of God. Also, we are all to be judged for our deeds having lived in the body that we had while we lived on earth. We have questions that need answers.

Nowhere in the Bible is it written or even suggested that a person's spirit is removed from existence. There are a few passages that state that the spirit goes somewhere.

I said in my heart, "Concerning the condition of the sons of men, God tests them, that they may see that they themselves are like animals." For what happens to the sons of men also happens to animals; one thing befalls them: as one dies, so dies the other. Surely, they all have one breath; man has no advantage over animals, for all is vanity. All go to one place: all are from the dust, and all return to dust. Who knows the spirit of the sons of men, which goes upward, and the spirit of the animal, which goes down to the earth? (Ecclesiastes 3:18–21, NKJV)

And the LORD God formed man of the dust of the ground, and breathed into his nostrils the breath of life; and man became a living being. (Genesis 2:7, NKJV)

Then the dust will return to the earth as it was, and the spirit will return to God who gave it. (Ecclesiastes 12:7, NKJV)

Where Does a Man's Spirit Go at Death?

What remains a mystery is what happens to a person's spirit when the body dies. We know that the spirit goes back to God, but what happens at that point? We do know two things that happen. The spirit does not enter into a final judgment at that point because the resurrection of the dead is for the final judgment of all people. We also know that the spirits of people are not allowed into the direct presence of God.

All these spirits of people who have died must go somewhere. Therefore, there must be some kind of determination for where they go. It is also logical to think that there must be two places separating those who served God from those who didn't serve God. It would not be just to have the wicked and the righteous to be mixed together in the same place.

What happens to a person's spirit when the body dies? Where does this spirit go? A few passages in the Bible give information about where these places are. In these next two passages, I'll use the Young's Literal Translation since it is more accurate in its use of words.

The Pit

All of them answer and say unto thee, "Even thou hast become weak like us! Unto us thou hast become like! Brought down to Sheol hath been thine excellency, the noise of thy psaltery, under thee spread out hath been the worm, yea, covering thee is the worm. How hast thou fallen from the heavens, O shining one, son of the dawn! Thou hast been cut down to earth, O weakener of nations. And thou saidst in thy heart: the heavens I go up, above stars of God I raise my throne, and I sit in the mount of meeting in the sides of the north. I go up above the heights of a thick cloud, I am like to the Most High. Only—unto Sheol thou art brought down, unto the sides of the pit." (Isaiah 14:10–15, YLT)

Sheol is translated as hell. Notice that scripture mentions *brought down*. The king of Babylon was assigned a place in hell. He was brought down to hell. Also notice the same use of *brought down* and *the sides of the pit.* Next, I'll give a more precise description of hell, which most of us have always wondered about.

17And it cometh to pass, in the twelfth year, in the fifteenth of the month, hath a word of Jehovah been unto me, saying, 18Son of man, wail for the multitude of Egypt, and cause it to go down, it—and the daughters of honorable nations, unto the earth—the lower parts, with those going down to the pit. 19Than whom hast thou been more pleasant? Go down, and be laid with the uncircumcised. 20In the midst of the pierced of the sword they fall, to the sword she hath been given, they drew her out, and all her multitude. 21Speak to him do the god's of the mighty out of the midst of Sheol, with his helpers—they have gone down, they have lain with the uncircumcised, the pierced of the sword. 22There is Ashur, and all her assembly, round about him are his graves, all of them are wounded, who are falling by sword, 23Whose graves are appointed in the sides of the pit, and her assembly is round about her grave, all of them wounded, falling by sword, because they gave terror in the land of the living. 24There is Elam, and all her multitude, round about is her grave, all of them wounded, who are falling by sword, who have gone down uncircumcised unto the earth—the lower parts, because they gave their terror in the land of the living, and they bear their shame with those going down to the pit. 25In the midst of the wounded they have appointed a bed for her with all her multitude, round about him are her graves, all of them uncircumcised, pierced of the sword, for their terror was given in the land of the living, and they bear their shame with those going down to the pit, in the midst of the pierced he hath been put. 26There is Meshech, Tubal, and all her multitude, round about him are her graves, all of them uncircumcised, pierced of the sword, for they gave their terror in the land of the living, 27and they lie not with the mighty, who are falling of the uncircumcised, who have gone down to Sheol with their weapons of war, and they put their swords under their heads, and their iniquities are on their bones, for the terror of the mighty is in the land of the living. 28And thou, in the midst of the uncircumcised art broken, and dost lie with the pierced of the sword. 29There is Edom, her kings, and all her princes, who have been given up in their might, with the pierced of the sword, they with the uncircumcised do lie, and with those going down to the pit. 30There are princes of the north, all of them, and every Zidonian, who have gone down with the pierced in their terror, of their might they are ashamed, and they lie uncircumcised with the pierced of the sword, and they bear their shame with those going down to the pit. 31Then doth Pharaoh see, and he hath been comforted for all his multitude, the pierced of the sword—Pharaoh and all his force, an affirmation of the Lord Jehovah. 32For I have given his terror in the land of the living, and he hath been laid down in the midst of the uncircumcised, with the pierced of the sword— Pharaoh, and all his multitude, an affirmation of the Lord Jehovah! (Ezekiel 32:17–32, YLT)

- In verses 18, 19, 24, 27, 29, and 30, notice the use of "going down."
- In verses 18, 24, 25, 29, and 30, notice the use of "the pit."
- In verse 23, notice the use of "the sides of the pit."
- In verse 19: "laid," 21: "have lain," 25: "appointed a bed," 27: "they lie not," 29: "do lay" and "do lie," 30: "they lie" 32: "laid down."

This is a description of hell for many of the kings of the earth at various times in history. The Prophet is now prophesying that Pharaoh is now going to join all these other kings. We have several descriptions of hell. There is the use of the phrase *going down* as mentioned in the previous passage in Isaiah. We can conclude that this place is somewhere in the interior of the earth. There is the use of the words *the pit* and *the sides of the pit*.

We can conclude that hell must look like a pit that has sides. "The sides of the pit" may look like a canyon with walls all around it. We are not told how big this pit is or how broad or narrow or deep this pit is. We are also given information that the spirits of all who are in the pit are assigned a place along the *sides of the pit*. We are given information that none of these spirits are allowed to wander from these assigned places along *the sides of the pit* because there is no mention of wandering. Instead, it is mentioned that each spirit must remain in that assigned place. It is also apparent that these spirits of former people are very much awake and aware of other spirits entering into the pit to their assigned places in *the sides of the pit*. We also observe that each nation that had a warring king on earth and is assigned a place to *the side of the pit* also has his army of those spirits placed around him on *the sides of the pit*. One last observation is that all these spirits of former people on earth now bear their shame. They have undergone some type of sentencing and are very much aware of their guilt.

How big is this pit or hell? We don't know. We don't know how big the spirits of the former people are. It could be that each spirit of a man is only a few inches in size (four to six inches), which would be quite reasonable to assume. And if this is true, then the pit may not be as large as we might imagine. The pit may be deeper than it would be in length. It would also stand to reason the pit of hell has an unknown depth. When you get closer to the bottom, it gets hotter and there is greater torment. Are there varying levels of torment within the pit? Might those who did a greater amount of sinning be more deserving of a greater amount of torment than those whose sins where minor?

Another point to contemplate about those who are in hell's prison is that they are also from the time of Adam till Noah (the antediluvian age). Those who went to hell first, such as in the antediluvian age, and all those who follow in consecutive order have missed out on all the events that have occurred at the time of their deaths up till the present. They have little information except what is passed on to them from others entering into the pit. It may even be that there is no communication among the residents of the pit. Thus the first spirits have either no information of what has transpired on earth or just bits and pieces of our present history if communication is allowed within hell. They know little—if anything—of what happened after Noah's flood. We don't know what the spirits are allowed to do in hell. We know that they are in a conscious state and are tormented by the flame. Are they allowed to communicate to each other? We know that one was allowed to see Lazarus; he was not permitted to speak to Lazarus, but he spoke to Abraham (Luke 16:19–31).

Here are some other passages mentioned in the Bible about the pit of hell.

> And when He came out onto the land, He was met by a man from the city who was possessed with demons; and who had not put on any clothing for a long time, and was not living in a house, but in the tombs. Seeing Jesus, he cried out and fell before Him, and said in a loud voice, "What business do we have with each other, Jesus, Son of the Most High God? I beg You, do not torment me." For He had commanded the unclean spirit to come out of the man. For it had seized him many times; and he was bound with chains and shackles and kept under guard, and yet he would break his bonds and be driven by the demon into the desert. And Jesus asked him, "What is your name?" And he said, "Legion"; for many demons had entered him. They were imploring Him not to command them to go away into the abyss. (Luke 8:27–31, NASB)

The abyss is the pit. Notice that even these demons know about the pit and do not want to go there.

> For thus says the Lord GOD, "When I make you a desolate city, like the cities which are not inhabited, when I bring up the deep over you and the great waters cover you, then I will bring you down with those who go down to the pit, to the people of old, and I will make you dwell in the lower parts of the earth, like the ancient waste places, with those who go down to the pit, so that you will not be inhabited; but I will set glory in the land of the living. (Ezekiel 26:19–20, NASB)

Here we find the prophet Ezekiel foretelling the inhabitants of Tyre of their coming fate. Notice that Ezekiel has knowledge of the pit and that it is inside the earth.

> He keeps back his soul from the pit, and his life from passing over into Sheol. (Job 33:18, NASB)

Job is telling his friends some of the things God does to help people from being judged. From this verse, we see that it is not God's desire to send people to the pit.

You will also notice that in almost every passage that deals with those who die and go to paradise or hell, they are described as *sleeping* or *resting*. Is this use of the word *sleeping* or *resting* referring to their death being temporary since they will all be resurrected, or is this one of the states that they are in while residing in paradise or hell? In paradise, are those spirits in an active or inactive state—such as sleep—or are they in a very active state and moving around? We know that the spirits in the pit are assigned to a single place and are not permitted to move about like in a prison cell, and they are conscious. Therefore I believe that they conscious.

Paradise

Let's look at some more passages in the Bible.

There was a certain rich man who was clothed in purple and fine linen and fared sumptuously every day. But there was a certain beggar named Lazarus, full of sores, who was laid at his gate, desiring to be fed with the crumbs which fell from the rich man's table. Moreover the dogs came and licked his sores. So it was that the beggar died, and was carried by the angels to Abraham's bosom. The rich man also died and was buried. And being in torments in Hades, he lifted up his eyes and saw Abraham afar off, and Lazarus in his bosom. Then he cried and said, "Father Abraham, have mercy on me, and send Lazarus that he may dip the tip of his finger in water and cool my tongue; for I am tormented in this flame." But Abraham said, "Son, remember that in your lifetime you received your good things, and likewise Lazarus evil things; but now he is comforted and you are tormented. And besides all this, between us and you there is a great gulf fixed, so that those who want to pass from here to you cannot, nor can those from there pass to us." Then he said, "I beg you therefore, father, that you would send him to my father's house, for I have five brothers, that he may testify to them, lest they also come to this place of torment." Abraham said to him, "They have Moses and the prophets; let them hear them." And he said, "No, father Abraham; but if one goes to them from the dead, they will repent." But he said to him, "If they do not hear Moses and the prophets, neither will they be persuaded though one rise from the dead." (Luke 16:19–31, NKJV)

There is no suggestion that this story of Lazarus is a parable. Jesus is telling this story as being a factual event that had taken place before his death and resurrection. The point of the story is that we ought to be helping the poor instead of living posh lives for ourselves. We also glean some information about hell and paradise from this account.

The rich man was sentenced to hell. He was alert and awake in his spirit form while in hell. He was able to see Lazarus with Abraham. He was able to carry on a conversation with Abraham. Verse 26 says, "Between us and you there is a great gulf fixed, so that those who want to pass from here to you cannot, nor can those from there pass to us." What is this *great gulf*? Also notice that Old Testament believers (Abraham) dwell with Lazarus.

There is some kind of expanse that separates the pit of hell from where Abraham's spirit is dwelling. Also notice that the rich man's spirit is in torment by *this flame*. Apparently, the spirits of people are able to feel. The rich man's spirit is in torment from the heat of the flame. There is a flame and heat in this pit of hell. Every spirit there is able to feel the heat produced from this flame, and they are in torment too.

There also exists a *great gulf* between the pit and where Abraham resides. This becomes a great mystery to us because there is no other mention of this *great gulf* in the Bible. Where is this place where Abraham resides? Is it someplace under the earth's surface? We can conclude that this place—the pit or hell—is underneath the surface of the earth. And it is active with flames of fire and heat produced from the flame.

It is my personal belief that this place is probably in the depths of a somewhat active volcano or close to a volcano. There is probably some molten lava that is still active but not erupting. There have to be some vents to allow oxygen into the interior of the pit to allow for flames because flames require oxygen. The pit therefore has to be a material place. The pit could be an opening from the surface of the earth from which humans can peer down into. Or the pit may be closed off from having an opening at the surface of the earth but still have vents for air passages. We may be able to find this place, but we would probably never know about the spirits of the dead who are there. It could also be that the pit has a small opening on the earth's surface that living people are able to find and gain access into. The vents may be just slivers in the ground that are only a few inches across or like pinholes in the surface of the earth.

What remains a mystery is where all the other spirits of the believers in God are assigned. There is no information about the whereabouts of this place. It could be in a location in physical heaven. It's my belief that it must be far away from the pit. I also believe that paradise is not in heaven but in another location somewhere in the universe. My own personal belief is based upon a few facts in the Bible. Since the rich man is able to communicate to Abraham, the other mystery becomes the *great gulf*. We know that no one is permitted to travel across or through this *great gulf*. The *great gulf* is the barrier separating the pit of hell from the other spirits of people wherever that place is. Is this place here on earth? What do the spirits of people who walked in the faith of Abraham do in this place?

For some reason, God chooses to keep this information from the living on earth. It is a mystery to us. Why?

> Then one of the criminals who were hanged blasphemed Him, saying, "If You are the Christ, save Yourself and us." But the other, answering, rebuked him, saying, "Do you not even fear God, seeing you are under the same condemnation? And we indeed justly, for we receive the due reward of our deeds; but this Man has done nothing wrong." Then he said to Jesus, "Lord, remember me when You come into Your kingdom." And Jesus said to him, "Assuredly, I say to you, today you will be with Me in Paradise." (Luke 23:39–43, NKJV)

Notice how verse 43 mentions *be with me in paradise*. This can't be heaven; otherwise, Jesus would have used the word *heaven*. Paradise literally means "garden" in Greek. This word paradise is the only name used to describe the place where departed spirits of the righteous go.

One more point to mention is that the spirit of every person who dies on earth is escorted to someplace where Jesus is. This could be outside of heaven itself. The point is that every spirit returns to God (Jesus) and at that point receives a sentence to either go into the pit of hell or to the place of paradise. This is not the final judgment—but two separate places of waiting for the final end of everything to happen on earth. It is at the final end that all are resurrected from the dead and receive eternal judgments. The pit of hell and paradise are merely places of waiting till the time of the resurrection of the dead.

What information can we collect about this place Jesus calls paradise? What else can we learn from the Bible about the resurrection of the dead?

> I have set the LORD always before me; because He is at my right hand I shall not be moved. Therefore, my heart is glad, and my glory rejoices; my flesh also will rest in hope. For You will not leave my soul in Sheol, nor will You allow Your Holy One to see corruption. You will show me the path of life; in Your presence is fullness of joy; at Your right hand are pleasures forevermore. (Psalm 16:8–11, NKJV)

> For David says concerning Him: "I foresaw the LORD always before my face, for He is at my right hand, that I may not be shaken. Therefore, my heart rejoiced, and my tongue was glad; moreover my flesh also will rest in hope. For You will not leave my soul in Hades, nor will You allow your Holy One to see corruption. You have made known to me the ways of life; You will make me full of joy in Your presence." (Acts 2:25–28, NKJV)

Does "he ascended" mean that Jesus also first descended into the lower parts of the earth?

> He who descended is also the One who ascended far above all the heavens, that He might fill all things. (Ephesians 4:9–10, NKJV)

> For Christ also suffered once for sins, the just for the unjust, that He might bring us to God, being put to death in the flesh but made alive by the Spirit, by whom also He went and preached to the spirits in prison, who formerly were disobedient, when once the Divine longsuffering waited in the days of Noah, while the ark was being prepared, in which a few, that is, eight souls, were saved through water. There is also an antitype that now saves us— baptism (not the removal of the filth of the flesh, but the answer of a good conscience toward God), through the resurrection of Jesus Christ, who has gone into heaven and is at the right hand of God, angels, and authorities and powers having been made subject to Him. (1 Peter 3:18–22, NKJV)

Here we learn that Jesus had to go into hell, but he does not stay in hell. We also learn that Jesus ends up in physical heaven at the right hand of the Father. Why did Jesus have to go into hell before he ascended into heaven? What events occurred with Jesus immediately following his death?

Jesus probably first went to paradise since he told this to the criminal who died that very day. He probably made the announcement to every spirit in paradise that his work was almost finished. Those spirits had been waiting all those years for that event to take place; it would only seem fitting that Jesus would first appear to them. 1 Peter 3:18 says, "That he might bring us to God."

Jesus continued on into hell. In 1 Peter 3:19, Jesus "preached to the spirits in prison." What was the message that Jesus preached to all those in hell? We are given no answer to that question; his message remains a mystery, but we can arrive at a probable conclusion. The Greek verb for *preached* is directly connected to the Greek noun "to herald." Jesus wasn't preaching the gospel; that would be a vain act since the gospel is intended for those who have yet to die. Just as someone is appointed to be a herald by a king they would make proclamations. Jesus probably made several proclamations. He may have set in place a more defined set of ordinances concerning the eternal judgment that is to come. Jesus was given lordship over all the rulers and souls of people. It would only follow logical reasoning that as the new ruler, Jesus was making proclamations to those in hell.

We also notice that Jesus makes proclamations to those who lived up till Noah's Ark (the antediluvian age). In the antediluvian age, there was no law or ordinance given unto people from God. Jesus was probably establishing many ordinances to these spirits because they had missed out on all that had happened from their time in hell—and so had the rest of the spirits in hell.

After this, where did Jesus go? He either returned to heaven or back to earth to rise up from the dead. What happened to all those in paradise? Did they go anywhere or just continue on in paradise? Some of them came back to rise from the dead just as Jesus did. We don't know how many others came back. Where did the rest go? Did they remain in paradise? Many people think that all in paradise went to heaven, and paradise was done away with. There is no mention of these spirits moving on into heaven. In all reasoning Paradise is probably still in existence.

> Your dead shall live; together with my dead body they shall arise. Awake and sing, you who dwell in dust; for your dew is like the dew of herbs, and the earth shall cast out the dead. Come, my people, enter your chambers, and shut your doors behind you; hide yourself, as it were, for a little moment, until the indignation is past. For behold, the LORD comes out of His place to punish the inhabitants of the earth for their iniquity; the earth will also disclose her blood, and will no more cover her slain. (Isaiah 26:19–21, NKJV)

> But now Christ is risen from the dead, and has become the firstfruits of those who have fallen asleep. For since by man came death, by man also came the resurrection of the dead. For as in Adam all die, even so in Christ all shall be made alive. But each one in his own order: Christ, the firstfruits, afterward those who are Christ's at His coming. Then comes the end, when He delivers the kingdom to God the Father, when He puts an end to all rule and all authority and power. For He must reign till He has put all enemies under his feet. The last enemy that will be destroyed is death. For "He has put all things under His feet." But when He says, "All things are put under Him," it is evident that

He who put all things under Him is excepted. Now when all things are made subject to Him, then the Son Himself will also be subject to Him who put all things under Him, that God may be all in all. (1 Corinthians 15:20–28, NKJV)

Notice that there is no mention of anyone in paradise moving on to dwell in heaven with Jesus.

All the Dead Must Return to Their Former Bodies

Jesus sets a pattern for all people who have died to dwell in the realm of the departed spirits. First, all spirits are to come back from the realm of the departed spirits. Second, all spirits are to enter back into their former bodies, having returned from the realm of the departed spirits. Where the righteous spirits reside remains a mystery. There are several beliefs about where they might be, but in truth, there is no mention of where they are.

My belief is that they are still residents in Paradise. I base this upon three facts. They have not been raised from the dead. They do not have bodies. All current residents in heaven have bodies. The final judgment has not occurred.

Why do all people need to be raised back into their former bodies? We know from scriptures that in this present dispensation, when people die, they are immediately taken into the presence of Jesus. They meet the Lord, but where does this meeting take place? The scripture never says we go to heaven to meet Christ in heaven. It only says that we meet with Jesus. Where a dead person meets with Christ remains a mystery. It is my belief that all people meet with Christ and are sentenced to wherever they are to go till the resurrection of the dead because Christ in now they're judge. It is also my belief that Christians who die are ushered to someplace outside of heaven to meet with Christ. There is no mention in the Bible that all Christians are ushered into physical heaven.

> Now as they said these things, Jesus Himself stood in the midst of them, and said to them, "Peace to you." But they were terrified and frightened, and supposed they had seen a spirit. And He said to them, "Why are you troubled? And why do doubts arise in your hearts? Behold My hands and My feet, that it is I Myself. Handle Me and see, for a spirit does not have flesh and bones as you see I have." When He had said this, He showed them His hands and His feet. But while they still did not believe for joy, and marveled, He said to them, "Have you any food here?" So they gave Him a piece of a broiled fish and some honeycomb. And He took it and ate in their presence. (Luke 24:36–43, NKJV)

> Now Thomas, called the Twin, one of the twelve, was not with them when Jesus came. The other disciples therefore said to him, "We have seen the Lord." So he said to them, "Unless I see in His hands the print of the nails, and put my finger into the print of the nails, and put my hand into His side, I will not believe." And after eight days His disciples were again inside, and Thomas with them.

Jesus came, the doors being shut, and stood in the midst, and said, "Peace to you!" Then He said to Thomas, "Reach your finger here, and look at My hands; and reach your hand here, and put it into My side. Do not be unbelieving, but believing." (John 20:24–27, NKJV)

In both occurrences, Jesus appears to the disciples and has to show them that he indeed has a body just like the one he had before his death. In fact, Jesus's body even bears the scars from the wounds that were inflicted during his last days on the cross. Jesus is pointing out during these two instances that just as he returns back into his former body at resurrection, so too will everyone return to their former bodies exactly as they were at some point during their lives on earth. It is my personal belief that we will all be returned to our bodies around the age of thirty years old. God will literally reconstitute our bodies exactly as they once were. It would not be of benefit to be reconstituted in a body of old age or that of an infant.

The resurrection of the dead was mentioned in the Old Testament in a few places. It was not an unknown doctrine in the Old Testament, but most people didn't know about or understand the resurrection.

For I delivered to you first of all that which I also received: that Christ died for our sins according to the Scriptures, and that He was buried, and that He rose again the third day according to the Scriptures. (1 Corinthians 15:3–4, NKJV)

Notice how verse 4 mentions "according to the scriptures." At that point, there was no New Testament. All they had for scriptures was the books of the Old Testament.

I have set the LORD always before me; because He is at my right hand I shall not be moved. Therefore, my heart is glad, and my glory rejoices; My flesh also will rest in hope. For You will not leave My soul in Sheol, nor will You allow your Holy One to see corruption. (Psalm 16:8–10, NKJV)

You who have shown me great and severe troubles, shall revive me again, and bring me up again from the depths of the earth. You shall increase my greatness, and comfort me on every side. (Psalm 71:20–21, NKJV)

For I know that my Redeemer lives, and He shall stand at last on the earth; and after my skin is destroyed, this I know, that in my flesh I shall see God, whom I shall see for myself, and my eyes shall behold, and not another. How my heart yearns within me! (Job 19:25–27, NKJV)

Your dead shall live; together with my dead body they shall arise. Awake and sing, you who dwell in dust; for your dew is like the dew of herbs, and the earth shall cast out the dead. (Isaiah 26:19, NKJV)

At that time Michael shall stand up, the great prince who stands watch over the sons of your people; and there shall be a time of trouble, such as never was since there was a nation, even to that time. And at that time your people shall be delivered, everyone who is found written in the book. And many of those who sleep in the dust of the earth shall awake, some to everlasting life, some to shame and everlasting contempt. Those who are wise shall shine like the brightness of the firmament, and those who turn many to righteousness like the stars forever and ever. (Daniel 12:1–3, NKJV)

Come, and let us return to the LORD; for He has torn, but He will heal us; He has stricken, but He will bind us up. After two days He will revive us; on the third day He will raise us up, that we may live in His sight. Let us know. Let us pursue the knowledge of the LORD. His going forth is established as the morning; He will come to us like the rain, like the latter and former rain to the earth. (Hosea 6:1–3, NKJV)

In the New Testament, we gain a lot of information and teachings about the resurrection of the dead. In fact, the resurrection of the dead is not any small doctrine that is taught in the first church.

Do not marvel at this; for the hour is coming in which all who are in the graves will hear His voice and come forth—those who have done good, to the resurrection of life, and those who have done evil, to the resurrection of condemnation. (John 5:28–29, NKJV)

Some people think that verse 29 refers to two separate resurrections. This is true, and I will point it out later in the chapter. This verse teaches us that there are two separations, classes, or groups that will be resurrected. At the time of resurrection, the resurrected spirits will be placed in two separate groups. One group is called the resurrection of life, and the other group is the resurrection of the condemnation. Thus the righteous are separated from the wicked. Are all who have died to be resurrected at the same time? This verse is in agreement with Daniel 12:3.

> For since by man came death, by Man also came the resurrection of the dead. For as in Adam all die, even so in Christ all shall be made alive. But each one in his own order: Christ the firstfruits, afterward those who are Christ's at His coming. Then comes the end, when He delivers the kingdom to God the Father, when He puts an end to all rule and all authority and power. (1 Corinthians 15:21–24, NKJV)

All Who Have Died Must Be Resurrected

Notice in verse 22 that *all shall be made alive.* All people who have died will be resurrected. Notice in verse 23 that there is an *order to resurrections.* Jesus is the firstfruits or the first to be resurrected. The next resurrection occurs "at his coming." Verse 23 says, "Then comes the end." This marks the end of the age of grace. This is the end of the Millennium Reign. There is no more death. No one grows old and dies. Christ the firstfruits are referred to as one of the ceremonies that God gave to the Israelites through the Law of Moses.

> And the LORD spoke to Moses, saying, "Speak to the children of Israel, and say to them: "When you come into the land which I give to you, and reap its harvest, then you shall bring a sheaf of the firstfruits of your harvest to the priest. He shall wave the sheaf before the LORD, to be accepted on your behalf; on the day after the Sabbath the priest shall wave it. And you shall offer on that day, when you wave the sheaf, a male lamb of the first year, without blemish, as a burnt offering to the LORD. (Leviticus 23:9–12, NKJV)

This is a picture or representation of Christ being raised from the dead. The waving of the first fruits is the acknowledgement of having reaped the first fruit of the first harvest. It marks a new beginning, having entered into the Promised Land. The sheaf is the first of the very first harvesting from seed that has been planted. The seed enters into the earth and dies, and then new life springs up to produce fruit.

Jesus died, was buried, and rose from the dead just as a seed dies, is buried, and rises with new life. The sheaf is waved to be accepted on your behalf. This was done so that the farmers would be blessed. It was also done as a picture of what God intended through Jesus. Also notice that the waving of the sheaf was done on the first day of the week, following the Sabbath day, which was the seventh day of the week. Christ was raised from the dead on the first day of the week.

So far, we have learned from the Bible that there will be a resurrection of everyone who has died. At this resurrection, the righteous will be separated from the wicked.

What Happens at the Resurrection?

What happens at this time of resurrection? What happens to the wicked, and what happens to the righteous?

> But each one in his own order: Christ the firstfruits, afterward those who are Christ's at His coming. Then comes the end, when He delivers the kingdom to God the Father, when He puts an end to all rule and all authority and power. (1 Corinthians 15:23–24, NKJV)

Verse 23 says, "Afterward those who are Christ's at his coming." Paul is showing us that we who are Christ's, are those who belong to Jesus. Paul is also writing about Jesus coming. The resurrection takes place at the return of Christ.

From the following passages of scripture, we find three events that take place at the time of resurrection.

> Let not your heart be troubled; you believe in God, believe also in Me. In My Father's house are many mansions; if it were not so, I would have told you. I go to prepare a place for you. And if I go and prepare a place for you, I will come again and receive you to Myself; that where I am, there you may be also. (1 John 14:1–3, NKJV)

- Jesus is returning to gather the believers together.

And then the lawless one will be revealed, whom the Lord will consume with the breath of His mouth and destroy with the brightness of His coming. (2 Thessalonians 2:8, NKJV)

• Christ will come to overthrow the Antichrist and all the wicked who have not died.

Then I saw an angel coming down from heaven, having the key to the bottomless pit and a great chain in his hand. He laid hold of the dragon, that serpent of old, who is the Devil and Satan, and bound him for a thousand years; and he cast him into the bottomless pit, and shut him up, and set a seal on him, so that he should deceive the nations no more till the thousand years were finished. But after these things he must be released for a little while. And I saw thrones, and they sat on them, and judgment was committed to them. Then I saw the souls of those who had been beheaded for their witness to Jesus and for the word of God, who had not worshiped the beast or his image, and had not received his mark on their foreheads or on their hands. And they lived and reigned with Christ for a thousand years. But the rest of the dead did not live again until the thousand years were finished. This is the first resurrection. Blessed and holy is he who has part in the first resurrection. Over such the second death has no power, but they shall be priests of God and of Christ, and shall reign with Him a thousand years. Now when the thousand years have expired, Satan will be released from his prison and will go out to deceive the nations which are in the four corners of the earth, Gog and Magog, to gather them together to battle, whose number is as the sand of the sea. They went up on the breadth of the earth and surrounded the camp of the saints and the beloved city. And fire came down from God out of heaven and devoured them. The devil who deceived them was cast into the lake of fire and brimstone where the beast and the false prophet are. And they will be tormented day and night forever and ever. Then I saw a great white throne and Him who sat on it, from whose face the earth and the heaven fled away. And there was found no place for them. And I saw the dead, small and great, standing before God, and books were opened. And another book was opened, which is the Book of Life. And the dead were judged according to their works, by the things which were written in the books. The sea gave up the dead who were in it, and Death and Hades delivered up the dead who were in them. And they were judged, each one according to his works. Then Death and Hades were cast into the lake of fire. This is the second death. And anyone not found written in the Book of Life was cast into the lake of fire. (Revelation 20:1–15, NKJV)

- The resurrection of believers occurs.

There are a lot details provided in this passage of scripture. I'll point out all the events that occur at this point. In Revelation 19, we read about Christ returning to earth. Jesus returns in the clouds with a great host of heaven. He doesn't set foot on the earth, but he is still in the sky.

In verses 1–3, we read that an angel from one of the returning hosts captures Satan and places him in hell where he remains for a thousand years. By mentioning a thousand years, we know that this is the beginning of the Millennium Reign. Also since an angel binds Satan, we know that the hosts that are accompanying Jesus's return consist of angels. There is no mention of saints or Christians. Just because there is no mention of previous believers does not mean that they are not raised at the return of Christ for him to begin the Millennium Reign.

In verse 4, there is mention of thrones with various people sitting on the thrones, having been given authority to judge. By that time, Jesus is probably not in the sky; he is now upon the earth. The thrones are probably establishing God's government on earth. Also notice that the thrones are already occupied by others. Who are these other people? Probably believers from the past being the first 12 disciples. Next we see all those who were slain during the time of the Great Tribulation with Jesus. All these people are resurrected from the dead.

In verse 5, we read that the rest of the dead are not resurrected. Who the rest of the dead are is a mystery. Are these the spirits that were in the pit or are they those of paradise or are they of both places? I assume that the "rest of the dead" are those who are in the pit. There is no logical purpose to raise the wicked back at this point in time.

Herein lies a difficulty. In verse 4, we see the establishing of God's government on earth to begin the Millennium Reign on the earth. Who is part of the Millennium Reign? We know that none of the wicked from the past are partakers in the Millennium Reign. The difficulty is with whether all the past believers in God partake in the Millennium Reign? There is no direct mention in the Bible of who partakes of the Millennium Reign except those who were killed in the Great Tribulation and those who survived the Great Tribulation. Do all those in paradise get to partake in the Millennium Reign along with those of the Great Tribulation?

It is my personal belief that all those in paradise will take part in the Millennium Reign. This is based solely on a few pieces of scripture and natural logical thinking. Revelation 20:4 says, "And I saw thrones, and they sat on them, and judgment was committed to them." There was also the promise made to the 12 disciples that they would rule with Jesus having 12 thrones. These people are from the first generation of believers of Jesus. They are involved with the Millennium Reign. They were in Paradise. I therefore assume that all in Paradise are to live in the Millennium Reign.

> So Jesus said to them, "Assuredly I say to you, that in the regeneration, when the Son of Man sits on the throne of His glory, you who have followed Me will also sit on twelve thrones, judging the twelve tribes of Israel. (Matthew 19:28, NKJV)

There Are Two Resurrections

For if we believe that Jesus died and rose again, even so God will bring with Him those who sleep in Jesus. (1 Thessalonians 4:14)

These few verses may be referring to those in paradise. In my logical thinking, I would assume that with the return of Christ, there is no longer a need for paradise thus paradise is done away with. I would also think that God's intention is for all the believers—from Adam through the Great Tribulation—to live upon the earth throughout the Millennium Reign. It doesn't seem fitting that all those who died and reside in paradise are not allowed to partake of the Millennium Reign. It would also not seem fitting for those who die in the Great Tribulation to go to paradise and then return in a resurrection to live in the Millennium Reign. It would not be fair for those who have been in paradise from Adam till the Great Tribulation. It would be fair for everyone in paradise to undergo the first resurrection together. Let's read these verses again—with the thought of there being two resurrections.

1Then I saw an angel coming down from heaven, having the key to the bottomless pit and a great chain in his hand. 2He laid hold of the dragon, that serpent of old, who is the Devil and Satan, and bound him for a thousand years; 3and he cast him into the bottomless pit, and shut him up, and set a seal on him, so that he should deceive the nations no more till the thousand years were finished. But after these things he must be released for a little while. 4And I saw thrones, and they sat on them, and judgment was committed to them. Then I saw the souls of those who had been beheaded for their witness to Jesus and for the word of God, who had not worshiped the beast or his image, and had not received his mark on their foreheads or on their hands. And they lived and reigned with Christ for a thousand years. 5But the rest of the dead did not live again until the thousand years were finished. This is the first resurrection. 6Blessed and holy is he who has part in the first resurrection. Over such the second death has no power, but they shall be priests of God and of Christ, and shall reign with Him a thousand years. 7Now when the thousand years have expired, Satan will be released from his prison 8and will go out to deceive the nations which are in the four corners of the earth, Gog and Magog, to gather them together to battle, whose number is as the sand of the sea. 9They went up on the breadth of the earth and surrounded the camp of the saints and the beloved city. And fire came down from God out of heaven and devoured them. 10The devil who deceived them was cast into the lake of fire and brimstone where the beast and the false prophet are. And they will be tormented day and night forever and ever. 11Then I saw a great white throne and Him who sat on it, from whose face the earth and the heaven fled away. And there was found no place for them. 12And I saw the dead, small and great, standing before God, and books were opened. And another book was opened, which is the Book of Life. And the dead were judged according to their works, by the things which were written in the books. 13The sea gave up the dead who were in it, and Death and Hades delivered up the dead who were in them. And they were judged, each one according to his works. 14Then Death and Hades were cast into the lake of fire. This is the second death. 15And anyone not found written in the Book of Life was cast into the lake of fire. (Revelation 20:1–15, NKJV)

In verse 6, we read that there are those who have part in the first resurrection. After the thousand years, we read about one more final separation of the righteous and the wicked that have lived on the earth during the thousand-year reign of Christ and how there will be many people who choose to become wicked even during the Millennium Reign. All these wicked people will try to destroy God's righteous people, but they will be devoured in their one massive attempt as revealed in verses 7–9. Notice also that none of the righteous are harmed, and there is no mention of any of them dying. At this point in time, all the wicked people are slain directly from God. They undergo death.

In verse 10, Satan is placed back into the pit of hell.

In verse 11, Christ has a great white throne, and Jesus is sitting on the throne. This is the beginning of the great judgment of all people who have ever lived.

In verses 12 and 13, we read about the second resurrection, which involved all the spirits that have died. The books of all the events of what each person did while on earth before their death are open. Everyone who has ever lived is being judged at this great and final judgment.

In verse 14–15, we read that there is no more mention of the pit; instead, it is a lake of fire. All the wicked are cast into this lake of fire—but not the righteous.

In verse 6, we also read that of all those who are resurrected at Christ's return will not ever die because the "second death has no power" over them. A second death must take place for all the wicked ones who will be cast into the lake of fire and brimstone. All these wicked people who are resurrected at the second resurrection for the final judgment will undergo a second death. We can conclude that every soul that ends up in the lake of fire will be reduced to just the spirit without a body. This judgment is for all eternity.

> 31When the Son of Man comes in His glory, and all the holy angels with Him, then He will sit on the throne of His glory. 32All the nations will be gathered before Him, and He will separate them one from another, as a shepherd divides his sheep from the goats. 33And He will set the sheep on His right hand, but the goats on the left. 34Then the king will say to those on his right hand, "Come, you blessed of my Father, inherit the kingdom prepared for you from the foundation of the world: 35for I was hungry and you gave Me food; I was thirsty and you gave Me drink; I was a stranger and you took Me in. 36I was naked and you clothed Me; I was sick and you visited Me; I was in prison and you came to Me. 37Then the righteous will answer him, saying,

"Lord, when did we see You hungry and feed You, or thirsty and give You drink? 38When did we see You a stranger and take You in, or naked and clothe You? 39Or when did we see You sick, or in prison, and come to You? 40And the king will answer and say to them, "Assuredly, I say to you, inasmuch as you did it to one of the least of these My brethren, you did it to Me." 41Then He will also say to those on the left hand, "Depart from Me, you cursed, into the everlasting fire prepared for the devil and his angels: 42for I was hungry and you gave Me no food; I was thirsty and you gave Me no drink; 43I was a stranger and you did not take Me in, naked and you did not clothe Me, sick and in prison and you did not visit Me. 44Then they also will answer Him, saying, "Lord, when did we see You hungry or thirsty or a stranger or naked or sick or in prison, and did not minister to You?" 45Then He will answer them, saying, "Assuredly, I say to you, inasmuch as you did not do it to one of the least of these, you did not do it to Me." 46And these will go away into everlasting punishment, but the righteous into eternal life." (Matthew 25:31–46, NKJV)

In this passage, we again read about Christ returning to the earth. When he returns, there will be people who have yet to die the first death. This is not the great "white throne" final judgment. This is when Christ is returning to begin the Millennium Reign. But this passage of scripture gives us a little detail about what happens when at the end of the Millennium Reign.

In verse 32, we read that everyone will be gathered together—from Adam to the last man to die—and these people will be separated into two groups.

In verse 34, we read that on his right side are those believers who are to inherit the kingdom of God.

In verse 41, we read that those on his left side are sent to the lake of fire or everlasting punishment.

From these two passages, we learn that there are two resurrections and two deaths. The first resurrection is at Christ's return to set up his Millennium Reign. This first resurrection is for those who died during the Great Tribulation, but it may also include all those who are in paradise. The second resurrection is for all those who died from the first death and were not raised at the first resurrection to partake in the great "white throne" final judgment. The second resurrection may only be for those who are in the pit of hell. The second death is for all those who are judged and cast into the lake of fire and brimstone for the remainder of eternity.

The one question that is raised that is somewhat mysterious involves the first resurrection. We know from scripture that all those who are slain during the time of the Great Tribulation are resurrected, but does this resurrection involve all those who are in paradise, some of those who are in paradise, or none of those who are in paradise?

> 13But I do not want you to be ignorant, brethren, concerning those who have fallen asleep, lest you sorrow as others who have no hope. 14For if we believe that Jesus died and rose again, even so God will bring with Him those who sleep in Jesus. 15For

this we say to you by the word of the Lord, that we who are alive and remain until the coming of the Lord will by no means precede those who are asleep. 16For the Lord Himself will descend from heaven with a shout, with the voice of an archangel, and with the trumpet of God. And the dead in Christ will rise first. 17Then we who are alive and remain shall be caught up together with them in the clouds to meet the Lord in the air. And thus we shall always be with the Lord. 18Therefore, comfort one another with these words. (1 Thessalonians 4:13–18, NKJV)

This passage in verse 16 reveals that all those who have believed in Jesus will be raised up from the dead. These people must be from the Great Tribulation. But are these believers also from paradise? Verse 14 would appear to suggest that everyone in paradise is also raised and returns with Christ as he begins the Millennium Reign.

In Revelation 20:4, we find thrones already established with people who are given authority to judge. These people had to first return with Jesus. Next we find the dead believers from the Great Tribulation being raised from the dead. Revelation 20:5 said, "The rest of the dead did not live again until the thousand years were finished." Are these spirits the wicked who are in the pit? Probably.

Another fact we learn from 1 Thessalonians 4:16–17 is that those that are resurrected are raised first from the dead. They receive their bodies and are standing in the sky with Jesus. Then all those believers who have not died the first death are caught up together with those who just rose from the dead and meet with Christ who is still hovering in the sky with all his angels and those raised from the dead. There is no mention that any of them returning to heaven. Do all the believers in God since Adam and Eve up to this future act join with Christ and the angels in the sky? There is no mention that any of the believers who are caught up with Jesus in the sky go to heaven. Everyone is hovering in the sky.

> Do not marvel at this; for the hour is coming in which all who are in the graves will hear His voice and come forth—those who have done good, to the resurrection of life, and those who have done evil, to the resurrection of condemnation. (John 5:28–29, NKJV)

We cannot rule out this scripture. It appears that everyone in paradise and in the pit will be resurrected at some point in time. All the wicked people will be resurrected at the Great White Throne Judgment. None of the fallen angels are resurrected (only mankind). There also is no mention of this all happening at once. It would appear that this verse refers to two separate resurrections.

> When the Son of Man comes in His glory, and all the holy angels with Him, then He will sit on the throne of His glory. All the nations will be gathered before Him, and He will separate them one from another, as a shepherd divides his sheep from the goats. (Matthew 25:31–46, NKJV)

The Great White Throne Judgment

Again, we read that all people are separated into two companies when the resurrection of the wicked occurs. One company is the believers in God. The second company is the unrighteous or the wicked. Whether this separation occurs on earth or in the sky and earth, there is no mention. But it matters that a separation occurs. Once the separation is finished, those in the company of the unrighteous are cast into a lake of fire. In these verses, there is no mention that returning into the lake of fire involves undergoing a second death. That does not mean that a second death will not occur. All these people may be sent into the lake of fire with their bodies as well.

From natural logical reasoning, I would assume that their bodies would not survive the flames. This would release their spirits from their charred bodies, and they would remain in the lake of fire in their spirits only. This is in harmony with Revelation 20:12 in that all again are brought before God from the pit to receive their final judgments. This is the second resurrection and the second death concerning the damned. To be resurrected, you must have lost your body through death. This second resurrection may also include some of the believers in God who may have died in accidents as well as being slain from the wicked during the Millennium Reign. Another difficulty is that there is no mention of any of the righteous dying during the Millennium Reign. Death is done away with for the righteous – so do any of the righteous die during the Millennium Reign?

The picture we have written to us is that Jesus is returning to earth to begin his Millennium Reign. He is returning at the peak of the Great Tribulation. He returns to earth's sky with all his angels. (Those in paradise may also be a part of this host of angels.) An angel binds Satan and casts Satan into the pit of hell.

Next, all the former people of the earth who died in the Great Tribulation are resurrected from the dead. The righteous who did not die in the Great Tribulation are then caught up with the present host who are still hovering in the sky. All the remaining wicked people who have not died are standing upon the earth, looking into the sky, and seeing Christ's return. The people of God have been separated in the sky from the unrighteous who are standing on the earth.

Next, all the unrighteous are cast into the pit of hell, removing all the wicked from the earth. They all die their first death at this point. The earth is now cleansed of all the wicked. Jesus and all those with him come back to the earth from the sky to occupy the earth for a thousand years. The angels return to heaven since they are not part of the Millennium Reign on earth.

During the Millennium Reign, man is again allowed to procreate. During these thousand years, even though Jesus inhabits the earth and has his believers, there will be those who will choose to live as unbelievers. At the end of the Millennium Reign, Satan is released for a short time to tempt these people. They will form an uprising against Jesus and his people. They will come to destroy all the believers in God.

During this attempt, God will intervene and "devour them." All these new wicked people undergo their first deaths and are placed into the pit of hell. The Great White Throne Judgment follows this event. There is no timeframe given for how much time passes from God placing the remaining wicked into the pit of hell till the Great White Throne Judgment. At some point all the wicked who are dead from the first death are resurrected. This is the second resurrection of the wicked. The wicked from the Millennium Reign are also gathered together with the wicked from the pit in the second resurrection. The Great White Throne Judgment occurs. Then all those who are condemned from God are sent to the lake of fire. This is the second death. Their bodies are forever lost, and all that remains are their spirits. The righteous will continue on with God in eternity. The wicked will continue on in all eternity in their judged state of damnation.

- Bible Truth: We do not go to heaven because there is no point in going to heaven only to have to immediately come back to earth to occupy with Christ in the Millennium Reign. The purpose of Christ's return is for his Millennium Reign.
- False doctrine: There is no such thing as a Rapture of the believers before Christ's return. It is appointed unto all people to die. Only those who are alive at the time of Christ's return do not undergo the first death. The false doctrine of a Rapture is not in harmony with the Bible.

CHAPTER 8

Eternal Judgment

This chapter starts with a statement that comes from my experience of walking with God in my life. Having a relationship with God, I have come to see that condemning judgments are one of God's least desired acts that he must administer unto people. For him, it's like condemning your own child to hell. It's the last thing you would ever want to do with your child. So it is with God and humanity.

God would rather see all people turn from their sins and not have them be condemned to hell. Since God is a just God, he has no choice but to condemn people to hell because of a refusal to turn from wickedness and rebellion. God has created each one of us just as most of humans have helped to create children of their own. Just as each child is precious to each parent so it is that each one of us is precious to God since he created each of us. God endures much grief and pain when he has to condemn anyone to the pit. If you think you have suffered, think again. You will never know how much pain and sorrow God suffers having to condemn people to the pit. God is a god of love and he also is a god of justice.

The word eternal is part of this judgment. That means that once the judgment is made, it is not modifiable. It is a final judgment that can never be revoked or changed. This judgment lasts throughout all eternity.

For God did not send His Son into the world to condemn the world, but that the world through Him might be saved. (John 3:17, NKJV)

The Lord is not slack concerning His promise, as some count slackness, but is longsuffering toward us, not willing that any should perish but that all should come to repentance. (2 Peter 3:9, NKJV)

The entire Bible is riddled with verses that reveal God as a judge. I will share some of these verses.

But you have come to Mount Zion and to the city of the living God, the heavenly Jerusalem, to an innumerable company of angels, to the general assembly and church of the firstborn who are registered in heaven, to God the Judge of all, to the spirits of just men made perfect, to Jesus the Mediator of the new covenant, and to the blood of sprinkling that speaks better things than that of Abel. (Hebrews 12:22–24, NKJV)

Notice how God is the judge of all. The general assembly is the nation of Israel; the church of the firstborn is the New Testament Christian. The spirits of just men and women made perfect are the Old Testament believers who placed their faith in God. Since God is the Creator of the earth and all living beings on earth, he thus has all responsibility to be the judge of all. In the New Testament, we find that God is reluctant to administer judgment.

> Far be it from You to do such a thing as this, to slay the righteous with the wicked, so that the righteous should be as the wicked; far be it from you! Shall not the Judge of all the earth do right? (Genesis 18:25, NKJV)

> Therefore, I have not sinned against you, but you wronged me by fighting against me. May the LORD, the Judge, render judgment this day between the children of Israel and the people of Ammon. (Judges 11:27, NKJV)

> Rise up, O Judge of the earth; render punishment to the proud. (Psalm 94:2, NKJV)

> For the LORD is our Judge, the LORD is our lawgiver, the LORD is our king; He will save us. (Isaiah 33:22, NKJV)

> And if anyone hears My words and does not believe, I do not judge him; for I did not come to judge the world but to save the world. He who rejects Me, and does not receive My words, has that which judges him—the word that I have spoken will judge him in the last day. (John 12:47–48, NKJV)

> And if you call on the Father, who without partiality judges according to each one's work, conduct

yourselves throughout the time of your stay here in fear. (1 Peter 1:17, NKJV)

Since Jesus has become the Lord of even death, God has made Jesus the Lord of all the earth. So now judgment becomes part of Jesus's responsibility. This is also due to the fact that Jesus is also the Word. And we will soon see that Jesus and the Word are one. So it is that the Word also is a measuring tool for judgment.

There must be a standard to measure all judgment. The written Word of God is the standard of measure for all judgment from the Father and through Jesus. No man or being can argue against this standard of law. It is very clear that everyone knows this standard, and they either choose to rebel against the law of God or to keep his standards of law. There are only two choices to choose from. There is no third option.

For the Father judges no one, but has committed all judgment to the Son, that all should honor the Son just as they honor the Father. He who does not honor the Son does not honor the Father who sent Him. (John 5:22–23, NKJV)

In these two verses, we learn the Jesus is the executer of justice and has been given the responsibility of being the judge of all mankind.

God's Standard of Measurement for Judging

Let's look a little more closely at the standard of measurement that God uses in judgment. Remember that Jesus must have a standard in which all judgments must be fair and unbiased. No mistakes can be made in making judgments.

1Therefore, you are inexcusable, O man, whoever you are who judge, for in whatever you judge another you condemn yourself; for you who judge practice the same things. 2But we know that the judgment of God is according to truth against those who practice such things. 3And do you think this, O man, you who judge those practicing such things, and doing the same, that you will escape the judgment of God? 4Or do you despise the riches of His goodness, forbearance, and longsuffering, not knowing that the goodness of God leads you to repentance? 5But in accordance with your hardness and your impenitent heart you are treasuring up for yourself wrath in the day of wrath and revelation of the righteous judgment of God, 6who will render to each one according to his deeds: 7eternal life to those who by patient continuance in doing good seek for glory, honor, and immortality; 8but to those who are self-seeking and do not obey the truth, but obey unrighteousness—indignation and wrath, 9tribulation and anguish, on every soul of man who does evil, of the Jew first and also of the Greek; 10but glory, honor, and peace to everyone who works what is good, to the Jew first and also to the Greek. 11For there is no partiality with God. 12For as many as have sinned without law will also perish without law, and as many as have sinned in the law will be judged by the law. (Romans 2:1–12, NKJV)

These verses contain the four main principles of God's judgment.

- In verse 2, notice "the judgment of God is according to truth."
- In verse 6, notice "will render to each one according to his deeds."
- In verse 11, notice "there is no partiality with God."
- In verse 12, notice "for as many as have sinned without law will also perish without law, and as many as have sinned in the law will be judged by the law."

In verse 1, most people make judgments according to whatever standard they have adopted, which is usually selfishness. But God uses a standard according to truth. God bases this standard on the knowledge that exists about him. This includes his kingdom and all righteousness. In verse 6, we see that God will judge each person according to his or her deeds. God is therefore keeping records of every person's deeds—good and bad.

And I saw the dead, small and great, standing before God, and books were opened. And another book was opened, which is the Book of Life. And the dead were judged according to their works, by the things which were written in the books. (Revelation 20:12, NKJV)

We read that God has recorded everything that every person has ever done. God has the ability to remember all these things, but he goes further to record them in books so that judgments are made from more than the ability of God. God is keeping a complete, flawless record of everything each human does. Also in verse 6—and many other verses in the Bible—we find the use of the word *deeds*. Deeds pertain to the outward actions that are performed by individuals. The Bible also reveals that God is the judge of the intentions of the heart.

- Bible principle: All deeds are first developed within the mind and heart of a person before they are performed as outward deeds.

In the day when God will judge the secrets of men by Jesus Christ, according to my gospel. (Romans 2:16, NKJV)

For the word of God is living and powerful, and sharper than any two-edged sword, piercing even to the division of soul and spirit, and of joints and marrow, and is a discerner of the thoughts and intents of the heart. And there is no creature hidden from His sight, but all things are naked and open to the eyes of Him to whom we must give account. (Hebrews 4:12, NKJV)

But the LORD said to Samuel, "Do not look at his appearance or at the height of his stature, because I have refused him. For the Lord does not see as man sees; for man looks at the outward appearance, but the LORD looks at the heart." (1 Samuel 16:7, NKJV)

Therefore, judge nothing before the time, until the Lord comes, who will both bring to light the hidden things of darkness and reveal the counsels of the hearts. Then each one's praise will come from God. (1 Corinthians 4:5, NKJV)

The eyes of the LORD are in every place, keeping watch on the evil and the good. (Proverbs 15:3, NKJV)

God has the ability to see our hearts and the thoughts of our minds. So this too is recorded. Just because men and women think these things or toy with them in their hearts does not mean that they are carried out in deeds. We are judged by our deeds. There are many deeds performed that go unseen by most people, but God is watching and will judge based upon the evil motive of the heart. An example is when someone plans a murder or an evil act but has another person carry out the deed. King David did this with Uriah in order to gain Bathsheba – Uriah's wife.

- Bible Principle: God has the ability to see the heart and thoughts of all beings he has created.

In Romans 2:11, we also learn that God is not partial when it comes to judgment. Most people are influenced into making partial judgments when the time comes to make decisions. They can be influenced by all kinds of external things, such as race, creed, religious beliefs, social status, physical appearance, wealth or poverty, education, circle of influence, and social circle. They can also be influenced by inward thoughts, such as promises, planned outcomes, end results, manipulative schemes, and cause and effect.

God judges according to people's deeds and is never influenced by anything. This makes God a very righteous Being. He also is fair to those who choose to not be involved in any wicked ways. For all the residents of heaven, there is never the fear that God will allow just one wicked being to dwell in their midst and create havoc for the rest.

In verse 12, we learn that God's judgments are also based upon the understanding that each person had while living on earth. No man will be able to have an excuse because everyone has a certain amount of knowledge of God and morality.

> For since the creation of the world His invisible attributes are clearly seen, being understood by the things that are made, even His eternal power and Godhead, so that they are without excuse, because, although they knew God, they did not glorify Him as God, nor were thankful, but became futile in their thoughts, and their foolish hearts were darkened. (Romans 1:20–21, NKJV)

God doesn't have just one standard for judgment. I count four standards that are part of God's nature. These four standards are not designed for God or his kingdom; instead, they are God's ways, based upon his character. Because of God's nature and abilities, rebels will not be able to have any excuse for their actions. Every being will be judged in the sight of everyone else. Everyone's deeds and thoughts will be exposed before all; they will bear their shame in hell.

Two Stages of Judgment

In the Bible I see two stages of judgment. One is in relation to time or the history of the earth and the other is in relation to eternity. Eternal judgment is mentioned in Hebrews 6:1–2. I will deal mostly with eternal judgment, but it will help to understand the first stage of judgment. This will also show the pattern of God's ways as we see how judgment operates in eternity. The stage of judgment in relation to time is when God doles out judgments to men and women while they live on earth.

You shall not make for yourself a carved image, or any likeness of anything that is in heaven above, or that is in the earth beneath, or that is in the water under the earth; you shall not bow down to them nor serve them. For I, the LORD your God, am a jealous God, visiting the iniquity of the fathers on the children to the third and fourth generations of those who hate Me, but showing mercy to thousands, to those who love Me and keep My commandments. (Exodus 20:4–6, NKJV)

You show loving kindness to thousands, and repay
the iniquity of the fathers into the bosom of their
children after them—the great, the mighty God,
whose name is the LORD of hosts. Jeremiah 32:18,
NKJV)

God is revealing a pattern among mankind. The first
generation usually makes the choice to engage in a certain
sin, and that sin becomes accepted to all involved during that
first generation. The next generation grows up accepting
this certain sin, but the sin is more of a natural occurrence
in their lives. The third and fourth generations grow up
without knowing that the sin is actually a sin.

God is saying that he will visit the sins of the first
generation all the way into the fourth generation and
beyond. How does God visit the sins into future generations?
God will either be a blessing to anyone who does right
and good—or he will become a curse to anyone who does
wrong. *God's Advanced Doctrines* explains how God does
this cursing. With this promise of blessing or cursing, we
see how God will visit whoever is engaged in right or wrong.

I call heaven and earth as witnesses today against
you, that I have set before you life and death,
blessing and cursing; therefore choose life, that both
you and your descendants may live. (Deuteronomy
30:19, NKJV)

So you shall keep His statutes and His
commandments which I am giving you today, that
it may go well with you and with your children after
you, and that you may live long on the land which

the LORD your God is giving you for all time. (Deuteronomy 4:40, NASB)

Because each generation continues on in the sin of the past generation, they inherit the same curse of God. This continues till people decide that they don't want any more cursing. These generational judgments are in regard to time, not eternity.

In Ezekiel's time, the people of Israel made a proverb as an excuse to continue in the sins of their forefathers. God rebuked Israel in attempt to get Israel to turn away from wickedness and rebellion. Again this judgment in regards to time, not eternity.

The word of the LORD came to me again, saying, "What do you mean when you use this proverb concerning the land of Israel, saying: 'The fathers have eaten sour grapes, and the children's teeth are set on edge?'" "As I live," says the Lord GOD, "You shall no longer use this proverb in Israel. Behold, all souls are Mine; the soul of the father as well as the soul of the son is Mine; the soul who sins shall die." (Ezekiel 18:1–4, NKJV)

The people tried to use the excuse of the principle in Exodus 20:4–6 that sinning was not their fault. They were implying that the present backsliding of Israel was due to the sins of their forefathers and that God could not justly hold them responsible for the current moral condition. God rejected this excuse because even though the moral decline was a result of the forefathers, that present generation still chose to continue in that immoral condition. God was using the second stage of judgment—eternal judgment. They will pay the price for being cursed—and will later be judged in eternity for their own conduct.

> The soul who sins shall die. The son shall not bear the guilt of the father, nor the father bear the guilt of the son. The righteousness of the righteous shall be upon himself, and the wickedness of the wicked shall be upon himself. (Ezekiel 18:20, NKJV).

God's pattern is to not accept an excuse for rebellion. For this generation of people, there is the judgment involving death. This is in regards to the resurrection of the dead—or regarding eternity.

> But when a righteous man turns away from his righteousness and commits iniquity, and does according to all the abominations that the wicked man does, shall he live? All the righteousness which he has done shall not be remembered; because of the unfaithfulness of which he is guilty and the sin which he has committed, because of them he shall die. Yet you say, "The way of the Lord is not fair." Hear now, O house of Israel, is it not My way which is fair, and your ways which are not fair? When a righteous man turns away from his righteousness, commits iniquity, and dies in it, it is because of the iniquity which he has done that he dies. Again, when a wicked man turns away from the wickedness which he committed, and does what is lawful and right, he preserves himself alive. Because he considers and turns away from all

the transgressions which he committed, he shall surely live; he shall not die. Yet the house of Israel says, "The way of the Lord is not fair." O house of Israel, is it not My ways which are fair, and your ways which are not fair? "Therefore, I will judge you, O house of Israel, every one according to his ways," says the Lord GOD. "Repent, and turn from all your transgressions, so that iniquity will not be your ruin. Cast away from you all the transgressions which you have committed, and get yourselves a new heart and a new spirit. For why should you die, O house of Israel? For I have no pleasure in the death of one who dies," says the Lord GOD. "Therefore, turn and live!" (Ezekiel 18:24–32, NKJV)

God is referring to eternity in Ezekiel's book. We can see the difference between the two stages of earthly time and eternity. An easy way to remember this when reading the Bible is to remember the word *death*. When God is using the word *death* or *dead*, he is referring to eternal judgment.

The Bible is full of examples of God's first and second stages of judgment. A few are listed below.

Now the two angels came to Sodom in the evening as Lot was sitting in the gate of Sodom. When Lot saw them, he rose to meet them and bowed down with his face to the ground. And he said, "Now behold, my lords, please turn aside into your servant's house, and spend the night, and wash your feet; then you may rise early and go on your way." They said however, "No, but we shall spend the night in the square." Yet he urged them strongly, so they turned aside to him and entered his house; and he prepared a feast for them, and baked unleavened bread, and they ate. Before they lay down, the men of the city, the men of Sodom, surrounded the house, both young and old, all the people from every quarter; and they called to Lot and said to him, "Where are the men who came to you tonight? Bring them out to us that we may have relations with them." But Lot went out to them at the doorway, and shut the door behind him, and said, "Please, my brothers, do not act wickedly. Now behold, I have two daughters who have not had relations with man; please let me bring them out to you, and do to them whatever you like; only do nothing to these men, inasmuch as they have come under the shelter of my roof." But they said, "Stand aside." Furthermore, they said, "This one came in as an alien, and already he is acting like a judge; now we will treat you worse than them." So they pressed hard against Lot and came near to break the door. But the men reached out their hands and brought Lot into the house with them, and shut the door. They struck the men who were at the doorway of the house with blindness, both small and great, so that they wearied themselves trying to find the doorway. Then the two men said to Lot, "Whom else have you here? A son-in-law, and your sons, and your daughters, and whomever you have in the city, bring them out of the place; for we are about to destroy this place, because their outcry has become so great before the LORD that the LORD has sent us to destroy it." Lot went out and spoke to his sons-in-law, who were to marry his daughters, and said, "Up, get out of this place, for the LORD will destroy the city." But he appeared to his sons-in-law to be jesting. When morning dawned, the angels urged Lot, saying, "Up, take your wife and your two daughters who are here, or you will be swept away in the punishment of the city." But he hesitated. So the men seized his hand and the hand of his wife and the hands of his two daughters, for the compassion of the LORD was upon him; and they brought him out, and put him outside the city. When they had brought them outside, one said, "Escape for your life! Do not look behind you, and do not stay anywhere in the valley; escape to the mountains, or you will be swept away." But Lot said to them, "Oh no, my lords! Now behold, your servant has found favor in your sight, and you have magnified your loving kindness, which you have shown me by saving my life; but I cannot escape to the mountains, for the disaster will overtake me and I will die; now behold, this town is near enough to flee to, and it is small. Please, let me escape there (is it not small?) that my life may be saved." He said to him, "Behold, I grant you this request also, not to overthrow the town of which you have spoken. "Hurry, escape there, for I cannot do anything until you arrive there." Therefore, the name of the town was called Zoar. The sun had risen over the earth when Lot came to Zoar. Then the LORD rained on Sodom and Gomorrah brimstone and fire from the LORD out of heaven, and He overthrew those cities, and all the valley, and all the inhabitants of the cities, and what grew on the ground. But his wife, from behind him, looked back, and she became a pillar of salt. (Genesis 19:1–26 NASB)

And turning the cities of Sodom and Gomorrah into ashes, condemned them to destruction, making them an example to those who afterward would live ungodly. (2 Peter 2:6, NKJV)

Look, this was the iniquity of your sister Sodom: She and her daughter had pride, fullness of food, and abundance of idleness; neither did she strengthen the hand of the poor and needy. (Ezekiel 16:49, NKJV)

Sodom became this way because of pride, abundance of food, idleness, and failure to help the poor and needy. Sodom later got into deeper sins of sexual perversion. In the end, the wickedness in Sodom and Gomorrah became so severe that God removed these wicked people from the earth lest other cities would follow their ways. God dealt with judgment in time and then judgment in eternity.

But a certain man named Ananias, with Sapphira his wife, sold a possession. And he kept back part of the proceeds, his wife also being aware of it, and brought a certain part and laid it at the apostles' feet. But Peter said, "Ananias, why has Satan filled your heart to lie to the Holy Spirit and keep back part of the price of the land for yourself? While it remained, was it not your own? And after it was sold, was it not in your own control? Why have you conceived this thing in your heart? You have not lied to men but to God." Then Ananias, hearing these words, fell down and breathed his last. So great fear came upon all those who heard these things. And the young men arose and wrapped him up, carried him out, and buried him. Now it was about three hours later when his wife came in, not knowing what had happened. And Peter answered her, "Tell me whether you sold the land for so much?" She said, "Yes, for so much." Then Peter said to her, "How is it that you have agreed together to test the Spirit of the Lord? Look, the feet of those who have buried your husband are at the door, and they will carry you out." Then immediately she fell down at his feet and breathed her last. And the young men came in and found her dead, and carrying her out, buried her by her husband. So great fear came upon all the church and upon all who heard these things. (Acts 5:1–11, NKJV)

We see here that again God is dealing with judgment in time and eternity. We also see that God deals with individuals as well as entire cities or nations.

But if you do not obey Me, and do not observe all these commandments, and if you despise My statutes, or if your soul abhors My judgments, so that you do not perform all My commandments, but break My covenant, I also will do this to you: I will even appoint terror over you, wasting disease and fever which shall consume the eyes and cause sorrow of heart. And you shall sow your seed in vain, for your enemies shall eat it. I will set My face against you, and you shall be defeated by your enemies. Those who hate you shall reign over you, and you shall flee when no one pursues you. And after all this, if you do not obey Me, then I will punish you seven times more for your sins. I will break the pride of your power; I will make your heavens like iron and your earth like bronze. And your strength shall be spent in vain; for your land shall not yield its produce, nor shall the trees of the land yield their fruit. "Then, if you walk contrary to Me, and are not willing to obey Me, I will bring on you seven times more plagues, according to your sins. I will also send wild beasts among you, which shall rob you of your children, destroy your livestock, and make you few in number; and your highways shall be desolate. And if by these things you are not reformed by Me, but walk contrary to Me, then I also will walk contrary to you, and I will punish you yet seven times for your sins. And I will bring a sword against you that will execute the vengeance of the covenant; when you are gathered together within your cities I will send pestilence among you; and you shall be delivered into the hand of the enemy. When I have cut off your supply of bread, ten women shall bake your bread in one oven, and they shall bring back your bread by weight, and you shall eat and not be satisfied. And after all this, if you do not obey Me, but walk contrary to Me, then I also will walk contrary to you in fury; and I, even I, will chastise you seven times for your sins. You shall eat the flesh of your sons, and you shall eat the flesh of your daughters. I will destroy your high places, cut down your incense altars, and cast your carcasses on the lifeless forms of your idols; and My soul shall abhor you. I will lay your cities waste and bring your sanctuaries to desolation, and I will not smell the fragrance of your sweet aromas. I will bring the land to desolation, and your enemies who dwell in it shall be astonished at it. I will scatter you among the nations and draw out a sword after you; your land shall be desolate and your cities waste. Then the land shall enjoy its sabbaths as long as it lies desolate and you are in your enemies' land; then the land shall rest and enjoy its sabbaths. As long as it lies desolate it shall rest—for the time it did not rest on your sabbaths when you dwelt in it. And as for those of you who are left, I will send faintness into their hearts in the lands of their enemies; the sound of a shaken leaf shall cause them to flee; they shall flee as though fleeing from a sword, and they shall fall when no one pursues. They shall stumble over one another, as it were before a sword, when no one pursues; and you shall have no power to stand before your enemies. You shall perish among the nations, and the land of your enemies shall eat you up. And those of you who are left shall waste away in their iniquity in your enemies' lands; also in their fathers' iniquities, which are with them, they shall waste away. But if they confess their iniquity and the iniquity of their fathers, with their unfaithfulness in which they were unfaithful to Me, and that they also have walked contrary to Me, and that I also have walked contrary to them and have brought them into the land of their enemies; if their uncircumcised hearts are humbled, and they accept their guilt—then I will remember My covenant with Jacob, and My covenant with Isaac and My covenant with Abraham I will remember; I will remember the land. The land also shall be left empty by them, and will enjoy its sabbaths while it lies desolate without them; they will accept their guilt, because they despised My judgments and because their soul abhorred My statutes. Yet for all that, when they are in the land of their enemies, I will not cast them away, nor shall I abhor them, to utterly destroy them and break My covenant with them; for I am the LORD their God. But for their sake I will remember the covenant of their ancestors, whom I brought out of the land of Egypt in the sight of the nations, that I might be their God: I am the LORD. (Leviticus 26:14–45, NKJV)

Here we see again the judgment in time. Notice that the judgments start out small; if rebellion continues, judgment becomes more and more severe. This actually occurred when the Babylonians took Israel captive and again about AD 70 with the Roman Caesar Titus.

We also notice that every time a person or nation repents of his or her sin, God will relent from cursing them. There are several examples of this in the Bible. We learn that God is a merciful Being and would rather not send any cursing upon anyone. All these things happen in time, but when the judgment calls for death, God will deal with eternal judgment.

I would like to add something that many people wonder about quite a bit. We see sin creep into people's lives or into a country's society. We wonder why God just doesn't administer judgment right away. Why is God so slow in doling out judgment? Why does it sometimes require one or two generations to see judgment come from God? This was even observed in the Bible.

> Some men's sins are clearly evident, preceding them to judgment, but those of some men follow later. (1 Timothy 5:24, NKJV)

> Because the sentence against an evil work is not executed speedily, therefore the heart of the sons of men is fully set in them to do evil. Though a sinner does evil a hundred times, and his days are prolonged, yet I surely know that it will be well with those who fear God, who fear before Him. But it will not be well with the wicked; nor will he prolong his days, which are as a shadow, because he does not fear before God. (Ecclesiastes 8:11–13, NKJV)

Remember that God is the Judge in time and in eternity. What we don't know is that God may be working in these people's lives in an attempt to bring them to a place to stop sinning. Most of us will never know what God is doing in a sinner's life. We do know that once God sees that a person is beyond recovery and is bent on wickedness, he will have no choice but to intervene with judgment. I do know that God will send lots of warning in hopes that the person or nation will stop sinning. It is not God's desire to pour out time judgments or eternal judgment. How difficult it is for God to send any kind of judgment.

A Closer Look at Eternal Judgment

Let's take a closer look at eternal judgment. In eternal judgment, each person has to answer before God for all his or her deeds on the earth. They will have to stand before God alone. No one can take his or her place of judgment. No one can be justified by the righteousness of another as in a marriage. No one person can be condemned for the wickedness of another. Each is held accountable for his or her own actions and deeds. How is this eternal judgment going to be carried out? I count three separate times of eternal judgment as do most Bible students.

- The Judgment Seat of Christ. This is for the judging of Christians, followers of God, believers of Jesus, and people who kept faith in God up through the age of grace.
- The Throne of Christ's Glory. These are the wicked who are alive through the Great Tribulation who have never died the first death.
- The Great White Throne. This judgment is for all those who died the first death and are resurrected after the Millennium Reign.

Many people find it difficult to believe that Christians will be judged. Notice that the Christians are the first to be judged. Why?

> For the time has come for judgment to begin at the house of God; and if it begins with us first, what will be the end of those who do not obey the gospel of God? Now "If the righteous one is scarcely saved, where will the ungodly and the sinner appear?" (1 Peter 4:17–18, NKJV)

Judgment begins at the house of God. Judgment begins with the believers of God.

> But why do you judge your brother? Or why do you show contempt for your brother? For we shall all stand before the judgment seat of Christ. For it is written: "As I live, says the LORD, every knee shall bow to Me, and every tongue shall confess to God." So then each of us shall give account of himself to God. Therefore, let us not judge one another anymore, but rather resolve this, not to put a stumbling block or a cause to fall in our brother's way. (Romans 14:10–13, NKJV)

Notice that the phrase *your brother* occurs twice and *our brothers* occur once. It is clear that these verses refer to a judgment for Christians. In verse 12, *each of us* again shows that this judgment is for the believers in God.

> Therefore, we make it our aim, whether present or absent, to be well pleasing to Him. For we must

all appear before the judgment seat of Christ, that each one may receive the things done in the body, according to what he has done, whether good or bad. (2 Corinthians 5:9–10, NKJV)

Again, this scripture is dealing with Christians and not sinners. Most of this judgment is dealing with those who walk in obedience of faith in God. Remember the chapter about faith? This judgment deals directly with the issue of faith.

Also notice that in both the above scriptures that *the judgment seat of Christ* is used. This judgment seat of Christ has an interesting description. The word *judgment seat* is from the Greek word *bema*, which describes a raised platform for public address. The raised platform denoted that the one on the platform had authority. The Romans used this idea of a raised platform for speaking or pronouncing judgments. The Roman in authority would place the chair on the platform and sit while pronouncing judgment. We can assume that "the judgment seat of Christ will be much the same way for his people.

What happens during this judgment of the Christians? Remember that only those who had faith in Christ are at this judgment. Those who never went on to live in the positive end of the number line are counted with the dead. Those people will not be resurrected with the living at this resurrection.

This judgment will not condemn believers to the pit. It not a judgment of condemnation; it is a judgment to render to each individual what he or she earned as a result of obedience to God. It is more of a judgment of rewards. It is a judgment in respect to service rendered to God. Of course, there will be some or many who will have obeyed in various areas and didn't obey in other areas. These judgments occur because our actions determine our ultimate rewards in Christ.

> For no other foundation can anyone lay than that which is laid, which is Jesus Christ. Now if anyone builds on this foundation with gold, silver, precious stones, wood, hay, straw, each one's work will become clear; for the Day will declare it, because it will be revealed by fire; and the fire will test each one's work, of what sort it is. If anyone's work which he has built on it endures, he will receive a reward. If anyone's work is burned, he will suffer loss; but he himself will be saved, yet so as through fire. (1 Corinthians 3:11–15, NKJV)

Notice that there is the contrast between gold, silver, precious stones, wood, hay, and straw. Quality is what is being emphasized in verse 12. In verse 13, Paul uses fire as the means for judgment. The fire will burn away the wood, hay, and straw, but it will not burn away gold, silver, or precious stones. Paul uses this illustration to explain this judgment. Throughout the Bible, fire is referred to as the testing source. In this use, it is not literal. It is used as an example of the testing source or judgment.

Upon reading this, many believers are going to wonder about the time of judgment when we appear before the judgment seat of Christ. Most believers are going to want the greatest amount of rewards instead of the least amount. This serves as fear for each believer to make sure you are doing all that you're commanded to do- this is the fear of God. This is why there is always a push in the New Testament to always be serving God to the fullest. For believers in God, you had better make sure you have repented from all your sins. You had better make sure you are doing all that God has asked of you. You had better make sure about every detail in your life—and do not become slack in any area of your life.

> And if you call on the Father, who without partiality judges according to each one's work, conduct yourselves throughout the time of your stay here in fear. (1 Peter 1:17, NKJV)

Now let's look at the second judgment which is the throne of Christ's glory. This second judgment is really the first judgment to occur at the time of the Great Tribulation. This judgment is not for each individual that involves opening the books of every event that each person did. It is merely separating the wicked from the righteous and then sentencing the wicked to the pit till the time comes for individual judging.

> When the Son of Man comes in His glory, and all the holy angels with Him, then He will sit on the throne of His glory. All the nations will be gathered before Him, and He will separate them one from another, as a shepherd divides his sheep from the goats. And He will set the sheep on His right hand, but the goats on the left. Then the King will say to those on His right hand, "Come, you blessed of My Father, inherit the kingdom prepared for you from

the foundation of the world: for I was hungry and you gave Me food; I was thirsty and you gave Me drink; I was a stranger and you took Me in; I was naked and you clothed Me; I was sick and you visited Me; I was in prison and you came to Me." Then the righteous will answer Him, saying, "Lord, when did we see You hungry and feed You, or thirsty and give You drink? When did we see You a stranger and take You in, or naked and clothe You? Or when did we see You sick, or in prison, and come to You?" And the King will answer and say to them, "Assuredly, I say to you, inasmuch as you did it to one of the least of these My brethren, you did it to Me." Then He will also say to those on the left hand, "Depart from Me, you cursed, into the everlasting fire prepared for the devil and his angels: for I was hungry and you gave Me no food; I was thirsty and you gave Me no drink; I was a stranger and you did not take Me in, naked and you did not clothe Me, sick and in prison and you did not visit Me." Then they also will answer Him, saying, "Lord, when did we see You hungry or thirsty or a stranger or naked or sick or in prison, and did not minister to You?" Then He will answer them, saying, "Assuredly, I say to you, inasmuch as you did not do it to one of the least of these, you did not do it to Me. And these will go away into everlasting punishment, but the righteous into eternal life." (Matthew 25:31–46, NKJV)

This judgment occurs at the Great Tribulation when Jesus returns to the earth with all his angels. This judgment is called the throne of Christ's glory and rightly so because we see all the glory of Christ returning with his angels. When the Millennium Reign is ushered in, and all believers from Adam till this event are the only people to occupy the earth.

The final judgment is the Great White Throne Judgment. This third and final eternal judgment is when all people are brought before God. It occurs at the end of the Millennium Reign. This judgment involves the second resurrection. It is during this short period of time that all men and women are judged. This also includes the righteous because all books are open—even the Book of Life. Remember that the righteous already underwent the first judgment, but now they have lived in the Millennium Reign and have made new choices. So they are in need of a second judgment. The first judgment was to determine who got to live in the Millennium Reign and what rewards they obtained.

This final judgment determines where each soul will abide in eternity. There has to be a final judgment for even the believers of God because there is the possibility that some may fall away and backslide into sin. This final judgment will determine if you live eternity in the lake of fire and brimstone or in the kingdom of God. After this, there are no more scenes of judgment. If you're assigned to the lake of fire and brimstone, there will never be another time of resurrection or meeting with God. If you're in the kingdom of God and you later rebel, then each case will be dealt with on an individual basis. There will be no need for another judgment in eternity that involves the entire community of heaven's subjects.

In concluding this chapter, I want to point out to the reader that it was never God's intention to have to be a judge for all mankind. It is a very grievous act for God to have to judge his creation of man. At the time of Noah, God was so stricken with grief that he said that it grieved him that he ever created man. God has a heart just like all beings. God created man for friendship and companionship—and to share all his goodness with a race of beings that he could love. But to his disappointment, most of mankind is not interested in walking with God. It is an extremely grievous act for God to have to bring judgment to any person. God has gone out of his way to provide ways for man to return to him. For those who turn to God and walk with him, he has great joy.

Chapter 9

Summing Up

These eight basic foundational doctrines are the main building stones that are needed to have a wonderful relationship with God. Having a good understanding of all eight of these doctrines will enable you to go on to full maturity in God. If you don't accept these—or only accept a few of them and believe in something else other than what is presented—you will never go on to develop into a mature person of God. God will never be able to use you—even in the smallest way. This will become apparent as you become older because of two outstanding fruits. You will never flow in the power of God, and you will never grow deeper in a relationship with God—and he will not talk with you. Inevitably, if you believe and build upon these eight doctrines, you will flow in God's power, and he will talk to you on a consistent basis. God will use you in his kingdom to do many works. You also will have entered into the kingdom of God. The big test that you can gauge yourself with is if you are having God speak to you on a consistent basis and you are moving in the power of God with signs and wonders. If neither of these fruits is occurring, there is something wrong with what you believe.

During the reading of this book, you have probably come up with a lot of questions that need answers. This is a good test to tell if you are on the right path. Truth always opens more doors to gain more knowledge. That which is false always confuses and clogs the thinking mind. Falsehoods never lead to more truth. That which is false will never lead you into a deeper, richer relationship with God. You will never experience more of God in all his fullness. That which is false always leads to a dead end.

In *God's Advanced Doctrines*, I touch on many of the questions you may have. In that book, I attempt to touch on many of the more difficult doctrines and other doctrines that relate to God and life in general. I would advise you to begin writing down all your questions. They don't have to be in any order—just write them down. This will help you as you increase in God. Go back and review them every few weeks. As you mature, these questions will slowly be answered. However, the answers may bring more questions.

As you develop in maturity, you are going to experience a lot of the strange ways of God. This can be confusing, but remember that there is a reason for everything that he does. It's a matter of understanding God's ways. He will reveal all his ways to those who seek a closer walk with him. Those who seek the Lord understand all things. (Proverbs 28:5)

God's mysterious ways will always remain that way to those who don't seek a deeper relationship with him. When you witness God doing something strange, you may not understand what or why he would do such a thing. Remain obedient, and you will understand his way later.

I was always told that I would never arrive at a full understanding of God, but I discovered that those people were wrong. As you mature and come to know God and believe the correct doctrines, you will arrive at a place of full maturity. This is such an awesome place to get to. It's like being in the swimming pool—diving and swimming and having a grand time—as opposed to just wading around in a toddler's pool. Full maturity is the most exciting place to arrive in God's kingdom. I'm amazed by how few people ever go on to full maturity or any amount of maturity. There are so very few grown-up Christians.

In addition, you will experience the outward blessings of God in incredible ways. God will always bless you in all your efforts. Even when you make mistakes, God will rescue you from your blunders. We all make mistakes and wish we didn't make them. But for those who know God and are maturing in him, he literally will rescue you from all these mistakes. And to top it all off, you will increase in wisdom from each rescue. There is no end to being blessed by God. I never thought I would ever be used by God through the power of the Holy Spirit as I see happening today. Things I use to dream of doing and never thought possible have become reality. I always wanted to see the whole world. I wanted to be able to photograph the whole world to be able to share with others what they probably will never see. This is all becoming a reality that I never thought would happen. And this is just a minor desire.

I've only made three blunders in my life. That's not bad compared to most people. There are the countless little mistakes we all make as we go through life, but I consider a blunder a major mistake. In those three blunders, I gained an immense amount of knowledge and wisdom. Now God uses me in a lot of counseling sessions with those who are going through these same struggles. I'm truly amazed by how God works in rescuing us from our blunders—and then we turn around and gain an immense amount of knowledge and wisdom from these mistakes. This is all part of becoming mature.

I never thought that I would be the author of several books. These books came as a result of maturing and learning the truth about God. As a result, I have been blessed in several ways. I'm financially blessed in that I don't need to lean on the financial support a church. I'm blessed in that I meet all kinds of people and am always making new friends when I visit the places that God sends me. Meeting and making new acquaintances is a wonderful blessing. I have a huge family of friends, which I never thought would ever happen. Maturity has its blessings.

Oh course, all this brings problems that arise from the blessings of God. I have more enemies than probably anyone on earth. I have to deal with a lot of whining because that's what babies do best. The increased attacks of Satan seem impossible to overcome, but I triumph in every attack that Satan presents. I get to see the vengeance of God upon all those who inflict harm upon me. This becomes a most wonderful time of victory.

I read about God's vengeance in the Bible, but witnessing it is incredible. This became an entire new revelation to me since I didn't know that God did such things to protect those who serve him. Any mature servant will tell you that God will send protection and vengeance. There are so many things that the church doesn't know about because most of them have never matured in God. How can they possibly know these things—let alone teach any of this—if they have never experienced full maturity? The truth is that they can't, and anyone who is under these leaders will never know any of these wonderful blessings.

I'm sharing a lot from my own experiences, and I'm still gaining more experiences. This will happen till the day I die. I have used very few scriptures to back up all that I've written in this chapter because I want you to see that there are many wonderful blessing to be gained by maturity in God. Most readers of this book probably have never heard this before, and it is all new for them. The church can't teach you any of this because it is not mature, but with God, it has always been there. As you read through the Bible, you will begin to see little mentions of what I'm writing about in this chapter. It would take an entire book to cover the mature life in God—and I may undertake this someday.

For now, know that the mature life in God is incredible. The blessings that await the mature Christian are far more than anyone can imagine. I wish there was a larger group of mature Christians upon the earth during my lifetime, but there are so few of us. I hope that all who read this will go on to full maturity in God. It would be wonderful to share all the glories of God with those who mature. There is nothing more exciting in life – next to hearing God's voice - than sharing with others who understand and have had the same experiences in God.

I write this final chapter as an encouragement for the reader to press on to develop a mature life in God. You will not be disappointed.

There are still many things that I haven't even mentioned in the mature life of a believer.

A Secret Insight

I will give you one insight or secret to what awaits a mature believer to show you one of many things that await anyone who achieves full maturity in God. Everything you build must be built upon the eight basic doctrines that are presented in this book. As you build, you will eventually come to see and understand this secret that I will now explain.

There is no limit on becoming a mighty man or woman of God. Anyone can become mightier than Moses, Elijah, or Paul. Nowhere in the Bible does God place a cap on this. There is no place that says that no one will ever be mightier than any of the Old Testament and New Testament saints. God poured out a great blessing upon Solomon with a gift of wisdom in that he was the wisest of all men at his time, but God never said that he would not make another man even wiser. There is no cap on Solomon. There is no cap on any of the mighty people in the Bible.

It is greatly desired by God that many people become mighty and powerful in the Holy Spirit. There is no set number for how many may attain this. Stephen in the book of Acts became a mighty and powerful man to the point that no one could argue against him. God did a lot of miracles through Stephen. He was on his way to being more powerful than the eleven disciples. And Stephen was just one of the seven chosen to administer to the needs of the church in Jerusalem.

There is no cap on how powerful you can become. God needs many mighty women and men. It's amazing that you will not find any women who aspired to become mighty women of God in the New Testament. There has been one mighty woman in the age of grace that I know about. She is from the previous generation named Kathryn Kuhlman, who became a mighty woman of God. Kathryn was used by God up till 1976 when she died of old age. God use her as a faith healer during the previous generation. I don't know of any others in history. Only one woman since Christ came and ascended to heaven has become a mighty woman of God that I know of. That's pathetic for the church. So now I will teach you about becoming mighty in God. First you have to grow up and become mature. What a concept!

Do you want to perform great exploits for God? Do you want to become powerful in the Holy Spirit? Do you want to be mightily used by God? Do you want to see miracles from God? Do you want to help the poor and sick and elders? Do you want to expand the kingdom of God? Do you want to destroy the works of Satan in people's lives? Do you want to become one of the mightiest people of God that the world has ever witnessed? All this is possible because God has never placed a cap on any of this. Who said that you can't do such a thing? Whoever said this is not powerful themselves. Too bad! What do they know? Never listen to anyone who says such a thing. Look at what I just revealed in the Bible—and see if I'm not speaking the truth.

You have tasted just one part of becoming mature. There are many more hidden things that only the mature will ever get to experience.

I hope that this last chapter will inspire the reader to go on to a fully mature, wonderful relationship with God. God's glory just keeps getting better and better. There is no end to it. Best of all, if the reader does pursue God, you will come to know a very gentle, loving, caring Being we call the Father. The closer I get to God, the sweeter he becomes to me. The Father, the Son, and the Holy Spirit are full of compassion and tender love. Just knowing them and being close to them is by far the greatest blessing in all existence.

Contact Caleb Ministries

You can contact Caleb at the e-mail address: Calebm@live.com
Phone numbers are listed on the website: ProphetCaleb.com
For speaking engagements, visit the website for calendar availability and other information.
For book signings, visit the website: ProphetCaleb.com

Monthly E-Mail Newsletters

We have two newsletters. A free monthly newsletter is a one-page letter that briefly covers topics of importance. A second newsletter costs $12 per year. This second newsletter covers in-depth topics as well as what is happening all over America and the earth, concerning the remnant. It provides prophecy updates as well as articles about the latest ideas and strategies of organizing the remnant and who God is adding to the leadership, the different remnants that are being raised up and what is happening within each remnant group, details of more revelations from God concerning America and the world, questions and answers that have been raised at speaking engagements, interviews with other men and women of God, discounts for other new books, and many other subjects of importance.

For more information visit Calebnewsletter.com

About the Author

Caleb is a remarkable man because of his walk with God throughout his life. His close relationship with God becomes evident shortly after you meet him. He has gone on to the depths of God where others have given up. He is a true servant of God. Caleb is now being sent from God to be a prophet to America and the rest of the world.

God's Basic Doctrines will help anyone walk with God. Caleb is also an award-winning fine arts photographer. He worked as a letter carrier for the US Postal Service for thirty-five years. God is calling Caleb to be a pastor at a church in Colorado where he resides. Caleb enjoys working out, hiking, traveling, and teaching others about the kingdom of God.

About the Book

The church is full of false teachings. For two thousand years, we have been lied to by the church. *God's Basic Doctrines* exposes many of the false doctrines concerning God and how to get to heaven once we die. After writing *America's Resurrection – A Modern-Day Prophecy*, Caleb dives into one of the main reasons why God is sending judgments.

The church is at fault and is the reason why the world is in such a wicked state. The author details what went wrong with the church doctrinally and exposes these false doctrines.

Part of a prophet's work is to expose all the lies and heresies that others are preaching. Therefore, being a prophet involves being bold enough to attack false doctrines that a church has incorporated into any culture. Caleb is now being sent from God to be a prophet to America. *God's Basic Doctrines* is the next step for anyone to gain a closer walk with God. Have you ever wondered why nothing ever works for you in God? Have you ever wondered why God never speaks to you as he does in the Bible?

God's Basic Doctrines spells out the truth as is presented in the Bible. Caleb uses large amounts of Bible verses to back up all that he explains. In the end, you are left to make your own logical conclusions based upon what is written in the Bible—and not what the church would have you believe. Caleb makes the Bible easy to understand. You will not be disappointed!